"<u>Where was this book when I needed it?</u> Answers all the questions I needed to ask ..."

Darlene Shidler, former Comp patient
Goshen, Indiana

"An excellent effort to portray the real world of Comp. A needed piece, easy to read, gives a perspective clearly based upon many years of patient-oriented understanding and concern."

John Moran, Director of Safety & Health,
Laborers' National Health and Safety Fund,
Washington, D.C.

"Right to the point in every chapter. There is really nothing left out. A good resource manual for anyone that is involved in Workers' Compensation."

Mike Wiemeri, Field Claim Adjuster,
Wausau Insurance Co.,
Ironwood, Michigan

"I would recommend this book as a reference for Qualified Rehabilitation Consultants, new Claim Adjusters, and Vocational Counsellors."

Fran Williams, R.N., P.H.N., Q.R.C.

GOING ON COMP

How to Get Through a Workers' Compensation Injury Without Losing Your Cool

by William P. Fleeson, M.P.H., M.D.

Med-Ed Books & Publishers
Duluth, Minnesota

6545396

Library of Congress Catalog Card Number 91-061688

ISBN 0-9629475-6-3
ISBN 0-9629475-7-1

Published by Med-Ed Books [SAN 297-4150]
324 W. Superior St., #510
Duluth, MN 55802 U.S.A.

Publisher's Cataloging in Publication Data

Fleeson, William P., M.D.
Going on Comp: How to Get Through a Workers' Compensation Injury
    Without Losing Your Cool / by W. P. Fleeson, M.D.
    Includes Index.
    1. Work.
    2. Workers' Compensation.
    3. Medical Care
    4. Self-care, Health.
    5. Workers' Compensation--Law and legislation.
HD 7103 1991   368.41--dc20   LCC 91-061688
ISBN 0-9629475-6-3 $26.95 Hardcover
ISBN 0-9629475-7-1 $17.95 Softcover

Printed in the United States of America   1 2 3 4 5 6 7 8 9 0   91 92 93

*Dedicated to the spirit of my grandfather,
George Paul Riedel, who spent his life trying to make
the world a better place to work.*

Acknowledgments

To the following people for their assistance:
My deepest gratitude to my extraordinary wife, without whom there would be no book and no joy in daily life;
Thanks to my patients who inspired everything in these pages; my appreciation to my reviewers for their in-depth evaluations and valuable comments and suggestions: Judge Gregory A. Bonovetz, Steve Charon, Dennis Egnatz, M.D., Ron Gut, Thomas Holm, M.D., John Moran, Dan O'Neill, Marilyn Peterson, Walt Plude M.S. of Arrowhead Psychological Associates, Darlene Shidler, Mike Wiemeri, and Fran Williams. Thanks to Dick Smith for unfailing computer advice, to Librarians Ann Jenkins and Vi Boder of the Duluth Public Library and to Faye Anderson of Blue Cross/Blue Shield for their time, interest and skill. And special thanks to Mary Prestage whose resilience and innumerable keystrokes transformed drafts into final product.

Contents

CHAPTER 1

A Book For Finding Answers

"They don't tell you anything when you go on Comp," a patient's wife told me once. "We didn't know <u>what</u> to do."

When I showed them how simple it would have been to keep her husband's benefits from being cut off, she was bitter: "I wish we'd known all these things. It would have been much easier for us".

I wrote this book for patients "On Comp" and for anyone who wants to know about Comp. If you have a work injury, an occupational illness, or a Workers' Compensation hassle I wrote it with you in mind. It's for patients with questions about their benefits, about injury, treatment, return to work, disability, rehab, settlement, about their future life.

I wrote it to provide a ready source of answers to Comp questions, answers that have never been available all in one place.

The Idea Is To Win

While you're recovering from a work injury, the Workers' Compensation system of your state will pay your medical bills, provide you with temporary income, and help you return to a job close to your previous income.

The way I see it, patients "win" when they get through their injury without feeling hassled, their case is settled fairly and they return to work smoothly. That's what almost everyone seems to want. But because the Workers' Compensation system doesn't always work this well, any Comp case has the potential to get bogged down, any patient on Comp can be frustrated and feel helpless because he doesn't know what's going on.

> *A machinist intent on his work doesn't see an overhead load start to slip. By the time he tries to get away it's too late: The impact crushes his shoulder. This injury is going to put him out for at least a year.*
> *During that time he'll almost forget he's a machinist. He's going to be a <u>patient</u>. He's going to be "On Comp".*
> *He doesn't know it yet, but this is going to change his life. He doesn't know it yet, but he's going to need help--a lot of help...*

For over 20 years I've treated injured employees from the workplaces of this country, and I've been impressed how often patients on Comp are in tough situations and need explanations. Things are expected of them, but they don't know what they are. Some patients don't even know how or what to ask, though they need the answers desperately.

I've watched as injured workers quickly find themselves in this bewildering territory. In only a few minutes or weeks they've gone from chasing the American dream of independence to being a dependent patient and a claim number. They lose control over their life. They're just not prepared to deal with the foreign problems of Comp.

Moreover, Comp is so full of pitfalls it's easy to mess up. Nevertheless, I've watched patient after patient come out of this mess and win. It happens when they find out how!

What This Book Does

I asked a compensation judge: What single thing would make it easier for an employee on Comp? "<u>Better information</u>", he said. "A patient should know more about his injury, his benefits, and what he has to do to get out of the system and back to work."

The judge was in good company: Physicians and healers since Hippocrates' time have known that patients recover sooner if they have good information about their problem. I think this book can give you that information. The book is structured to show you what happens to you when you go on Workers' Compensation, and what you can do about most situations that come up.

This book presents the answers to, and explanations of problems that I've found my patients needed the most. I've tried to include information about every part of Workers' Compensation from A to Z. This should help you know what you're getting into, how to find your way through it, and how to get out of it at the end.

The chapters take you in sequence from the time of injury through typical treatment, return to work and case settlement. Many people--insurers, lawyers, and even physicians--could probably benefit from reading these perspectives. But I've written primarily to give information to the injured employee.

How To Find The Answers In This Book

It's OK to read the book in any order, depending on your current needs. For almost any situation that you might come up against, I've tried to provide something to help you deal with it. For example, in the first section I give you advice on filing a claim, how to choose a doctor, and how to prepare for medical examinations. There are explanations of special tests, and why doctors need them. And I show you how you can read and evaluate your own medical records to see if they help or hurt your case.

If you've already gotten the feeling there's more to Comp than simply collecting checks--and you're certainly right--you'll probably want to just start with the next chapter. In Chapters 2 through 5 you can find out all about Comp, what it's supposed to do for you, and how to get the most out of it.

In Chapter 4 you'll see how to write down a few simple things that could be worth their weight in gold at the end of your case.

The second section covers all kinds of treatment, and Chapter 14 shows you how to get the most help from your rehab consultant. The psychological and family aspects of Workers' Compensation are in Chapters 17 and 18.

The third section covers the end stages of a Comp case. Maybe you haven't gotten your last four Comp checks, or your benefits have been cut off: You can turn to Chapter 24, How To Find Help, for practical suggestions. If you've already recovered from injury but the process of return to work is getting you down, you could start at Chapter 20, Return To Work, to read about how others faced the same difficulties and handled them. Disability is in Chapter 22, and preparing for your next job is in Chapter 26.

I've even attempted to explain permanent partial disability, financial awards, and the use of an attorney in Chapters 22, 23, and 25.

There are special end Bonus Sections that cover hundreds of types of occupational injuries and illnesses. There are eight sections in this portion (A through H) that describe the most common workplace medical problems and diagnoses, and many of the more exotic ones too. If you've been only recently injured, you could start by looking up your type of injury to find out about it and to see what you can expect in the long run.

Suppose you hurt your back last year and you've had six months of treatment, but you still hurt too much to ride in a car, put on your socks, or have intercourse. Then you could start at Chapter C on Back Problems. Same for neck problems, lung symptoms, etc. If you think you have a skin injury or a toxic exposure, look up the name of the problem or toxin in the index and refer to the chapter where it is covered.

Use the table of contents: The title of each chapter tells you what it's about. For a more detailed search, use the index at the end of the book. The emphasis throughout is on showing you what to expect. Every state's Comp system is slightly different, but the guidelines here should be helpful to everyone.

STAY ON TOP

If you have information--the right information at the right time--you can keep control on Comp even though you're a patient. You can stay on top.

You can make the system work in your favor. You <u>can</u> win over Comp and not lose your cool doing it.

I offer this book to you. I hope you use it every day 'till you're off Comp, and then give it to a friend who isn't.

Notes: Throughout these pages I've usually written "he" instead of "he/she". I've disguised names, changed circumstances, and "fictionalized" details so no patients or cases can be recognized. And of course medical advice in a book can't cover everything, so check out your own situation with your own doctor.

And last, if there's a problem about being on Comp that you think I missed, write me c/o the publisher and I'll consider it for the next edition:

Med-Ed Books and Publishers
324 West Superior St., Suite 510
Duluth, MN 55802

T

CHAPTER 2

Your Benefits Under Comp

"The burden of the wearing out and destruction of human, as well as inanimate machinery, should be borne by industry just as other costs of production and assumed by the employer...."

from a 1918 court ruling

This chapter tells you what your Comp benefits are. Every state is slightly different in details, but all Comp systems are similar in their broadest respects.

Your Coverage And Benefits

You have both financial and non-financial benefits under Workers' Compensation. When you get hurt on the job and make a claim for injury, Workers' Compensation will automatically 1) pay for your medical care, surgery, therapy, and the cost of rehabilitation treatment, and 2) pay you regularly to partially make up for wage loss until you recover. Death benefits also exist.

Workers' Compensation legislation now exists in all 50 states and Canada. Though each state is different, the laws all generally do the same thing: Provide you with financial assistance to recover.

Not only will you receive checks, your doctors and hospitals and pharmacies will have their bills paid at no cost to you. If you have to travel to see the doctor, you will receive mileage payment, also meals and lodging in some cases.

In addition, the whole Workers' Compensation system will be operating to get you back into your old job if possible, or into another job that matches your capacities and with similar income. This is the basic purpose of Workers' Compensation.

You should be aware that there are some things Comp will not cover. Some states' laws cover all occupational illnesses and injuries, others cover injuries but only a few of the common occupational <u>diseases</u> such as asbestosis or skin diseases. Businesses with less than ten workers sometimes aren't covered, neither are farm workers or casual or household employees.

In most states you will not be covered if the injury occurred because you were intoxicated, if you injured yourself on purpose, or if you were attacked by another employee. In some states (for example Alabama or New Jersey) you cannot apply for compensation benefits if you were negligent, refused to use a safety appliance, or if you were injured due to misconduct.

Most states do not pay Comp benefits if you miss only a few days due to an injury: Anywhere from 3 days in Minnesota to 14 days in Mississippi.

But if you have a bona fide and more serious work injury, you have the right to receive Comp.

FINANCIAL ASPECTS OF COMP

Your weekly benefits will generally be about 2/3 of your regular wages. These are called payments for "Temporary Disability". States differ and there are some dollar maximums. For examples, in California the maximum is now around $250 per week, in Minnesota $400 per week, but as high as $1,200 in Alaska and as low as $170 in Tennessee.

> *"No one wants to be hurt on the job and when it happens most people are not prepared to meet the crisis...There is help for the injured worker..."*
>
> *Mississippi Comp pamphlet*

Your weekly payments will be tax-free. This makes them worth about 30% more to you. This is how the Workers' Compensation system attempts to keep your income at near the same level as before you were hurt.

Comp benefits end when your injury is healed and you return to work. Benefits can also be terminated for non-cooperation: Missing doctor or therapy appointments, not cooperating with a rehab consultant, going on vacation without notice, even being put in jail for drunk driving.

However, you might also receive cash at the end of healing, depending on the severity of injury and your recovery. For example, if you lose a thumb, sustain permanent lung damage, have a severe facial scar, can't lift heavy objects or can't climb ladders and so on, in most states you will have a "permanent injury". With many injuries like these you probably will still be able to work, though perhaps not at your old job.

In such situations, Comp would pay you for a "Permanent Partial Disability". The Comp insurer would ask your doctor to estimate how disabled you are. Based on his statement you would then receive a cash settlement, anything from a few hundred to several thousand dollars, based on the specific formulas in your state's laws (see Chapter 23).

If it turns out that you're totally unable to work at <u>any</u> available job because of a work injury (unlikely these days), this is "Permanent Total Disability", and you'll probably get a larger cash payment (disability ratings and payments are explained further in Chapter 22). In such cases you would probably apply for SSDI (Social Security) but that system is complicated and very different from Comp and not covered in this book.

But cash settlement or not, the point is that your state's Workers' Compensation machinery is there for you. It's in place to help you financially while your injury heals.

How do you ensure that you get your benefits? Follow the rules (Chapter 4), know the pitfalls so you can avoid them (Chapter 5), and learn the facts of doctor visits, treatment, rehab and return to work (Chapters 6-20) so you know just how to make Workers' Compensation go smoothly for you.

THE WORKINGS OF WORKERS' COMP

Workers' Compensation operates like insurance: Your employer buys a policy for his business and everyone in the plant is covered in case of work injury or some occupational illness. (I buy one that covers all my office employees, for example.)

The Comp insurance company administers the policy, and your state monitors all claims and the handling of them.

> "Workers' Compensation is a type of insurance covering injuries and disabilities which are work-related. The full cost of this insurance is paid by the employer."
>
> Colorado Comp booklet

The legal principle that you should be compensated if someone harms you, as it applies to "the actions of the employer", is behind Workers' Compensation. Our system is largely based on German civil law, modified by the English legal code, and then adapted to the U.S. Each of the 50 states has its own set of laws that govern Comp, each one different from the others.

I've found that many people, even many doctors, still think Workers' Comp is some kind of government benefit. It's not: Workers' Compensation is insurance. Your employer has to pay for it. It's true that some states such as Nevada do run the whole program themselves, but it's still not a government benefit.

In fact, Workers' Compensation is often a large expense for a small company. For example, coverage for clerks and secretaries might only cost the employer about fifty cents for every $100 of wages. But coverage for roofers, loggers, and windowwashers may cost as much as $50 or even $150 for every $100 of wages.

So we have a Comp system in the U.S. where workers don't carry the financial burden of injury. That risk is carried by industry and passed on to customers just like any other cost of doing business. Of course the result is that some small operators and contractors can't afford the rates and they go out of business. But the ones that stay are required to have the coverage.

Employers usually buy the policy from a large insurer such as Aetna, Fireman's, Liberty Mutual, St. Paul, Travelers, or Wausau. The policy protects the employer from lawsuits by injured employees. Some large employers have enough assets to simply insure themselves. Then the state oversees companies' compliance with the Comp laws.

In some states the laws are more oriented to the injured workers, and in those states claims are more readily accepted and paid. But other states can be more oriented toward employers, and benefits are more often withheld. It depends on what the political mood was in the state when the laws were written.

Not only are the laws different, the companies that administer the claims also vary in their attitudes. Some are very oriented toward friendly service to the patient, others are hardnosed and can be difficult for employees to deal with (see Chapter 6). In every state, it's important for you to know that:

   a) all claims and disputes are ultimately reviewed by state-
      appointed compensation boards;
   b) an insurer can try to get any decision changed to its
      benefit, and so can an employee;
   c) the burden of proving disability is <u>always</u> on the worker.

If you aren't sure what the Workers' Compensation climate is where you live, you'll find out soon enough. If it's worker friendly, things are more likely to go smoothly for you. If it's not, you'll need to learn all you can about it. Either way, the more you know about the system, the more comfortably you'll get through your time in it.

This Is A Big System

How big? 50 states ... thousands of laws ... hundreds of thousands of doctors and adjusters and attorneys...

Gas plant explosions, construction accidents and truck rollovers and factory injuries every day ... toxic solvents ... lung injuries ... new occupational skin problems ... 6,300,000 total injuries last year ... 3,000,000 of them with lost time or restricted work ... seven thousand workers killed every year on the job ... and if every state were the same there could be 520 serious work injuries in each one every day Monday through Friday because there are <u>26,000 work injuries a day in our country</u>!

The Comp system takes them in...chews on them ... processes them ... costs are rising 7 to 10% all the time and expected to double in five years ... and there aren't fewer injuries but more each year.

Those injuries go on Comp and they all get medical treatment. Our nation's medical professionals do their jobs successfully, mostly, and injured workers are likely to get well. The 50 Comp systems see thousands of successful outcomes every day.

It's true that Workers' Compensation can turn from rosy to thorny. I see patients all the time that find this out after only a few weeks. But Workers' Compensation still works most of the time, and it's a reasonably effective and fair system. Most of those 6,000,000 injured workers eventually get very close to appropriate compensation for their injury.

Sure, there are still "a few little problems" here and there--some people might say everywhere. I think everyone in Workers' Compensation would admit it's far from perfect, because no system this big can always run smoothly. Patients do get lost or ignored, and not everyone gets what they deserve. But most people do get paid, they do get back to work, and in my opinion the majority get treated right.

Looking At Your Own Situation

You'd like to say that the Comp system might be smooth and fair for some, but it isn't so great for you? That it's possible to get the runaround, or get lost in the cracks, or not get your medical bills paid? That you've had little smooth sailing and you've already been on Comp for months?

Well, in spite of the problems, Comp now is like the brightness of day compared to the dark ages of work injury just a few generations ago. Getting compensated for a work injury used to be a <u>very</u> rough road.

In the next chapter I tell you what it used to be like to have a work injury. I'd bet that after a few pages you'll agree that it's good to be living now instead of a hundred years ago.

WRAP-UP

How to do yourself some favors when you're on Workers' Compensation:
1) Remember Comp coverage is only a temporary benefit, to help you financially while you recover;
2) Remember, you don't have to pay any tax on your Comp benefits;
3) Remember that your employer pays for a Comp policy, state laws govern how Comp works, an insurance company administers your benefits;
4) It's not realistic to count on lots of cash from a disability award, because no one ever got rich from a Workers' Compensation settlement. I've found the patients who do the best are those who keep one goal uppermost: They want to get <u>out</u> of the Comp system and get back to their work and a normal life.

R

CHAPTER 3

Workers' Compensation: Better Now Than It Ever Was

"...There were those who worked in the chilling rooms, and whose special disease was rheumatism; the time limit that a man could work in the chilling rooms was said to be five years."
Upton Sinclair, 1906

Workers' Compensation now--in all 50 states--might be cranky and frustrating at times. But it's so much better than it used to be, there's almost no comparison. No matter what hassles you might be experiencing on Comp, you've got more in your favor than an injured worker before you ever did. I think it will help your perspective to know where our Comp system came from.

It Used To Be Rough

We take good work injury coverage for granted now, but it wasn't always this way. There wasn't always an injury compensation system--not in the U.S. not anywhere.

In fact, if your great grandpa had been seriously hurt on his job there's a good chance you wouldn't have made it into the world--things were that rough. Here's how it was long ago:

For thousands of years "work" was done at home, in the fields, or in the landowner's army. All labor was dangerous, safety was a luxury. If a worker was injured and didn't recover fully he was either dead or remained crippled and helpless.

People faced injuries alone for most of mankind's history. Some families absorbed a few maimed relatives and gave them work at light tasks, but the rest of the injured became beggars. There was no such thing as weekly benefit payments. No disability awards, no light duty.

As towns and craft guilds grew, actual "industries" and large employers came into being. People flooded into factories in the 1700's and 1800's: Dim, stuffy, treacherous places of 14-hour-a-day toil by men, women and children. Because nineteenth century property rights were more compelling than human rights, conditions only deteriorated. No- one had heard of industrial safety practices. Injuries and deaths and crippling accidents were frequent and terrible, even as late as 1890.

But there was still no general compensation system or Comp laws. Some factory owners did care for the injured as if they were family, but most did nothing. They considered industrial accidents to be inevitable byproducts of "progress".

Pressure For Change

Public pressure for reform mounted in the U.S. by the late 1890's. There were some successful lawsuits against the largest employers; a few of the largest realized it would be better to share the risk throughout industry. Muckraking books such as The Jungle by Upton Sinclair in 1906 dramatized the horrors of industry:

"The pelts of the sheep had to be painted with acid to loosen the wool, and then the pluckers had to pull out this wool with their bare hands, till the acid had eaten their fingers off...

...Some worked at the stamping machines and it was seldom that one could work long there at the pace that was set, and not give out and forget himself, and have a part of his hand chopped off."

The public pushed for reform, and things began to change around the world. Child labor laws eventually came into being in Europe.

But everything improved slowly. Workers' Compensation law still didn't exist. Labor-management relations were often brutal. Workers' demands for compensation even for the most serious injuries were ignored. Few workers got very far with claims.

Anyone who tried to sue their employer found out quickly just how much the cards were stacked against them. To know what it was like in 1906, imagine Emil Jokanovitch, an injured worker, shifting in pain in his chair while his wife pleads for help from a big-time eastern attorney. Emil had worked for a steel mill, mostly on the trains, until he was hurt:

"Please, Sir, please help us and take our case. Emil can't do no work no more because of that leg he lost."

Emil starts to daydream of the sunny, blue skies he saw from the boxcars, the long pleasant trips through winding river valleys. Even the bad days were good: the cinders and soot, long hours, numb ears and icicles. There was always the warm feeling of having a good job and doing it well.

People looked up to me then, he remembers. But then his smile fades. He remembers the broken rung, the missing grab iron, the fall, his hip on fire. He can still hear the screaming never-ending locomotive whistle as he fell under the wheels...

"I'm sorry, Missus. A case like this in any county could take years, but here where that company is so strong? Almost impossible! You just don't have enough for my legal fees. Not without many hundreds, even thousands of dollars."

"But we'll find it somehow, Sir. The kids and me have been working. And we've got some relatives that might help..."

The lawyer was kind, patient. "No, Missus. I'm sorry. The company will do things you can't fight against no matter how much money you have."

He picked up three fat Cuban cigars and leaned them against a book. He knocked the first over as he spoke gently. "First they're going to claim--nay, they'll find a way to <u>prove it</u>--that one or other of your husband's fellow workers was negligent. They'll say someone didn't fix *the step, someone didn't warn Emil, or the engineer was going too fast. That's called <u>fellow worker defense</u> and just that will be enough."*

Emil murmured, almost to himself: "I'd give anything to walk out the door again with my lunch pail. But I can't and I think they ought to pay me something." "

The lawyer didn't look at Emil, he just knocked over the second cigar. "Next they'll claim your husband himself was at fault: He didn't look, he was in the wrong place, he didn't hold on, he should have been doing something else. They call this <u>contributory negligence</u>. If they prove it--and they always do--you'll lose on that count."

He looked directly at her and knocked over the last cigar. "And last, they'll simply point out that he <u>assumed the risk</u> when he took the job. After all, everyone knows brakework is dangerous. That's their most common defense tactic."

The cigar rolled off the desk to the floor. No-one spoke. Emil had had dreams of getting somewhere himself, of seeing his children maybe even go to school. But that was over.

Finally Emil pulled himself painfully out of the chair. "Come, Mama, there's nothing for us now. It's time to go home." As they left she was still talking, still trying: "What will we do, Sir? No one will take him, he can't care for horses, he can't even pick up rags. Mr. Esquire, we're going to starve!"

Emil's shoulders slumped. He pulled at her hand and shuffled out, gripping his homemade crutch. He had nothing else left.

There was no safety net for people like Emil, for people that had worked hard and done their job but had the misfortune to be injured. They, like Emil, were on their own, discarded as if they were a machine that had broken.

America Gets A Better Deal: 1920 To 1990

It was cases like Emil's, coal mine accidents, railroad injuries, foundry burns, and garment factory fires that spurred demand for improvement. Even so things changed slowly and the U.S. still lagged far behind Europe.

Then by 1911 New York State had passed the first Comp law. It required employers in 12 hazardous industries to carry responsibility for injuries on the job. 19 more states passed laws the next year. The worker had finally succeeded in getting some coverage.

Workers' Compensation went down in american history as The Great Compromise.

Both sides, employers and employees, gave up something to get Comp. Workers abandoned their right to sue an employer, but in return they received a guarantee of payment for injury. Employers gave up their right to charge a worker with negligence, and in return they were guaranteed that awards would not be above fixed amounts.

This compromise was the start of our present Workers' Compensation system, where injured workers must be automatically covered according to state law. But there were fits and starts. For a while Workers' Compensation was actually declared unconstitutional: Employers claimed it deprived them of their property without due process.

But the delays didn't last long. The public remained concerned and by 1917 the Supreme Court ruled that Workers' Compensation was in fact proper law. By 1920 there were Workers' Compensation laws in 40 states. Now all 50 states have compensation laws; it's taken over half a century.

But for many years the laws didn't provide anywhere near our present system of Workers' Compensation benefits. For years not a single occupational disease was covered. If employees had lead poisoning or coal miner's lung or brain damage from chemicals, they were simply out of luck.

And injuries continued, because there were still few safety measures in the workplace. Safety practices were costly and factory owners somehow figured that the new Comp laws ought to lead to fewer accidents! In the depression everyone further neglected the few safeguards that did exist.

Only with World War II and war technology did the use of safety practices catch up with the availability of Workers' Compensation. Then finally in 1970 the Occupational Safety and Health Act (OSHA) came into being "to assure so far as possible every working man and woman in the Nation safe and healthful working conditions".

Yet, there's still a long way to go. Workers' Compensation covers occupational injuries and illnesses, but OSHA still doesn't have enough clout to eliminate all unsafe work practices. And the criminal provisions in the law are still terribly weak: As of 1990 an employer who causes a worker's death by violating safety laws could spend 6 months in jail. By comparison, what's the penalty for copying a rented video movie? Only 5 years! Nevertheless, we've reached the point where Workers' Compensation always is there for you in time of need, and if it weren't for OSHA you'd need it even more.

SO WHAT'S THE PROBLEM?

If the system is so much better than it was, why can it be so frustrating for patients? What's responsible for the irritations and the hassles that some people experience with their Comp claims?

I'll tell you what I've noticed: Some people have a tough time with Workers' Compensation simply because they don't take it seriously, and they expect it to solve all their problems and always operate flawlessly.

They don't understand what they're up against when they go on Comp. They don't realize that Comp is a system that's been crafted over time, and altered again and again, as legislators changed their ideas about what might give injured workers a better shot at recovery and return to normal life than Emil had. They don't realize how much our Comp system was forged from a compromise, and an uneasy one at that.

And I've also been amazed at how often injured workers neglect some simple measures that will help them get the most from Comp and also prevent most problems. The next chapter shows you how to take six basic steps to avoid the most common pitfalls of Comp.

WRAP-UP

How to do yourself some favors if you're on Workers' Compensation and frustrated:
1) Remember how bad it could have been, and was, for those who came before;
2) Don't forget that Comp is not a way of life, it's only temporary. It's only income replacement until recovery. You'll get out of it.

P

CHAPTER 4

Cover Your Basics:
3 Musts & 3 Shoulds

A woman on Comp tells her husband as he walks in: "Now I'm getting a big hassle from the claims people at work. They're telling me to use vacation days for all these weeks I been off. Saying they won't pay all the doctor bills."

He stops and looks at her: "How can they do that? You had that injury at work. They should pay. Right?"

"Well, they're not. Telling me it's because I never reported it. Saying I didn't go see the doctor till 2 months later. I <u>did</u> turn it in, but they say they can't find the slip."

There are few things a patient absolutely must do when on Workers' Compensation. However, I've found that when patients do the six simple things in this chapter their cases can move along much more smoothly and they'll avoid or eliminate 90% of Comp problems.

Any case could turn difficult if a patient neglects these things. There are so many ways to get in trouble on Comp, from having minor hassles all the way to losing benefits, that it's worth it to learn these few simple precautions.

#1: You Must Report Your Injury

If you're hurt at work, report that injury immediately. This may seem obvious, but you'd be surprised at how many of the patients I see don't do it--and at the problems that causes.

It's required that you report an injury within a few days in virtually every state. Whether you fall, strain something, break a bone, cut off a finger, or get struck by an object at work immediately report it to your foreman or supervisor, personnel department, or whoever in your company keeps track of Workers' Compensation. If in doubt, ask your foreman or union representative. They will know who it is.

What happens if you neglect to report an injury within the time limit set by your state? That's simple: It won't be covered.

Next, make sure you fill out an injury or accident report. Put down the date of the injury, and then be sure to keep at least one copy. Put your claim number on it and keep that copy safe. Reports do get lost from even the best offices, and your copy may be the only proof that you reported the injury.

What happens if you don't keep a copy of the report? Several months down the road there might be an argument over whether or not it was filed on time or filed at all. If you have the copy, you win the argument.

Two other things are important when you report your injury. First, find out the name of the Workers' Compensation insurer. Second, find out the name of the person who will handle your claim--the claim adjuster--and get your claim number from that person.

If you work for a large employer it may act as its own insurer. But other employers will have Workers' Compensation insurance companies such as Aetna, Fireman's Fund, Liberty Mutual, Lumbermen's, St. Paul,

Travelers, Wausau, and so on. Find out from your company, or your union, then get the address and telephone number of the person who will handle your claim. Keep them handy.

Use the simple forms at the end of this chapter to keep track of your Workers' Compensation claim. If you have all this information in one place and at your fingertips it can save you a lot of time and worry. Keep all your notes at home in the same safe place as your accident report copy.

If you don't have a traumatic injury but you think you have an occupational illness, report this as soon as you have good reason to suspect it. For example, suppose you've gotten sick from exposure to a chemical, or have difficulty breathing because of fumes or dust. These would be occupational "illnesses" and should be reported.

But occupational illness problems aren't usually as straightforward as injuries. And claims of such illness can make employers touchy. So I recommend you first get your symptoms checked out on a preliminary basis by a doctor to make sure you don't have some other health problem that is causing them. Afterwards you can report that you have a suspected occupational illness. Fill out an injury report, turn it in to the right person, and keep your copy.

Remember, under Workers' Compensation law you are not supposed to be penalized by your employer if you report an injury and apply for compensation. And the law also says there is no need for you to prove that you were not to blame for the injury. So get any injury reported right away.

Lastly, make sure you take advantage of a publication made just for you. Virtually every state's Workers' Compensation office (see Chapter 24 for how to call and write yours) puts out a booklet that explains the laws and benefits of Workers' Compensation in that state. It will tell you about details of your wage replacement, special requirements, selection of a doctor, and so on.

#2: You Must See A Doctor Early

I can't stress enough how important it is for you to start medical care right away. I've seen scores of patients who had no end of trouble with their

Comp systems just because they didn't see a doctor early. These people tell me "I thought it was just a bruise" or "I didn't want to put in a claim because the boss might get back at me". Many say they thought the problem would get better on its own.

With typical minor off-the-job problems this could be a good plan. But you'll see in the next chapter how different work injuries are: They're really part of a legal system, not merely a medical one. <u>So for a work injury, see a doctor</u> or forget about making a claim.

> *I've seen patients who didn't see a doctor for weeks or months and no-one at the plant knew they were hurt. Then when they never did get better, the insurer denied that a serious injury had ever occurred.*
> *"He reported it but never sought medical care," they assert, "so it couldn't have been significant." These patients then have to prove that they've been hurt all along, which is sometimes difficult and the result is further delay in getting coverage.*

I saw one patient recently who had back surgery, recovered, and went back to work. Then two months <u>later</u> he wrote to his employer: "My back problem was caused by work." No report of injury, no claim, no medical care showing an injury. And as you can imagine, no coverage.

<u>Don't use health insurance</u> for the first office visit, because that would muddle up billings for your whole case. If you use your health insurance, the Comp insurer might claim you "didn't put it on Comp because there really was no work injury". Workers' Compensation should pay the bills if you have a true injury from work, and you've filed a Comp claim, and have seen a doctor.

When you call the doctor's office to schedule an appointment be sure to tell them it's a Workers' Compensation injury. Have the Workers' Compensation billing information (including the insurer's address and your claim number) ready to give them. Expect them to call Workers' Comp to get authorization before they give you an appointment date.

If for some reason your claim is denied by Comp, go directly to Chapter 24, How To Find Help.

HOW TO CHOOSE A DOCTOR

In many states you can see any medical doctor or chiropractor you choose. For example in Maine you could go to anyone who claims to be a "healer". That includes medical doctors, chiropractors, nurses, prayer healers and others--and the insurance company has to pay.

But in others, for example South Dakota or Mississippi or Missouri, your employer or insurer will choose the doctor--you can't. In many states you can change treating doctors but it will have to be approved, and once it's done you can't change again.

In some instances you might see two doctors: The employer may send you to their choice, but you could also see the doctor of your choice. To know if this applies in your state you'll have to check with the Comp insurer or state office.

How do you pick a good doctor? You may simply want to see your family doctor who's known you since the diaper stage. For many or even most minor on-the-job injuries you can easily be treated by the plant nurse or doctor, or perhaps by a local emergency room or health service. Of course, if you had a life-threatening injury you would be taken to a hospital and emergency room; only afterward would you have to choose a physician.

For other injuries or occupational diseases you might only start with your family doctor, they let him refer you further. For the semi-serious injuries (shoulder, knees, bones, back, lungs, etc.) or complex toxic exposures you might see the company's recommended specialist or an Occupational Medicine specialist. If your injury is serious, I recommend you see someone who is skilled at treating your type of injuries and dealing with the Workers' Compensation system.

Is there anything wrong with seeing a company physician? Perhaps in the past there was. And maybe in some parts of the country there still is. But thankfully the days are mostly long past when people were sewed up in a little cubicle at the end of the assembly line by a shaky old retired surgeon.

Most small employers will arrange with a local physician to see injuries. This will usually be a private doctor practicing in town. When employers are larger, often over 20,000 employees, they may actually employ their own physician at the plant.

These days the "company" physicians are mostly very good and many of them are specialists trained in the problems of work injuries. The American College of Occupational and Environmental Medicine now has several thousand well-trained member physicians. In most cases these doctors provide the best treatment you could get anywhere for a workplace injury.

Nevertheless, many employees still think any doctor that the company chooses won't give them a fair shake. This is not true, and in some ways the term "company doctor" can be sort of an insult to those of us who give the highest quality care we can and provide it without bias regardless of who pays the bill.

> *There can be benefits to seeing "company" doctors: We often know one another. This recently paid off for a patient of mine whose employer was denying his claim, refusing to pay any bills for tests or rehab or surgery, etc. It didn't seem right to me, because he had an obvious injury. His employer is a Fortune 500 company and I know their national Medical Director. So I just called him up and asked him to look into the case, he did the next day, and straightened it out.*

My advice is, no matter what doctor you see, simply watch to see if a) he spends enough time with you, b) you feel he shows interest in your problem and conducts a detailed exam, c) it seems he knows what he's doing, and d) you like him. If so, then trust and continue seeing that doctor. If not, you could ask your state or insurer about changing physicians.

Later, your employer or insurer always has the right under Workers' Compensation law to send you to a physician of their choice for an additional or extensive examination, if they feel that will provide them more information. It means they'll actually be paying double, but that's their choice and their problem. Usually, it's likely to be to your benefit as well as theirs: Two heads on a problem can be better than one.

After your treatment is started, don't miss work unless the doctor gives you an off-work excuse in writing. Turn in a copy of the slip to your employer the same day and be sure to <u>keep your own copy</u>.

Later, when the doctor sends you back to the job, don't stay home any longer. If he's released you for work and you don't show up at that plant door, you'll probably lose your benefits.

#3: YOU SHOULD VISIT YOUR EMPLOYER AND INSURER

While you're recovering from your injury it's to your benefit to keep in touch with your employer. This isn't a "must do" but it's just one of those things that really pays off.

By keeping in touch I mean calling every few days or every week. Or stop in and visit the plant and tell your foreman how you're doing. This lets people at work know that you're interested in getting back to your job, not just collecting Comp checks. It also lets them know how your injury is progressing.

Visiting will take you out of the abstract category of "Comp claimant" and let them see you. This can make a world of difference.

> *I saw a young girl that the employer didn't know much about, in fact they thought she was faking and they were a little surprised when I started treating her and took her off work. But I told her she had to go visit them in person.*
>
> *She did visit, and later the manager called me to say how much they appreciated her coming in. They saw for themselves how much difficulty she had even walking. They understood her symptoms were real. After that visit she no longer had to live with her employer's suspicions.*

Remember, your employers are under no legal obligation to keep your job open. In actual practice, particularly in the construction industry, the job doesn't always stay open. But if they know you're healing up quickly and will probably be back soon they're very likely to keep the job for you. It's much better to let them know what you're doing to come back. (I just heard about an employer in Mississippi who absolutely prohibited an injured worker from setting foot on the premises. But even that unusual rule wouldn't prevent a phone call.)

You will also benefit from keeping in touch with your claim adjuster and the insurance company and by playing squarely with them. Let them know you're following what the doctor said, show them you're keeping your appointments, and let them realize you're doing your best to recover. Your insurance claim adjuster can be the biggest help that you have in the Workers' Compensation system and it will pay you many times over to talk with him or her once a week (see Chapter 6).

#4: YOU SHOULD WORK HARD TO RECOVER

The goal of Workers' Compensation is to return you to normal life as soon, and as near to your old job status, as possible. You can make things go quicker by doing your best to recover.

I recommend my patients get it in their mind early on that Workers' Compensation is not something like a "benefit to which every worker is entitled". Comp is wages that you earn by doing a tough job: Healing. Comp truly is a "job", not a vacation.

After all, when you go on Comp it's as if your employer is saying to you: "We're going to pay you every week while you're injured because you're a valuable employee to us. We want you to come back as soon as you can".

Just like any money you earn, it wouldn't be fair to take it without doing any work. Your job on Comp is to be a diligent patient. Workers' Compensation isn't a free fun ride, it's a system to pay you while you're injured so you can get back to what you were doing with minimal interruption to your income.

Suppose you had a tendency to not follow your doctor's advice, to slow down your healing by not doing the exercises or taking the medication he recommends: You wouldn't be doing your Comp job. You would expect the insurance company to then naturally be just as slow and hesitant to pay you.

The doctor does his best to prescribe treatment that will help you recover. So I recommend you follow what he advises. If he recommends physical therapy or medications, follow his treatment exactly. If he gives you advice on exercise, take the advice. If he says you'll do better losing weight, go on a diet. This is wise not only because his treatment is designed to help you recover. If you were to not cooperate with treatment, you could also jeopardize your compensation benefits.

What if your doctor is giving you what you think is bad advice? Can this happen? It can and I see it happen, though not frequently. If something doesn't seem right to you, read in this book about your specific injury and also read Chapter 9 on followup visits. If something still looks amiss to you, follow the recommendations and steps in Chapter 24, "How To Find Help."

#5: If You're Sent To Another Doctor You Must Show Up

The insurer needs to know what a doctor is doing, just as you would with any service you buy. If he's treating you and they're buying his expert services, they need medical records they can understand.

So you'd better hope that your doctor keeps detailed, objective and readable records (see Chapter 10 to learn how to tell) and that they're easy to understand. A Comp insurer always needs to know: a) is there a loss of function or any permanent injury? b) how severe isthe injury? c) what treatment is needed? d) what progress is being made? e) can you go back to work? and f) how soon?

The insurer absolutely must have this information at every stage of treatment. If they aren't getting it they'll send you to another doctor that can provide it. They'll also send you to get another doctor's advice if they see no progress in your case, or insufficient treatment.

> *I recently saw a patient whose medical records make it seem he'd had low back pain for 15 years when in reality it was neck pain. There were at least two other serious errors in his records, one of his doctors had refused to answer requests for information, and the other was unhelpful. Of course the insurer sent him for another exam to find out what was going on.*

I've seen hundreds of patients who have chosen to go to a medical doctor or chiropractor, but after six months they're still in pain, still off work, and the notes give no indication of their progress. Their doctor hasn't given them even the most basic treatment--they just seem to be "on hold". If your situation is like this with nothing happening and no forward motion, I guarantee you the insurer will send you to another doctor to find out what's going on.

This usually does not mean they're suspicious of you, or that they don't trust you or your doctor. It doesn't mean they're going to deny your claim. It simply means they're sending you to a doctor that they know from experience will provide information in language they can understand. And insurers do have the right to do this by law.

So if you do get sent by the insurer for another opinion (Chapter 12) or an I.M.E. (Chapter 21) you must go to the appointment. The evaluation will probably help your treatment. Moreover, if you fail to show up your benefits will probably be cut off faster than you would believe.

#6: You Should Keep Your Own Records

This again isn't a "must-do" but keeping notes or records about your case can prevent a lot of problems for you. Your own copy of records can clear up all sorts of misunderstandings and might even keep your benefits from being cut off. So I recommend you keep Comp records.

This means that every time you get a Comp check note it down with the check number, date and amount. Write down every time you see a doctor, his name and the date and a few words about his recommendations. Keep track of your mileage to all visits.

Keep track of each phone call: Who you called, the date and about what. Make a note every time you talk to your claim adjuster, even the times you visit your employer, when you talk to your rehabilitation specialist if you have one, and so on.

Use the form I've provided on the next page. In fact, tear it out of the book or make some copies to keep track of all your Compensation matters, and keep it safe. One patient of mine kept track of his daily symptoms on paper and it helped him.

You aren't required by any Comp law to keep these notes. And certainly no-one is going to keep them for you. But if there's ever conflict about your case, a hassle about your claim or your benefits, or an argument about whether or not you reported the injury, have been going to the doctor, etc., your notes will resolve the differences. This form could be worth a hundred times its weight in gold to you in any argument.

WRAP-UP

How to do yourself some favors by covering the 6 basics of Comp:
1) Report your illness or injury and file a report as early as possible;
2) Call your state's Workers' Compensation office (see Chapter 24 for the telephone number) and ask for their pamphlet for employees on Comp;
3) See a doctor right away and follow his advice;
4) Keep in touch with your employer and deal squarely with your claim adjuster;
5) Do your best to get well quickly;
6) Cooperate if you're sent for another opinion;
7) Keep your Comp records accurate and safe!!!   M

My injury date:__/__/__. The date I reported my injury:__/__/__.
Date of occupational <u>illness</u> onset __/__/__. Date I reported symptoms
__/__/__. I reported my injury to _____.
My claim # is _____. The Workers Compensation
insurer is_____
The Claim Adjuster is Mr./Ms._____,
Telephone number ___-____-_____, His/her address: _____
_____.

Date	Call or Visit	To Mr./Ms./Dr.	What We Discussed

My injury date:___/___/___. The date I reported my injury:___/___/___.
Date of occupational <u>illness</u> onset ___/___/___. Date I reported symptoms
___/___/___. I reported my injury to _____.
My claim # is _____. The Workers Compensation
insurer is_____
The Claim Adjuster is Mr./Ms._____,
Telephone number ___-____-_____, His/her address: _____
_____.

Date Call or Visit To Mr./Ms./Dr.   What We Discussed

___ _____ _____ _____
___ _____ _____ _____
___ _____ _____ _____
___ _____ _____ _____
___ _____ _____ _____
___ _____ _____ _____
___ _____ _____ _____
___ _____ _____ _____
___ _____ _____ _____
___ _____ _____ _____
___ _____ _____ _____
___ _____ _____ _____
___ _____ _____ _____
___ _____ _____ _____
___ _____ _____ _____
___ _____ _____ _____
___ _____ _____ _____
___ _____ _____ _____
___ _____ _____ _____
___ _____ _____ _____
___ _____ _____ _____
___ _____ _____ _____
___ _____ _____ _____
___ _____ _____ _____
___ _____ _____ _____
___ _____ _____ _____
___ _____ _____ _____
___ _____ _____ _____
___ _____ _____ _____

CHAPTER 5

Being On Comp
Is No Picnic

"Things aren't the same any more. I stop by to see my friends from work and they say "Hey, Easy Money! How ya' doin'?" Maybe it sounds like they're joking, but I know they're looking down their noses. It's getting to me, I'll tell you that."

Many obstacles can besiege a person on Workers' Compensation. This is an unusual system: Hundreds of thousands of people are on Comp, new cases go on every day, and everyone depends on Comp, but virtually. But no-one likes it.

The patient on Comp can bear the brunt of everyone else's resentment and start to think it's something that he's done. But it usually isn't. The truth is, Comp is a prescription for conflict. This chapter explains why.

BEING A PATIENT ON COMP

Patients usually don't like being on Comp. Sure, it can seem okay at first--
"free money for staying at home" -- but patients tell me it gets old fast. For
many people it's a drastic change from their accustomed life of going to
work, doing their job, seeing their friends, etc. Merely this change in routine can be disorienting, and so can the loss of regular paychecks. It's true
that wages are partially replaced by Comp benefits, but many patients start
to feel they're on the dole, dependent with no control, and they lose self-
esteem quickly.

Comp patients also start to perceive changes in their relationships
with friends, co-workers and family. Because they also have the discomfort of their injury, the combination is often really irksome to them. Innumerable patients have told me, "I'd rather be back at work with pain
than go through this" and "Sure, it'd be fine to be on Comp if you're feeling good, but you're not. Even if you were feeling good, people are looking over your shoulder all the time telling you what to do."

The part of being on Comp that probably gets to people the most is the
feeling that everyone is suspicious about them. Patients have told me
their employers don't believe they're injured, that the Comp insurer always checks up on them, and that even their own doctor doesn't seem to
believe their symptoms are real. They often feel labeled as a "Comp
claimant", rather than a patient trying to get well.

DOCTORS AND COMP

Most doctors don't particularly like getting involved with Comp cases.
"Why should I?" doctors have said to me. "When I see a Comp patient,
all my work is second-guessed, my decisions are often challenged, and
there's too much paperwork. And to tell the truth, I've seen too many
Comp patients that didn't <u>want</u> to get well."

> *"Doctor, what's taking this case so long?" the claim adjuster asks.*
> *"Well, he's still having a lot of trouble with that leg, and I think
> that he..."*
> *"Doctor, you do realize that we pay benefits every week that your
> patient stays away from work, don't you?"*
> *"Yes I do, but that doesn't change my ...".*

> *"Doctor, our statistics show that a broken leg should have been healed by now. Don't you think you should release your patient to work this week? We think this treatment is taking too long."*

One doctor complains that in Comp there's no patient-doctor confidentiality because all records have to go to the insurer and employer. Another doctor doesn't like having to make controversial decisions about disability or permanent impairment: He feels that with Comp he's always in the middle of a controversy. Other doctors would cross a freeway on foot to avoid an attorney, and they know that patients on Comp can get embroiled in legal battles.

Many doctors echo one doctor's perception that "Comp patients are different from other patients. I've read the studies that show they take twice as long to recover. And I have noticed that these patients can spend as much time on anger and blame as they do on getting well. I'd rather treat patients that <u>want</u> to recover."

EMPLOYERS AND COMP

Most employers think of Comp as a necessary part of business--but I don't believe any really welcome a Comp claim. Employers usually regard Comp "benefits" as only one thing: Temporary pay to an injured employee for doing the tough job of recovering. But they think that some employees consider Comp as "free benefits to which everyone is entitled", as vacations at the company's expense. They've seen this attitude and it rankles. It can make them resent Comp.

> *"Hmmmm. He didn't look so bad when I saw him at the store. Why can't he be back at some work by now? After all, we're paying him his benefits. He might as well be at the plant doing something."*

Employers may not understand the uncertainty, frustration, and bewilderment of being thrown into a medical/legal and bureaucratic system all at once. To the employer, many Comp cases simply drag on too long. "We question some employees' motivation to get better", they'll say. "We've seen disgruntled employees use Comp as revenge against our supervisors. We've never had much success with using substitute employees, but we've had too many hassles from light duty programs." Employers often feel left out: It's a rare employee who takes the time to visit their workplace during recovery and employers often take this as a sign of not caring.

INSURERS AND COMP

Many Workers' Compensation insurers have seen so many bad Comp claims they become cynical about them. They've seen fraud (a 1990 study by the State of Washington found that one out of 20 Comp claims involved some kind of fraud), they've seen delay, they've had to fight too often. This colors their perception: They naturally become suspicious of every claimant with a prolonged problem.

Insurers are certainly pleased when a Comp claim turns out well, but they have to spend most of their time on the others. They have a generally thankless job, and no-one likes to be involved in controversy day in and day out.

IS ANYBODY LEFT?

If patients, doctors, employers and insurers don't like Comp much, who else is there? Attorneys may be the only group left. But I can't tell if they really like Comp or not. My general impression is that most don't, and most tell me they don't.

Attorneys tell me that Comp cases are often complex and tedious to sort out, they have a hard time getting medical records, and getting doctors to communicate with them is like pulling teeth. They find the whole system frustratingly slow-moving with delays, dead ends, and built-in inconsistencies. Many attorneys--both plaintiff and defense--seem to complain that the other side always has the advantage.

IS THERE A SILVER LINING?

Sort of. If you feel uncertainty or perceive resentment from employer or doctor or friends, it is real. But it's comforting to know that the source of the difficulty isn't you. You can learn how to operate in the world of Comp, you can minimize your time and frustration, you can win.

I do actually enjoy seeing Comp cases. They are always a challenge, an opportunity to teach patients about their injuries and themselves and to sort out complex matters. I enjoy seeing patients come to grips with their problems and put Comp behind them. It can happen and does.

So don't get the impression that the outlook is all bleak. Many patients get through Comp quickly and with few hassles, despite these prejudices about Comp. There's help available from every direction. There are people ready and waiting to give helpful information to Comp patients, to assist them with paperwork, to give them good medical treatment and to help them get back to work.

WRAP-UP

How to do yourself some favors on Comp:
1) Realize it's a system no-one likes;
2) Learn the system, recover quickly, get on with life.

J

CHAPTER 6

Your Claim Adjuster: A Potential Ally

Two friends meet in the supermarket. Both their husbands are on Comp. The first says: "What a time Mark and I are having with Workers' Comp. It seems like one hassle after another, like the insurance company is just against us."

"Really? Don't they answer your questions? Didn't some guy come out, you know, a claims guy? One came out to see Chuck, he told us what to expect. We talk to him about once a week. He's been really helpful, pays us on time, helps with the forms, all that..."

When an employee goes on Workers' Compensation he needs all the help he can get, right from the start. But many people unfortunately overlook one person who could help them the most: The insurance company's claim adjuster.

If you have a good relationship with this person you can receive no end of valuable help. I've always recommended that my patients make special effort to get acquainted with their adjuster early. This chapter shows you how to work with claim adjusters so you get through a Comp case with less hassle.

WHAT CLAIM ADJUSTERS DO FOR YOU

Your claim adjuster will probably be the most visible and authoritative person to you in the whole system. When you file a claim the adjuster is the one who looks over the report of injury, calls the employer to verify what happened, reads the doctor's notes, decides if the claim looks genuine and then authorizes Comp checks.

The claim adjuster's job is to <u>explain</u> to you your benefits and payments, your rights and your obligations under Comp. If he does his job well, you should feel well-informed: Of all your benefits, of what's expected of you and of your future your job possibilities. Your adjuster should then <u>pay</u> you: On time and the full amounts. He should be available to <u>help</u> you: If your checks are late, if your forms are too overwhelming, if your doctor isn't doing much for you or if your rehabilitation isn't going well.

Your claim adjuster should be able to get you a <u>second opinion</u>, to eliminate bureaucratic hassles with doctors, to get medical records for you if necessary, and to act as your representative if things get tough. At the close of your case your claim adjuster should help <u>get your job back</u>, or help you find a new one, or even show you how to retire early if your injuries are so severe you can't work again.

So from beginning to end of your case your adjuster is your link to the entire system of Workers' Compensation. Because of this, a good relationship with him can be one of the biggest assets you have--if not the <u>biggest</u>--as your case progresses.

If your employer is self-insured then someone in your company will be acting as the adjuster. This would be someone in the personnel department or in employee benefits or "claims". Usually these people are also very helpful: They like to talk to people or they wouldn't be in the job they're in. In some ways having an adjuster right inside your company is even easier for some patients because of personal acquaintance with him or her.

WHAT CLAIM ADJUSTERS SAY ABOUT PATIENTS

I know some sharp adjusters, and one of the sharpest told me: "I always make an effort to establish good rapport with a new claimant ASAP, because that's when I can help them the most. We try to help them all along, but that initial contact is the most important, and you have to make it early."

This adjuster personally visits, at home, every newly injured worker as soon as she receives a claim. She told me: "Some claimants just accept that easily, they ask me questions about their benefits, and then I send their checks every two weeks. But with some people there is often a barrier. They're suspicious at first, maybe they've been told they shouldn't trust an insurance company, but generally I can overcome that when they see that my job is to help them get whatever they deserve."

Another very successful adjuster in Chicago told me: "I find that if I explain what we do and why, people settle down and realize we can help them. It smooths the way for them over the next few weeks of their injury, and really all along afterwards".

"We make such an effort to establish a good relationship right at the beginning, because we know that it pays off in an easier time for them and a smoother claim for us all along. It just means everybody's happier."

That claim adjuster always tells a newly injured employee how benefits will be calculated, when he will be expected to return to work, and what to do if he feels something is going wrong. "I just bring the law book with me and show them what it says. When they see that I'm serious about helping them, they usually relax."

This is a very forward thinking--though hardly exceptional or rare-- approach. Perhaps not all adjusters are as knowledgeable about the system and how to get it to run smoothly. But if you give yours the opportunity, things could go very smoothly indeed.

One top-notch adjuster, very popular with patients, told me: "We try to keep in personal touch with every claimant, usually meeting him or at least talking to him weekly. We also try to suggest that they keep in touch with the employer just as often. And we also talk to the employer frequently. That helps increase the probability that their job will be there waiting for them when they're healed."

I saw a good example of how many adjusters feel about claimants. This was the case of a woman with a long-standing right elbow problem. It severely limited her, and it had defied ten doctors consult-

ations. Nothing had helped, and she was just beside herself with frustration. Everyone involved had run out of ideas.

Distraught, she spoke once again with her claim adjuster. He told her, "Don't give up on this thing yet. We're not going to abandon you out there. If this thing can be fixed, I'll do whatever I have to to get you well". And sure enough, after we put our heads together a few more times, we did eventually get her to a surgeon that helped her a lot. This adjuster was Mike Wiemeri of Wausau Insurance Company. I asked him about his outlook and he told me: "I think we have to do it this way. I always say that the claimant is as much a customer, and just as important as, the employer, and we have to go to bat for them when they have something wrong that we can help them with."

Another patient of mine came from pretty far away, and every time he was in town for an office visited he also visits his claim adjuster. This way he kept her informed of his progress and his abilities. Because she knew how he was doing, she in turn kept him informed. And he felt it was worth the time to listen carefully to her advice.

The result? This man always got his checks on time and he's never gotten a nasty letter from the insurer. When his case had been bogged down going absolutely nowhere and he continued to hurt, his adjuster arranged a second opinion with me to try and move things along.

Because of his frequent contact with his adjuster, when he eventually had surgery she was there to assure him his checks would not be interrupted. Later when I prescribed home exercise equipment, she didn't have a problem writing the check for it. I suspect that when his case is over, and he's back to whatever work he can do, he's going to have no trouble getting his permanent partial disability check from her.

The Secrets Of Working With An Adjuster

To take the most advantage of all the things a claim adjuster has to offer, this is what I recommend to my patients:

1. Keep in touch with your claim adjuster weekly, at least by phone. But <u>a hundred times better is visiting in person;</u>

2. Sound out your adjuster for advice on Comp problems;

3. Don't try to deceive an adjuster or threaten to get an attorney. This never speeds up benefits, usually the opposite;

4. Keep your claim adjuster appointments, be on time, and try to be cooperative.

You should also realize that the lines of communication between you and your adjuster will be interrupted if you retain an attorney. This is not the case if you merely consult with an attorney to verify that your case is going along satisfactorily, or to determine if the adjuster is playing straight or to find out exactly what your rights are. But in virtually every state, once you have representation by an attorney the adjuster and insurance company are not allowed to talk to you or even write you a letter directly. The adjuster may naturally begin to to view you as a distant adversary, and that can hardly help your benefits or your claim.

Fair But Firm, And Only A Few Bad Apples

The overwhelming majority of adjusters tell me they receive clear instructions in training not to be hardnosed. They're in their jobs to help the injured worker get through his injury with all his checks, to provide him the best medical care available, and to get him his old job back or a new one as close to the old salary as possible.

"But we can only do it if they play square with us", they all tell me. "If a claimant doesn't return our calls, misses appointments with us, skips his therapy visits, and conceals prior injuries or claims from us, it's a bad sign that things aren't likely to go well and we do have to get tough on occasion."

One adjuster told me: "I look at the situation like this: I'm paying him and if I do my part conscientiously he ought to do his. Those Comp checks aren't gifts out of the sky, they're just like a salary for doing his job of getting well. I'll never deceive a claimant and I always start out by trusting every claimant. I'd like to think they realize they can trust me too".

Fair and firm often have to go together. I heard about one adjuster with a reputation for being really tough and hard. But then when I got to see her at work I saw she was always open, honest, and most helpful to claimants. She seemed to have seen it all, she knew every trick in the book, no-one got anything by her but she was even-handed with everyone. She was cool. I always wondered how she did it, and I eventually

found out. She'd seen Comp from both sides: Her husband had been
totally disabled from a work injury many years earlier.

You might be wondering, are there ever any "bad" or obnoxious claim
adjusters? Yep, some adjusters--a small minority thank heaven--seem to
be victims of job stress or burnout or cynicism. Over the years, and after
contact with hundreds of claims people, I've found a dozen or so of these
bad eggs.

If you have one of these adjusters he could truly make your life mis-
erable. These people are cold, they don't give a new claimant any benefit
of the doubt, they're suspicious of everyone and everything. If there is a
gray area they decide in the patient's disfavor, and they seem to be trigger
happy to deny a claim. They play only one game and it's hardball using
their rules.

The bad ones I've seen: I know a couple of adjusters that have the
reputation of being unpleasant to everyone they meet. I know of two that
have lied to my face and then covered for each other. I know two or three
more that I can't trust. I know two others that act as if they don't understand Comp, or are just plain stupid, or both.

I knew one claim adjuster with a large firm who was obstinate with
most patients. His response to any but the smallest claim was to deny it.
He stonewalled everything. "Let them take us to court," he'd say. His
claimants that I saw were frustrated and angry. But he lost most cases in
court, and I think his behavior hurt his company's reputation. Eventually
they lost a lot of business in this area.

I know another adjuster who still doesn't think any claimant is honest, who believes every employee is out to milk the system, and that everyone should work whether they hurt or not. I knew another who was
simply rude to most of her claimants. Though she was generally fair, no-
one ever enjoyed talking to her or felt they got any help from her.

I find that these unhelpful, mistrustful, unknowledgeable adjusters
complain the most about "bad claimants". I've also found that things
don't go well for this kind of adjuster in the long run. And fortunately
there aren't many of them: After all, my experience of only 10 or 12 out of
several hundred isn't too bad.

What if your adjuster is one of these bad ones? You may still get
through your case all right. But you're likely to need the advice later in

this chapter about disputes, and also in Chapter 24 on How To Find Help. You may even need an attorney's help (see Chapter 25).

ARE YOU BEING WATCHED?

Claim adjusters don't always have a pleasant job. At least one state (Washington, 1990) has estimated that at least 1 out of 20 Comp claims will involve fraud of some sort. So they have to investigate. It's some-times just in the nature of the system. It's going to be done, and it's not necessarily something you should feel insulted by. And it certainly shouldn't threaten you if your injury is bona fide and your claim is appropriate.

I know that some patients know they're being investigated and they don't like it. I asked a knowledgeable and experienced adjuster about this. She said: "Of course they don't like it. But part of our job is to investigate for any prior injury or claim, because it might affect the new claim. If a person has a back injury today, naturally I'm going to ask him if he had back problems last month or last year or if he ever claimed a different back injury at work. I think everyone does understand that--it means that we're supposed to be suspicious people."

Adjusters are perfectly capable of backing up suspicions of fraud with investigations and solid documentation. It's not at all uncommon for me to receive a videotape in the mail with a letter that goes:

> *Dear Dr. Fleeson:*
> *A private investigator filmed your patient last week. This film shows him lifting truck tires, working under his car, and loading equip-ment into his boat. Please review the film and advise us if his activities are appropriate considering the degree of injury he's claiming and the treatment that you have been recommending for him.*
> *Sincerely,*
> *ABC-Comp Insurance Co.*

The truth is, once in a while someone does fake their disability, and a tape like this will catch them at it. Insurers use surveillance to root out the fraudulent claims, the claimants taking advantage of the system.

But faking is <u>not</u> common. I think most patients get into trouble like this because they just never thought about it. It never occurred to them that some of their activities were against doctor's orders. But there they are on a private investigator's videotape and they're in hot water.

The same adjuster told me: "If we think something doesn't look right, for instance a claimant is off work with a supposedly serious injury and we get an anonymous phone call that he's out playing football or waterskiing, you'd better believe we're going to look into it right away. And you can't imagine how often that happens."

> *If you were to ask any adjuster, he'd probably tell you just what one told me: "Workers' Compensation isn't a paid vacation. Injured employees aren't supposed to be doing those house projects, or taking those fishing trips that they've been putting off. This just isn't the time for that."*
>
> *"On a regular job, their off hours are all their own. And no-one's watching what they do then. But when a person's on Comp, they're supposed to be getting well, following their doctor's orders. That's their job, and they better stay on it. 24 hours a day."*
>
> *"Sometimes we do have to deny claims. But we always try to explain why, and tell the person what our investigation showed up. It's not an enjoyable job, but we do it."*

You can avoid these problems. It's easy: Just ask your doctor what kind of activities you can be doing. Many's the time I've written in the chart "Walking and bike riding OK, but no softball" or "Fishing from shore OK, no pulling boat or lifting motor, no house painting", etc. Once it's in the chart, it's that clear your activity is in line with your treatment and you shouldn't have any hassles from investigations.

Close attention also works both ways. It could usually be to an employee's advantage to have a claim adjuster watching things like a hawk. The same adjuster who told me about denying claims also told me: "If I think something out of the ordinary is happening, say their leg's been giving out and they're falling but the doctor's notes don't show he's looking into it adequately, I'm going to try and get them to another doctor for a second opinion. Maybe I can find them someone that can help them more."

So I wouldn't worry too much about being watched. If you're straightforward and follow your doctor's recommendations for recovery, even surveillance won't have any negative effect on your claim or your checks.

IF THERE'S A DISPUTE WITH A CLAIM ADJUSTER

If you and your claim adjuster just can't seem to get anywhere, if you don't get the help from him or her that you should and you've been playing fair and square, all is not lost. You only need to do two things, or perhaps three:

STEP #1   First examine your own situation and your outlook. Ask: Am I truly trying to get well? Have I kept myself on track? Am I really playing fair and square? Have I asked the right questions? Have I cooperated? Have I avoided making any threats? If you can answer YES to all these things, and you've been keeping good notes and records (see Chapter 4) then move on to Step #2.

STEP #2   Put down on a piece of paper--I mean literally on a piece of paper, not just in your head--the exact questions that you need answered. List the attempts you've already made to get them answered. Call the insurance company and ask for the name of your claim adjuster's supervisor. That person might be in another city or even another state. Then when you're not angry (this is most important) call that supervisor and ask your questions.

STEP #3   If you still don't get anywhere, then read Chapter 24 and follow the steps there. There are very few people that will have to go this far. If you follow the advice in this chapter and the rest of this book, it's far more likely that your claim will be problem-free, that you'll get off Comp, and you'll get back to work without any disputes.

*   *   *

One last thing about claim adjusters. You have to realize that these people work in positions where no-one is ever going to say anything nice to them. Can you imagine what it would be like to live like that? No one thanks them. I doubt they get many pats on the back or attaboy's. They take telephone abuse from patients, doctors, and employers all the time. They have unpleasant and stressful conversations every day of their lives.

So give your adjuster a break. Treat him or her like you would any other professional--with a little consideration. You'll probably stand out as one in a thousand.

WRAP-UP

How to do yourself some favors with claim adjusters:
1) Meet your claim adjuster early in your injury, then often and on a friendly basis;
2) Ask questions, ask advice, play fair and square;
3) Keep track of your visits; use the form in Chapter 4;
4) Remember, once you are represented by an attorney your claim adjuster can't talk to you and you mightl alienate a potential source of help and also the person who pays you every two weeks.

K

CHAPTER 7

Seeing The Doctor, Making The Diagnosis

"Yeah, I saw a doctor. Sure, he did an exam, but it seemed kind of brief to me. Yeah, he put me on some kind of treatment--some pills and things..

No, no, I don't know what's wrong. To tell you the truth, I don't think he figured it out..."

Whatever your injury, the doctor will try to treat it and make you better. But he has to know what's wrong with you first. <u>This means that getting the correct diagnosis is the most fundamental requirement of your Workers' Compensation case</u>.

This chapter shows you how you can help the doctor get the diagnosis, and get it right. The more you can anticipate what the doctor needs during his evaluation of you, the more you can help him to help you (see Chapter 4 for how to choose the doctor you actually see).

The Start of an Exam

My first patient looked uncomfortable, perched on the edge of her chair and bracing herself with her arms. Her name was Laurie McGregor, she was 26, and her employer had sent her to me because over the years I've treated many of their plant's back injuries. Watching her made <u>my</u> back hurt.

In order to make a diagnosis, doctors have to ask all sorts of questions, then perform an exam and tests and afterwards sort through the findings and come up--we hope--with the right answer. At least the best answer we can, anyway. Then we start treating the problem.

In practice it isn't always easy. But the key to getting a good diagnosis is to obtain an accurate history.

She was reserved in the examination room, in fact standoffish and skeptical. But I understood. Sadly, this is pretty routine. After all, here she was in the office of a doctor she didn't know, in pain, and surely worried. She was here by her employer's choice, not her own, and of course most patients are suspicious of a "company doctor". Maybe she thought I'd just tell her there was nothing wrong and send her back to work with some aspirin.

I begin exams as I think all doctors should: With the Medical History. Because I'm an Occupational Medicine physician, I think it's important to first ask "What kind of work do you do?" A patient's occupational background is important. If a patient with back pain had worked for years as a nurses' aide doing heavy lifting every day, it would be significant--more than if that patient had been a sales clerk. Similarily, if a patient comes in with lung disease I need to know if he used to be a grain miller, welder, sandblaster--or an indoor salesman.

This is the pattern most doctors follow. First a history: How did the patient get hurt? What were the circumstances? How did he feel then? What makes it feel worse or better now?

I do some teaching at a medical school, and I tell my Physical Diagnosis students that if they're good and the patient is cooperative they can get 90%--sometimes 100%--of the diagnosis by history alone.

This patient worked on an assembly line, lifting and transferring five to ten pound objects from side to side all day long. I asked her about her past jobs; she used to work as a seamstress. She acted impatient as I collected all this preliminary information, perhaps thinking it was only small talk.

She remained impatient, even when I asked about her current problems: "Tell me what happened, from the beginning". She glanced at me once, then looked back at the wall. She spoke in a clipped monotone.

"I hurt my back."

"It does look like that. When did this happen?"

"A couple of days ago, maybe--I don't know." She still wasn't looking at me.

"How did it happen?"

"I lifted something I suppose. That's how people hurt their back, isn't it?"

"Yes, they can. Did you have some pain right away, or later?"

"Right away--I guess. Or later. It doesn't make any difference, my back is hurting now. Look, why are you asking all these questions? They sent me here to be examined, and you haven't done anything yet. Why don't you look at my back?"

Sometimes it's difficult to get a clear history. Some patients are more touchy, perhaps because they're hurting. But I always explain that the road to good diagnosis begins with history.

After my explanation some of Laurie's reserve started to thaw. She told me: "I picked up this extra-heavy piece that was on the floor and I lifted it to put it up on a shelf on my other side and I felt something go in my back. It got worse that day but I kept working. The next morning I could barely get out of bed. When I did get up it started to go down my left leg. That's when I really got scared, so I went to the emergency room."

"What did they tell you there?"

"They just examined me and told me to rest and call my doctor in a couple of days. They took some X-rays and gave me some pills, but nothing has helped."

"Is it still hurting down your leg?"

It was.

"Does it hurt when you cough or sneeze?"

It did.

"How about when you put on your socks? Is sitting worse than standing? Does it wake you up at night? Does it hurt when you bend?" All these things hurt.

"Is there anything that makes it feel better?"

"Nothing helps, not even the Codeine, my foot is starting to go numb, too. This feels like fire down the back of my leg. I wish I could cut it off."

It would have been clear at this point to any medical doctor that this patient had sciatica from a probable lumbar disc herniation.

History questions are designed to rule out certain problems, rule in others and point the doctor to a specific cause of symptoms. More general questions about past medical history help us predict how well a patient is likely to heal from an injury or surgery by indicating their general health status. We ask about past surgery, smoking, exercise habits, other diseases, etc.

I asked further but there was no pertinent past medical history, she'd never had surgery, she was a nonsmoker, and she usually did not exercise. That wrapped up the history.

THE EXAMINATION

We doctors do our work in steps. We let the history point us to the diagnosis--and establish it for us if possible--and then we do an examination to really nail it down. Later we may need to do other tests, lab work or X-rays or scans (see next chapter) to clinch the diagnosis, but the combination of history and exam is often enough.

It's odd, but patients often think the exam is <u>all</u> there is to an evaluation, even the most important part. The reality is that the best medical diagnosticians of the past did their work from clues on the history and the symptoms--as if they were Sherlock Holmes's of medicine.

It was time for the exam.
"Let's take a look at your back. Afterward we'll look at your X-rays."
She had difficulty getting onto the exam table. Though it was her low back that was injured, I also examined her neck for stiffness and pain, and her arms and shoulders for strength. Everything was normal. Then I palpated her mid and low back; she was tender in the lowest part of the spine.
She had pain when I asked her to bend forward, and when I tapped her knee and ankle reflexes her left foot didn't move. This confirmed that she likely had pressure on the large (sciatic) nerve that runs from the low back to the foot. She also had pain when I asked her to push forward with her leg muscles, and when I tested her sensation with a pin she didn't feel it over the foot.
When I asked her to lie down she had to roll sideways, and it hurt her to lie flat. When I raised her right leg up slowly in the straight leg

raising test, it was stiff but not very painful. But when I raised her left
leg, I only got it about 12 inches off the table and she had so much pain
I had to stop. This indicated again that the sciatic nerve was irritated
from impingement by a lumbar disc herniation.

When I asked her to stand up and bend forward, she hurt. She was
able to walk on her heels but not toes, and her back remained rigid. She
told me she hurt more afterwards.

With a few other tests the exam was complete. I left her to dress
while I got her X-rays, then I came back to discuss the next steps of
evaluation with her.

You can see how we start sorting out a problem: We ask enough questions to get a clear understanding of the injury, symptoms and course of illness and then we do the examination. We not only examine the parts of the body that are involved (the low back in Laurie's case) but also uninvolved areas. For example, some neck problems could cause low back or leg symptoms so we evaluate the neck too.

We test strength, motion, and other normal functions of the involved area to make the diagnosis. After any other tests we need, we start treatment and observe the patient's response. Then later we modify our treatment as we see changes.

This is "the scientific method of medicine". Our diagnosis and treatment are based on a) what we can observe; b) a vast collection of scientific medical knowledge over many years; and c) the outcome as treatment progresses.

Whether you see your own doctor or a "company doctor", the first visit should generally follow the pattern as with Laurie. A very simple injury would of course require only a short exam. But any more complicated or serious problem should receive an in-depth evaluation.

WHY YOU REALLY SEE A DOCTOR

Why do you really see the doctor? When it's for a work injury there are actually several reasons:

1) First, for yourself. So you can find out what's wrong. Sometimes people never look beyond this; they feel better just knowing what's

wrong.   The diagnosis reduces the anxiety of having pain that's unexplained. But there are more reasons, too;

2)   So that your <u>employer and insurer</u> can find out what's wrong.   In work injuries there are other players in the game besides you.   They need to know the diagnosis just as much as you do in order to start your Comp checks coming, process your claim, etc;

3)   For treatment.   So you can recover and eventually return to normal life.   (In the case of a work injury, "return to normal life" means returning to work if possible);

4) To determine the diagnosis and prognosis.   You, your employer, and the insurer need to know what to expect in the future, how long you'll be off work, if it's likely you'll return to your full job, and so on;

5)   To learn how to prevent the same kind of problems in the future. For example in the case of back injuries, your doctor should make sure that you eventually learn how to keep your back in good condition and how to use it safely.

STARTING TREATMENT

Treatment has to follow diagnosis. It has to match the problem. It should be logical, and your doctor should explain his treatment recommendations to you.

> I put Laurie's emergency room X-rays up on the box, but it was obvious I needed more views. I told her, "I'll have to send you upstairs for more films that will give me a better view of one area in your spine. But I can tell you now that I'm pretty sure what's wrong with your back."
>
> I handed her a model of the spine, pointed out the discs and nerves and explained why I was going to look for a disc herniation.
>
> She seemed to appreciate the visual explanation with the model. I told her, "There's a chance that you'll improve with bedrest. You should be on medications to relieve some of the discomfort, and it may turn out that physical therapy will help, too. But I can almost guarantee that we're going to need to get some further studies, in particular a CT scan or MRI. However, you're in so much discomfort now, let's just see how you do with a few days of rest."
>
> I told her, "This is the conservative way to treat your problem. Physical Therapy will come a little later, in a week or so. I want to see

you in three days. But I have to warn you, it's likely that this won't get better on its own. It's probable you're going to require surgery".

We discussed this a bit more until she was somewhat reassured. "Now let's take you out to Jane to make another appointment, she'll set you up for X-rays."

As most patients leave they appear a lot less anxious than when they came in. I think this patient realized she had gotten a thorough examination, that the diagnosis was already partly made, and that she knew more about the cause of her symptoms than she did earlier. Patients that have this experience can be confident that, for better or worse, their injury is going to get attention. These patients know a little of what might be ahead. Knowledge is a great pain reliever indeed, and I think you should expect the same kind of explanations from your doctor when he recommends treatment.

How You Can Get The Best Exam

GIVE A CLEAR HISTORY

When you see a doctor, <u>use simple language</u> to tell him how your problem started and just what hurts. If there is any uncertainty or miscommunication, it's going to make the diagnosis difficult. I would recommend you write down this information ahead of time.

Some patients are much better historians than others. They come in and tell what happened, when it happened, and how they felt. You wouldn't believe how many people simply say "It's my lungs, Doc" or "It's my back", but this isn't enough to make a diagnosis.

We need to know just what hurts and where--all the facts, just the facts.

My next patient gave me facts. His name was Bennie Berkemeyer, and he was short of breath. He was short of breath even when he sat at rest, and he was worried about his job as an ironworker. He said he thought he had been exposed to toxic gas.

"It doesn't hurt when I breathe, Doc, but I can't seem to get enough air. It started about a week ago and I think I'm getting worse. I've been coughing, and I don't feel so good."

His wife had come in the room with us, and she added "He's afraid he's going to die, Doctor. He didn't want me to tell you that, but he really is worried."

Bennie told me he started having a moist cough and then did cough up some reddish stuff a few days later. He had a headache, and he thought he'd been wheezing. And he felt weak all over, "like a baby" he said. He'd had a fever for four days. By the time he saw me he was too short-winded to tackle stairs.

He admitted he was a smoker (two packs a day for 40 years) and for years he'd been exposed to heavy dusts at work. He described an exposure to some clouds of dust or fumes that he thought were toxic about a month before his symptoms started.

"Take off your shirts and sit on the table" I said. I saw that his fingers were thickened, blueish and shaky and even with the little effort of undressing he was puffing. He was sweating too. I didn't say anything, but Bennie's diagnosis was probably made without doing another single test.

"Doc, I'll be able to go back to work, won't I? Ironwork is all I know." I told him we'd go over everything after I was done.

I examined his ears and nose, had him open his mouth and say "Ahhhhh" and thumped his chest. Then I listened to his lungs, had him breathe in and out through his mouth and say "E-E-E-E" while I listened to his chest. I examined his heart and his abdomen when he lay down. I looked at his skin color (which was normal but pale), I felt his pulse (fast), and took his blood pressure (low). With a few other tests, that completed his examination.

I told Bennie he would have to have an X-ray and some blood drawn from both vein and artery. But first I wanted to do a breathing test.

"This machine tests lung function, Bennie. I want you to fill your lungs as full as possible, then when I say "Go" you should blow into this tube as hard and as fast as you can and don't stop until I tell you." He did it, but he almost passed out from coughing. We tried three times, but he didn't have much lung power that day. I sent him up to the lab and X-ray. "Good try, Bennie. Come back in an hour and we'll go over your tests. We'll have all the answers for you then."

USE A PICTURE

When you see the doctor, make sure he can't misinterpret what you tell him. If your problem is that your low back hurts so much it's painful to walk, show him where the pain is and tell him exactly where it hurts. A doctor will look at your hip joint if you tell him your "hip" hurts--but if it's really your sacroiliac joint area that hurts, point to it and he'll look there.

A lot of patients say their "shoulder" hurts. But they don't really <u>mean</u> their shoulder joint: Almost all these patients actually have pain in the trapezius, the large upper back muscle between the neck and shoulder.

If you don't describe your problems clearly to your doctor it can lead to an incomplete or even inaccurate diagnosis. This can cause you a lot of trouble, both early and later on.

I've seen many cases where patients did not describe the problem clearly to their doctor and later suffered for it. In one chart I reviewed, the patient had simply told the doctor that his "back" was hurting. The too-busy doctor only did a <u>low</u> back exam, ordered an X-ray of the low back, and treated the low back. It went this way for eight or ten months. Finally the patient saw an orthopedic surgeon who recorded the true complaint of <u>upper</u> back, neck, and trapezius pain, he examined the right area, and treated it appropriately. Not surprisingly, the insurer denied the claim for neck problems and said they weren't related to the injury. They said "It wasn't for a year that the patient complained of neck pain". But in reality he had the upper back and neck pain all along, he just hadn't told the doctor the right thing. (And that doctor must have done a pretty sloppy exam, too.)

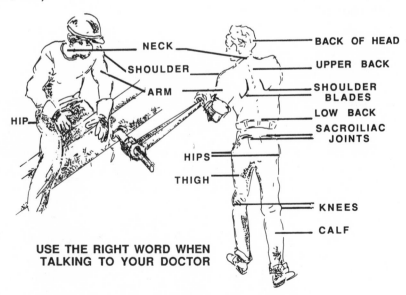

NECK — SHOULDER — ARM — HIP — BACK OF HEAD — UPPER BACK — SHOULDER BLADES — LOW BACK — SACROILIAC JOINTS — HIPS — THIGH — KNEES — CALF

USE THE RIGHT WORD WHEN TALKING TO YOUR DOCTOR

So tell your doctor exactly <u>what</u> you feel and show him exactly <u>where</u> your problem is. I've included a picture of the areas of the body most commonly hurting after a work injury.

You can use this picture when you see your own doctor and it will probably make things easier for you both. Draw on it, take it right out of this book if you want, and hand it to your doctor.

USE WORDS THAT CAN'T BE MISUNDERSTOOD

When you tell the doctor what hurts, be as precise as possible so you don't confuse him. Use words he will understand easily and that mean only one thing.

For example, aching and burning are two different things. So if the muscles of your upper back have a dull steady pain, tell the doctor they ache. But if you feel a hot burning, then describe it as a hot burning. Tell him more than just saying "It hurts a lot". Use these words:

Aching: A dull steady pain, long-lasting, not sharp.
Throbbing: A dull pulsating or pounding pain that may be accompanied by an ache as well.
Burning: A sensation of heat, usually in a muscle.
Stabbing: A sharp short painful sensation.
Pins and Needles: A prickly feeling like when your hand or foot comes back after being asleep. Not numbness.
Numbness: A feeling that skin or tissue is asleep, or like wood, you cannot feel anything when it's touched.
Weakness: Less strength when you use a muscle. (This is not the same as fatigue.)
Paralysis: You cannot use a muscle at all; your hand or arm or leg hangs limp.

And tell the doctor when you have the pain: Is it all the time (continuous) or does it come and go (intermittent)? Is it more in the morning or evening? Are you stiff until you move around a little, or is it worse after you've been up all day?

Tell the doctor what brings it on: Do you have more pain when you raise your shoulder or arm to do your hair, lift a bag of groceries, or sit in a deep sofa?

Give the doctor an accurate description and he's more likely to identify the correct diagnosis. Few injuries are simple enough to diagnose without a good description.

MAKE SURE YOU TELL THE DOCTOR ABOUT OTHER INJURIES AND MEDICAL PROBLEMS

Most doctors will ask about smoking, particularly if you have a lung injury. But a busy doctor may not ask about your hobbies, sports, or previous jobs. For example, if your hobby is auto bodywork and spray painting, you could possibly have a chronic toxic lung exposure that he should know about. If your hobby is racing mud trucks or building stone walls, you might have a chronic wrist or back problem that he should know about.

And for heaven's sake if there are old injuries or complicating factors, let your doctor know. For example, I treated a patient with a back strain for months. She just wasn't getting better, though it seemed to be a minor injury. I couldn't understand why my treatment wasn't effective. I subsequently found out that a) she was being regularly beaten up at home, and b) she had told a few other employees that she would never get better because she had been in a car accident two years earlier that gave her a permanent back injury. So give the doctor the information he needs, and he can help you better.

Another example was a patient I recently saw after neck surgery. He had severe headaches and neck pain. I eventually found out--only through some old and obscure records--that he had fractured his neck 10 years earlier when he dove into a lake, and had neck and headache problems for years. I found out that he also had had six or seven motorcycle accidents and concussions. (He said he just forgot to tell me about all of these when I had asked about old injuries.) No wonder I was having difficulty treating his headaches!

So if your history is at all complicated, make sure you can describe it clearly. What effect would such information have? It might not help your claim for work injury, but it will lead to better treatment. If you conceal it, the effect on your claim will be worse when the facts eventually come to light.

You might also want to look at the Timeline method in Chapter 12 and use that when you see the doctor.

What You Should Expect At The End

The bottom line with a work injury is that your doctor has to get the diagnosis, and get it early. There's just no time to waste pussyfooting around; there's a lot riding on making your case progress.

So I recommend that you urge the doctor treating you to do whatever testing is necessary to get your treatment and rehabilitation started without delay. If he doesn't do anything, suggest (tactfully at first) that he get moving--because it's your life he's holding up.

Though most doctors these days are extremely conscious of medical costs and try to hold back on ordering diagnostic tests, that kind of scrimping and delay is usually out of place in the early stages of a Workers' Compensation injury. Because on Comp, the clock starts ticking as soon as the patient stops working.

It's just plain false economy to be reluctant to order tests that could speed up the diagnosis. Every day or week that goes by is hard on the injured employee and costs the employer (and the public and consumers) money. The diagnosis has to be made quickly so that treatment can be instituted as soon as possible.

I've often noticed that patients are smarter than doctors about this. When I see them for a second opinion they complain to me that "My own doctor didn't even take X-rays", or "He didn't spend even two minutes with me," or "Nobody seems to be doing anything" after they've been off work for several weeks and don't see any progress. The patients themselves want action because they don't like being a Comp case and having pain.

Unfortunately, as I review charts I count far too many cursory exams, at least half of them in fact. If that's all you've gotten, try to get another doctor. There's no reason you should be shortchanged. I seems to me that you should expect the best, and that always means a thorough and full history and exam.

And as for explaining things to patients, my observation is that doctors are almost universally poor at this too. Every day I'm amazed at how many people have been seeing their own doctor for months and then tell me "I've never even seen these and they're my own X-rays".

Maybe some doctors are just too rushed to explain, or maybe it's just difficult for them, I don't know. But it has to be done, and I know it can be done because I always do it, even in the rush of a busy day. If your doctor doesn't do it, and you don't suceed in getting him to, you might ask to see another doctor. After all, it's <u>your</u> body, <u>your</u> pain, <u>your</u> life.

> *Three days later Laurie had not improved one bit. We did an MRI and she had a huge disc herniation that pressed on a spinal nerve root. After one more week of conservative treatment she was still no better at all.*
>
> *So I found her a surgeon, he operated, and she did fine. Her leg pain disappeared after four months of recuperation and appropriate exercise, she went back to work and she hasn't had any problems since then.*
>
> *And Bennie? I saw Bennie an hour later and showed him the simple pneumonia (not a work injury or illness) on his chest X-ray. He was better after 10 days of antibiotics and went back to work in three weeks; he never had any toxic exposure at all.*

WRAP-UP

How you can do yourself some favors when you see a doctor:
1) Tell the doctor about your medical history, your work and your hobbies, and old injuries if you have any;
2) Give a clear description of your problems and point to the places that hurt. Use the diagram in this chapter;
3) If you don't get a thorough exam, ask about another exam or opinion;
4) If the doctor won't tell you what he thinks is wrong and how long it will take to recover, try to see someone else that will. Remember, the diagnosis and prognosis are fundamental in Workers' Compensation. If the diagnosis isn't clear to your doctor, expect him to tell you why not and what he's going to do to try to make it more clear.

L

CHAPTER 8

X-Rays, Scans, & Special Tests

"A test? What kind of a test? Will it hurt?"

"What are they going to do to me?"

History and examination alone may not provide enough information to make a diagnosis. When there is a severe work injury or illness a doctor often needs additional X-rays, lab work, or special diagnostic tests.

This chapter is a guide to the most common testing procedures doctors use to establish a firm diagnosis.

X-Rays

X-rays are the most common diagnostic procedure in work injuries. They're simple and painless; the only discomfort an injured patient might experience is in positioning for the film.

Most people are probably familiar with having an X-ray: You put on a gown, go into a small dark room and either lie on the table or stand against a film cassette. The X-ray technician takes the film and the radiologist reads it later, usually with your own doctor. With plain X-rays we look at the positions of bones and joints. We can examine for fractures. We can also evaluate for arthritis, some types of lung injuries and some heart problems.

X-rays don't show the discs in the spine, but they do show the spaces occupied by discs. By evaluating these we can draw conclusions about the discs themselves (Special sections C and D).

Medical doctors always have to keep in mind ways to limit radiation exposure to patients. Shields and limited X-ray areas are important. With modern equipment and good technique, excessive X-ray exposure is rare.

CT And MRI Scans

A <u>CT (Computerized Tomography) scan</u> is a complex kind of X-ray study. It is relatively new--developed in the past 25 years. While you lie inside a short tunnel-like machine, the X-ray beam actually swings around you in a circle. Signals are fed into a computer and the result is a series of X-ray pictures that show parts of your body (for example your spine) as if they're displayed in cross-section. Occasionally an injection in your arm will precede a CT.

CT studies allow doctors to evaluate for damage to the bones, discs, spinal cord and nerves, abdominal organs and structures, pelvis area and so on. CT scan images provide doctors with considerably better detail about parts of bones and some soft tissues than we could get from merely reading plain X-rays.

Your doctor may send you for an <u>MRI (Magnetic Resonance Image)</u>, for example to study an injury of the spine or head, shoulder, knee, etc. This is a newer high tech way of "looking inside" any area of the body.

MRI's are some of our best evaluation techniques and they give us better diagnoses of some things than almost any other test. The MR scans give us extraordinarily clear and helpful images of bones, joints, muscles, tendons, abdominal organs, large nerves and other parts of the body.

The MRI scanner is also a tunnel-like apparatus, but a little smaller than the CT unit. The MRI images look somewhat like X-ray pictures, but there is absolutely no X-ray or radiation used in MRI's. The images are made by a powerful magnet.

There's no discomfort having an MRI, though the scanner is noisy. Some people with large shoulders feel cramped and some people become a little claustrophobic in the scanner. We can usually help this with medication, though I've found that 99% of patients do fine without any.

For many problems MRI is much more helpful than a CT scan, though both may be needed in some cases. They both show different detail than plain X-rays. There are no known side effects or dangers from MRI, unless you have metal somewhere in your body which could be moved around by the magnet. If your doctor orders an MRI and <u>if you think you might have metal in your eyes or anyplace else, make sure you let the MRI staff know</u>. Dental fillings are no problem. If you're pregnant, discuss it with your doctor.

OTHER IMAGES

<u>Bone scans</u> and <u>lung scans</u> are not like CT or MRI scans. For these, an X-ray doctor or technician will inject a small amount of radioactive isotope (not risky to you) into one of your veins. The isotope could also be inhaled for a lung scan. The material then distributes throughout your body and concentrates in any area of bone or tissue that has been recently inflamed or damaged in some way. The scan image is then taken shortly after the inhalation, or a few hours after the injection. Later your kidneys will eliminate all the isotope in urine.

We would order an isotope scan to evaluate for a recent fracture, a bone or disc infection, recent lung damage, joint injury or disease, etc. Scans are also used in other circumstances to detect cancer. We use them with work injuries mainly to search for injured tissue.

Thermograms are colored images of the infrared (heat) on the surface of your body. They're taken simply by using a camera-like apparatus that records heat. Many people claim thermograms can help diagnose nerve or spine problems. But a recent (1990) FDA report found no evidence to support the use of thermograms in this way. The national radiologist's organization considers them to be non-standardized and unreliable for diagnosis.

As of this writing, thermograms are controversial and adjunctive screening tests only--though they're probably helpful screening for breast cancer. Many attorneys seem to like to use them, and the images are attractive and impressive--but they're not diagnostic and not acceptable yet as hard evidence of injuries.

BLOOD AND OTHER TESTS

We call on laboratory blood tests to help us toward the diagnosis when a patient has a suspected occupational illness. For example, the effects of some toxic exposures such as lead, chemically-caused diseases such as pesticide exposure, and so on can often be picked up in blood. Most laboratory tests are done simply by drawing some blood from a superficial vein in the arm in front of the elbow.

However one test, the measurement of Arterial Blood Gases, is different. ABG's are drawn from an artery, usually at the wrist or sometimes near the elbow. When people complain of difficulty breathing we use ABG's because this test measures the amount of oxygen in the blood. Most patients don't like this test because drawing the blood hurts, but the results can help us immensely.

We do a couple of other special tests that use needles. One is an arthrogram, done for suspected injury to joints such as the shoulder or knee. In an arthrogram the doctor injects a small amount of fluid into the joint space. If the fluid leaks around a joint from a torn joint capsule or ligament, it shows on X-ray. Most people find arthrograms very uncomfortable.

Another needle test is an EMG (Electromyogram) or NCS (Nerve Conduction Study). Both of these are tests for nerve damage. They are commonly done in the arms after neck injuries or in the legs after low back injuries. These tests use small needles placed on the skin and in the muscles. An attached monitor can measure tiny electrical impulses along the nerves that run from the spine down through the arms or legs. If there is nerve damage, the impulses will be slower at the site of the injury. EMG's and NCS's can be painful, but not terribly so, and they take about 20 minutes. Most people get through them just fine.

WHEN TO DO SPECIAL TESTS

Time is of the essence in Workers' Compensation. If special tests can speed up the diagnosis, then the tests should be done as soon as they're needed.

I've heard prominent physicians lecture that a CT or MRI is only needed when all other conservative treatment has failed. That these expensive tests should not be used "just to make a diagnosis". That simple tests should be used first.

But they're dead wrong, at least when it comes to Workers' Compensation. We need the best diagnosis we can get and we need it early. If special tests help make it, they should be performed early on rather than waiting.

To hold back on testing while employees languish off work and doctors go with a "best guess" about the diagnosis helps no-one. Workers' Compensation cases have to move forward from the start, and the best possible diagnostic information is essential. If your doctor is delaying tests that could establish the diagnosis, discuss the delay with him.

WARNINGS

Testing is like all medicine: A combination of art and science. Making the diagnosis is never a "cookbook" procedure.

Can doctors differ in how they interpret X-rays, CT's and MRI's? You bet they can. You will have to judge for yourself if the explanations you get fit your symptoms and seem to make sense. If your doctor clearly explains to you the findings on your X-rays, if his description correlates with what you see on a diagram or a 3-D model, and it seems to explain your symptoms, then his treatment is likely to be right on too. If it doesn't all hang together, you may want another opinion.

Another thing to remember: Under Workers' Compensation the employer or insurer pays the bills for these tests, as long as they're ordered to evaluate only your work injury and not some other condition. If you should start receiving bills from the lab or X-ray department or hospital, let your claim adjuster know right away.

WRAP-UP

How to do yourself favors during diagnosis and treatment of your injury:
1) If your doctor recommends additional diagnostic testing, get it done as soon as you can--his diagnosis and treatment will be more on target;
2) If your doctor hasn't given you a firm diagnosis, ask if there are some other specific tests that might point toward the right diagnosis and treatment.

L

CHAPTER 9

Followup Medical Visits

An injured worker and a friend are talking. The friend asks, "How's it going, Robbie, that leg and arm getting any better?"

"Beats me--doctor doesn't say much."

"Aren't you getting some kind of treatment though? Therapy or something?"

"Unh-Uh, afraid not. Doesn't seem like much is happening, really."

"At least you got any idea when you might get back to work? Doesn't he say something about that when you see him?"

"Nope, he hasn't. Nope. He hasn't said nothing at all..."

What happens on followup visits--and what your doctor writes down about them later--is the backbone of the Workers' Compensation benefit system and the key to evaluating your progress. To avoid wasting time and to keep your Comp case humming along on track, your followup visits should be focused and productive.

This chapter tells you what to expect on a followup visit, what it should accomplish and what you need to do from your side.

The Purpose Of Followup Visits

Followup visits in a Workers' Compensation case have a specific purpose: <u>They must move your recovery forward</u>.

You'll probably have followup office visits at regular intervals as you recover. They should:

1) Gauge your progress;
2) Confirm the correctness of the diagnosis or lead to a modified diagnosis;
3) Produce an updated treatment plan; and
4) End with a prognosis (the doctor's prediction) about how fully you will recover and when you will return to work.

<u>If any visit to your doctor doesn't accomplish these four things, that visit is a waste of your time and of the Comp insurer's money</u>.

Why is it so important that you have an effective followup visit? Because, quite simply, your medical care is supposed to be getting you well and if it's not then you're stalled. Evaluation of your progress shows you and your doctor whether his treatment plan is working.

The combination of an updated treatment plan and a fresh prognosis lets you and everyone else involved in your case make plans. And the purpose of it all is to move your case ahead in such a way that you can eventually get off Comp, get back to your normal life and your normal income. This is why you want your followups to be as effective as they can be.

The Exam Is Everything

In many ways every followup medical visit should be similar to the first evaluation you had.

The exam is all-important. You should expect to go through not only some of the same kind of history taking, but also the same kind of examination of your shoulder or neck or low back or knee or lungs or skin as you did when you saw the doctor the first time.

On a patient's followup visit I ask him: "How have you been do-ing? Still having the same discomfort in the back? Any side effects from the medications?"

"No, no problems. I guess I'm doing pretty well. It still bothers me quite a bit in the mornings though."

"Do you have any of the same symptoms as before? Anything new?" I ask, and the interim history-taking goes on.

Your job on the followup visit is simple: Tell your doctor how you feel. Show him where you hurt. Tell him your symptoms accurately, make sure he knows if you have any side effects, and tell him what hurts when he does his exam.

It's as important on followup as on the first visit that you tell the doc-tor your symptoms precisely, just as if you were helping him come to the right diagnosis all over again. Use the drawing in Chapter 7 if you want to show him what hurts and where, and use the list of terminology in the same chapter: Aching, throbbing, burning, stabbing, pins and needles, numbness, etc.

The doctor needs this information because on a followup visit he has to literally rediagnose or verify his previous diagnosis. Without accurate data from you he would be groping in the dark.

So your doctor will probably ask questions about your ongoing symp-toms and your response to the treatment. He should ask if you've experi-enced any unpleasant effects from medications, or if you've had any new problems or new symptoms.

Then he'll likely do a repeat physical examination and perhaps fur-ther testing.

I say: "Let's take a look at the range of motion of that low back. Try to bend forward at the waist." He tries but he only gets to 60 de-grees. Still, that's better than on the previous visit. "Any tenderness? Does this area hurt more than this one?"

"No, all that tenderness is gone, Doc. Feels like it's moving a little freer now too."

"Seems to be. How about if we have you try leaning backward now. Any pain with that?" and we go through all the same type of testing I did on the first exam and on every other visit too.

I think it's best to put patients through a full reevaluation of the injured part, back, extremity or joint. I do range of motion and strength testing--every time--and even a new X-ray in a few cases.

For example, if a patient only bent forward 20 degrees when I first saw his back injury, and then on a followup visit I measure his motion at 90 degrees or more, then I have objective evidence that the medication and therapy are working. On the other hand, if he were to bend only 10 to 20 degrees on the followup, I'd see that treatment wasn't being very successful and I'd have to consider new testing to improve my diagnosis, or perhaps start some different therapy or a change in medications.

For musculoskeletal injuries, the followup tests and maneuvers specifically measure joints, muscle groups, nerves, muscle functions and spinal integrity. This is the best way I know to determine how well they've responded to treatment. Abnormal tests point to unresolved problems or lack of response to treatment.

For other types of injury, laboratory work or special testing (see Chapter 8) might be necessary. For example, a patient with a healing lung injury might have serial pulmonary functions or lung scans on each followup visit. Or a patient with some other toxic injury might have repeat blood work.

THE BOTTOM LINE OF EVERY VISIT

Once the examination and tests are completed, the doctor should make a diagnostic conclusion and tell you how you're doing. You should expect on every visit that he takes time to discuss his findings with you and tells you whether or not you've improved.

After I finish an exam I always sit down with a patient to go over the progress he's made since his last visit. I show him exactly what's better and what's not. Then I adjust the treatment and change or decrease medications as necessary.

The exam is over, X-rays are back in their jacket, and things look good. So I say exactly that: "Things look good, Steve. You tell me your leg pain is gone, I see that your reflexes are OK and back motion is better than ever, you're walking normally, and your X-rays are fine. It looks like that surgery did the job it was supposed to do."

All Steve does is smile—he was so tired of sciatica he would have done anything to get relief.

"I think things will continue to go well. I'd like to start you on some gentle exercises now and see you in about 3 weeks. You'll probably be at Light work again inside of 2 months."

I feel no exam is complete until I also go over the prognosis with a patient. I usually also estimate how much longer before he's likely to be ready to return to a more normal life and go back to work. I feel you should expect the same.

Lastly, at the completion of a followup visit the doctor should give you some idea of how fully he expects you to ultimately recover.

Depending on your injury, the first few followups may be too early for this kind of a prognosis or prediction, but after a few more visits it should be part of every followup.

If you have a Rehabilitation Consultant or a QRC, it's good medical practice for your doctor to also discuss your progress and prognosis with you and your rehab consultant together at the end of the visit. Not all doctors will do this, but they should. If yours doesn't, ask why not. For an explanation of rehab consultants and QRC's see Chapter 14.

As you leave, your doctor should also give you a duty slip that either keeps you off work until the next visit, or allows you to work with some restrictions until then. A duty slip might read: "Able to occasionally lift up to 15 pounds" or "No exposure to fumes or dust" or "Must be able to change positions frequently", etc. The specific restrictions would depend on your injury. <u>You should get an updated slip every visit</u>.

You should keep a copy of the duty slip for your files and also take a copy to your employer as soon as your followup visit is over. Then keep your copy safe.

IF YOU'RE NOT IMPROVING

Occasionally things are not so clear. There are occasions when I've had to say, "I'm not sure why you haven't seen improvement." But then I make plans for further workup or consultation.

So if <u>your</u> doctor doesn't know what's wrong with you, or is uncertain how to treat you, I think you should expect him to tell you that too. In that case I'd recommend you ask for a referral, if he <u>doesn't</u> make plans for further testing or evaluation.

At some point your doctor may tell you he's done all he can for you, that no further improvement is likely from medical treatment. If he has no other recommendations for consultation, then there are other ways he could move your case forward.

He could recommend a second opinion or consultation (see Chapter 12) to help him out, vocational testing (see Chapter 14), a search for alternative jobs, counselling (see Chapter 17) or a pain program (see Chapter 19). Or he could test your physical capacities and suggest a trial of return to light work (see Chapter 20).

OPTIONAL: TESTING OF CAPACITIES

If you are recovering well and a return to work might soon be feasible, then one other thing may occur on a followup visit: Testing of your capacities for work. To do this the doctor should make some arrangement to test you on how much you can lift, push, pull, etc. This is particularly important for musculoskeletal injuries.

In my practice I do this myself right in my office. I have a testing room with weights, push and pull apparatus, a balance walking beam, exercise equipment, and so on. But more commonly the testing will be done in a separate facility or a physical therapy department.

> I say to my patient: "Follow me into this other room and we'll try to simulate some of your tasks at work". First I have him push and pull various weighted objects to determine what he can do safely.
> If it looks as if he's straining I ask him about it: "Are you having some back pain with that weight?" I'll take some weight out and then have him give another try at the same activity.
> I do other testing to measure his lifting strength from waist level or floor level. I have him work overhead to simulate using a heavy tool, and so on.
> "Let's just strap these weights on your wrists and have you work overhead for a few minutes. This is a lot like what you do on your job, isn't it?"

The reason for doing physical capacity testing on a followup visit is simple: We want to determine whether it's safe to send a patient back to work at light duty or in any other capacity. (See Chapter 20 for more on this.)

HOW TO EVALUATE YOUR OWN VISITS

It's clear that when you're on Workers' Compensation, having followup visits is not "just going to the doctor": You're going for specific results. Those results have to be clear to anyone who reviews your chart later: The insurer, employer, rehab consultant, or some other doctor. And followups should occur at regular intervals without long gaps during which progress can lag.

If a visit adheres to the format I've laid out here (history, exam, revised diagnosis and treatment, discussion and prognosis) the visit will produce results. Anywhere in the country, no matter what the local Workers' Compensation laws, the way I've laid it out here is the way I think your followup visits should be done to give you the best chance at recovery.

Does it always happen this way? Hardly. I see plenty of problems with how followups are conducted in offices all over the country.

I review lots of medical charts every week, and at least half of them reflect doctor's care that neglects one or two, if not four or five of the components of good followup care.

Sometimes there are gaps of weeks and even months between visits. These are probably some of the reasons that Workers' Comp becomes a problem for so many patients: Their doctors don't do good followup care. How can you check to see if your followup visits have been adequate? First, just watch how each visit goes and whether it follows the pattern I've given in this chapter. Then think over your last visits. Did the doctor take an interim history? Did he do an exam and then compare your symptoms and findings with what they used to be? Did he continue or alter his treatment plan? Did he discuss it all with you? Did you leave his office understanding how you're doing?

If he didn't do these things, then what <u>did</u> he do? If you don't really know, then it couldn't have been a very effective followup, could it?

How do you make sure your followup visits go well? First, do <u>your</u> job of accurately telling your symptoms. Then remind the doctor (if you have to) to do an exam, ask him about his conclusions, and ask the prognosis. If this gets you nowhere try to go to another doctor, one who will live up to his responsibilities when he sees a Comp patient.

You could also try this: There's an even easier way for you to evaluate the quality of your own followups. Part of a doctor's job in Workers' Compensation is to keep medical records of each followup visit and send them to the Comp carrier. Obtain copies of your records (in the next chapter I show you just how to do it) and review them.

WRAP-UP

How you can do yourself some favors on followup medical visits:
1) Remember that the purpose of a followup visit is to update your diagnosis and treatment and move your case forward;
2) Make sure that your doctor sees you on a regular and frequent basis, and keep your appointments;
3) When you go for a followup tell your doctor exactly what you think is still wrong and describe just how you've responded to his treatment;
4) If you see that your progress bogs down, ask why and ask what to do about it. You should see some kind of progress on every single visit;
5) You can use your medical records to determine how effective your followups are.

M

CHAPTER 10

You & Your Medical Records

The Workers' Compensation carrier has denied a patient's claim because they feel it's actually an old injury: "It's here in your own doctor's notes from last year: Right shoulder strain."
"But that was when I strained my <u>neck</u> muscles, not my shoulder. And it was on the <u>left</u> side. <u>My doctor's notes are wrong!!</u>"

You'd be amazed at how important your medical records can be. First for day to day use, and second in a dispute.

Memories fade or change, doctors and even entire clinics come and go, so the chart notes that document your care remain the life-blood of Comp. Medical records stay around for years. Everyone involved in your case from beginning to end will depend on them to show the tracks of your care with accuracy and completeness.

It's not unusual to have a dispute in a Workers' Compensation case. If you have one, everyone will look to your medical records for resolution of opposing opinions. If your chart is unclear or contains inaccuracies, your claim could be in jeopardy. This chapter shows you how to obtain and evaluate your own medical records and shows you how to proceed if there are any inaccuracies in them.

Most Medical Records Aren't Good Enough

Most people never have a reason to even think about their doctor's records. It's taken for granted that they're adequate. This might be OK for a non-work injury, where even haphazard record-keeping bothers no-one but the doctor who has to use the file. But when you have a work injury and go on Workers' Compensation things are vastly different. The records need to be useful.

I've reviewed tens of thousands of charts over the years. But I still get disgusted when I see months and years of followup visits on a single page and little or nothing of substance in the notes.

I often see scribbled notes that read "Not doing well" followed by an illegible signature. I see handwritten notes--not much better--that read "Patient still has pain--back". Some of the worst ones just say "Same treatment" over and over and over. I've even seen "same treatment" written three times a week for a year!

Everyone in Comp needs good notes, and everyone has trouble with notes like these.

An insurance adjuster for a large company told me: "We see doctors' records all the time that are hopelessly inadequate for our purposes. They don't document the patient's symptoms. Sometimes there's not even an exam recorded! Notes like that just don't tell us what we need to know."

What does he do about it? Simple: "Often we simply have to suspend benefits until we get some info. Of course that inconveniences the claimant terribly and it's not his fault, but it's all we can do. If we can't find out what's going on medically, the claim stops cold."

On the next page are just a few examples of the notes I've come across lately. Sad to say, they weren't hard to find. They are typical of charts made every day in clinics, health services, medical doctors' and chiropractors' offices all over the country.

You can see why insurers and employers get frustrated: It's difficult for even trained medical professionals to get anything out of them. No one likes to rely on notes like these to find out how a patient is progressing.

It takes a lot of nerve to send notes like these to an insurer and call them "medical records". No-one can use these to evaluate treatment.

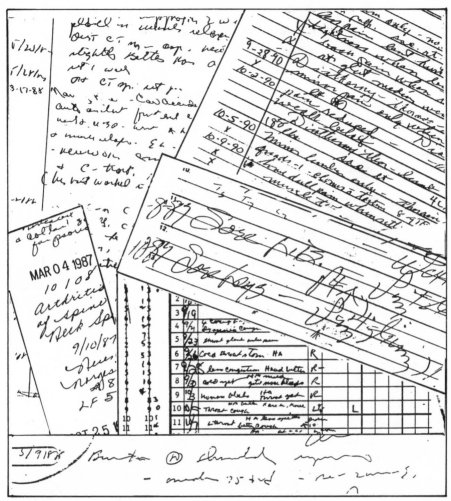

These aren't medical records--they're no more than notations. Notes like these don't document care. They mean little to anyone who's looking for information. For the purposes of Workers' Compensation they aren't worth the paper they're written on. I'd bet that if you asked the doctors who wrote them what they mean they wouldn't even know!

The problem with these notes is that they lack the most basic information. Sometimes they don't even have the name of the patient or the doctor, which could even make them legally worthless. They certainly don't tell what happened on a followup visit, or give the diagnosis, or record the patient's status or physical capacities or the prognosis. These notes provide literally nothing to anyone who needs to rely on them.

If these were your medical records, their effect would be to shroud your claim in fog and frustrate any insurers, rehab people, employers, or consulting doctors who try to use them.

How many Workers' Compensation medical charts are not adequate? In my experience at least half, probably more like two-thirds. Not all are as bad as these examples but at least half of the records I see neglect to record two, three, four or even five of the components of good initial or followup medical visits.

What if **your** medical records are wrong? Simple.

A consulting doctor could make a wrong conclusion or decision about you. An insurer could cut off your benefits when he shouldn't. Your employer might not hold your job. Your attorney could file a hopeless claim. A Comp judge could deny your request because it appears invalid.

And all because of wrong information.

Medical Records Should Use SOAP

It won't be on memory or opinion or even your doctor's recall that your case will be judged in the end. Workers' Compensation decision-makers and administrators use the written facts to make decisions.

So as a Comp patient, you'd better hope **your** records are good ones. Is there one format for medical records that's better than others? There certainly is: It's called "using SOAP".

In my experience I've found that the best medical records use the SOAP format: S for Subjective Complaints, O for Objective Findings, A for Assessment and P for the Plan. Chart notes of office visits should show these four parts clearly.

Here's how it goes. A doctor finishes an exam and then dictates notes about the visit:

> The doctor thumbs the switch of his recorder and speaks into it: "*Subjective*: Patient returns for reevaluation of neck pain. Symptoms continue to be..." and he goes on to record the patients' subjective complaints just as he heard them from the patient. He uses the patients' own words and also his own summary.

Then he dictates the next part: "<u>Objective</u>: On exam there is a limited range of motion, flexion to only 30 degrees, spasm and tenderness over the ..." He records everything he found on the exam as these are objective findings, things he could measure and document.

Next he dictates: "<u>Assessment</u>: Persistent cervical strain or sprain, minimal improvement" which is his updated diagnosis of the problem.

Last he dictates: "<u>Plan</u>: Obtain MRI to rule out disc herniations, continue PT with traction and massage, add Flexeril for muscle relaxation. Recheck in 7 days. Exercises at home."

The resulting notes are easy to read. They follow a logical pattern and there's no ambiguity. Typical SOAP'ed notes look much more inviting to read, they're simple to follow, and they're infinitely more useful. They look like the ones in the figure below.

Anyone can read SOAP'ed chart notes, anyone can tell how the patients were feeling and responding to treatment. Anyone could tell what I found on exam (the notes in the figure are from my charts) and can determine if I'm on the right track or not with the patient.

```
●●●●n, Steve
1/27/91


Subjective:    Steve returns with less low back pain, better tolerance
               activity.  Has been swimming and walking without side
               effects.  No pain on cough or sneeze.  No problems with
               traction.  No new symptoms--feels "80 % better".

Objective:     Gait normal, no limp.  No muscle spasm and minimal low bε
               tenderness.  Sitting exam shows flexion of 90°, standing
               the same.
               Normal refexes now at knees and ankles.  Straight leg
               raising is painful at 70° on left, normal on right.  Low
               extremity strength is good in quads and toes.
               Standing exam show no difficulty with heel or toe walk,
               normal lateral bend to right and left.

        Assessment:    Resolving L4-5 disc with radiculopathy

        Plan:          Continue PT with heat, massage and traction,
                       continue exercises and increase daily activity
                       Recheck in 3 weeks.  Expect to return to work
                       if very light duty--lifting under 10 # and no
                       bending--is available.  Should eventually
                       recover fully.
```

It's obvious from a SOAP'ed note just what the doctor is treating and why he's treating it as he is. It may turn out the doctor is right, or he may be wrong. But at least it's clear where his patients are at and what he's thinking. This kind of note also predicts, for everyone to see, how long he expects a patient to be off work, and why. The records show anyone who reads them the status of a case, the results of treatment, and the degree of progress.

Good SOAP'ed notes help a doctor to stay on target with his treatment. It's hard to imagine that any doctor wouldn't write his notes this way. But unfortunately, though the SOAP note was invented 30 years ago by Larry Weed, M.D. in Vermont, good examples of it are still not as widespread as they should be.

Perhaps this is because using SOAP is almost like taking a mini-exam on every patient. Records written in the SOAP format show up both detailed and skimpy exams. They show up good and unsuccessful treatment equally clearly. So using SOAP, a doctor has to constantly ask himself as he dictates: "Have I examined the right areas? Do the findings explain the patient's complaints? Have I made a diagnosis that I can back up with my exam? Has my treatment tied it all together? Could I have done anything better?"

This is really self-discipline and accountability. It should be part of Workers' Compensation, but in Comp, so many people are looking over a doctor's shoulder that SOAP'ed notes may just be too open to scrutiny for some doctors' liking.

Some doctors say SOAP isn't practical, it's too cumbersome, they'd be spending all their time dictating records if they used it. To them, all I can say is that I have a busy practice too and I use SOAP without any difficulty. In fact I find it easier than the old way.

In my opinion SOAP is a must in Workers' Compensation records. Any chart without it is inadequate. I recommended that you look to see if your chart has SOAP or not.

How To Get Your Own Records

Probably every state has a slightly different twist or interpretation on the ownership of Workers' Compensation medical records. They're not like the records of a personal medical problem, which technically belong to you and your doctor alone because of confidentiality.

But it doesn't really matter. Under Workers' Compensation you do have the right to get a copy of your own records.

Medical records are typically in the doctor's chart or file at his office. He will also always have sent one copy to the insurer--he has to do so because they won't pay him until he does. And almost anyone else who has to be involved in your claim--rehabilitation consultant, employer, Claim Adjuster, etc.--will also have the right to get your comp records (but not your personal medical records).

The best way for you to obtain a copy is to request them in writing. Send the doctor's office a brief letter such as this:

Please send me a copy of my medical records.

> *Your Signature*
> *Date*

It's important that you sign and date your request.

Just showing up at the doctor's door and demanding your records "Right now!" will probably not get you anywhere. Making copies of medical charts can be a time-consuming process for doctors' already overworked office staffs. So be patient but also don't hesitate to politely insist--in writing by mail--if it's necessary.

It will usually cost you something to get the copies. Typical charges may be $5 to $10 for retrieval fee, plus 25c to 75c per page. Every time. Expect to pay these fees in cash, because this is a cost to you personally and the insurer won't cover it.

If you ever go for a second opinion or consultation (see Chapter 12) the same rules of ownership, access, and procedure will apply.

But if you ever go for an Independent Medical Examination the rules are going to be different (see Chapter 21). Usually you won't have access to the doctor's report. The doctor doing an IME is not allowed to send it to you or even your family doctor. He's required to send his report only to the requesting source, either insurer or employer or attorney.

Sometimes the person who requested the IME will send an IME report to you, some never will. If you have already retained your own attorney at that point, he would definitely have the right to get a copy and presumably he will give you a copy.

Do Your Records Have The Right Stuff?

Do your medical records actually show what happened to you: How your problem started?   Whether you still had symptoms on followup? Whether you were following the treatment? Do they record your range of motion?   Or your lung function, or blood lead level, or skin condition? What was the doctor's diagnosis, his prognosis, his plan? What did your doctor write down?

Did your records get all this down, written in a form that everyone involved, including non-medical persons, can understand and use?

Because your records can affect your case and ultimately your claim so significantly, I recommend that you find out if they are accurate. To do this, first review them.   Second, take steps to correct any major inaccuracies.

Here are the steps you take. After getting hold of the records from every clinic or doctor you've been to (see previous page for the method) look at them to make sure they clearly reflect what you told your doctor or doctors about your injury and your symptoms. Check to see if they:

1) Record your complaints, a description of how you felt and any side effects;
2) Document exams of the area that was injured;
3) Contain diagnostic conclusions;
4) Include a treatment or workup plan, and;
5) At least some of the notes should end with a prognosis.

If your particular case is complicated or difficult, and if the best course of treatment is a little uncertain, look to see if your notes point that out. The doctor's Assessment could be "Undiagnosed back pain, uncertain how to proceed", but at least that would be stated clearly. It should be so stated in the notes because it's valuable information.

What if you find a misstatement in your own records, something that you think could mislead anyone who reviews your file? Can you "correct" the notes if you see such an inaccuracy?

No, medical records can't be "corrected" by changing them. No M.D. can ever alter or change his records. But they can be added to. You can discuss your concerns with the doctor, and afterwards he'll probably do an addendum for his chart, noting your concerns.

IT WOULD BE SAFEST TO ALSO WRITE THE DOCTOR A LETTER CLEARLY EXPLAINING THE PROBLEM, because your letter will go in his chart as additional evidence. Save a copy of your letter for yourself, of course--it could be worth its weight in platinum later. Keep it in your Comp files (see Chapter 4).

What if the chart notes don't look very orderly or logical? Well, I have to admit that most doctors probably wouldn't be too happy to have a patient come in and tell him the notes are messy. But if your doctor's notes don't read like you think they should, and don't seem to follow logical formats, you could give him a copy of this chapter. Show him that I'm saying he ought to get his act together and move into the 1990's. Keeping good records is just part of the price of admission to this field. Workers' Comp cases need reliable medical information, and only he can create it.

WRAP-UP

How you can do yourself some favors with your medical records:
1) Never underestimate the importance of having medical records that tell the whole story accurately. You'll never know how much you need them until the end of your claim;
2) Get a copy of your office notes, even if it costs you something. Make sure that they reflect what you told the doctor and what he told you, each visit;
3) Check to see if your doctor SOAPs his notes, or make sure they at least make good sense. Months or years from now when your case is closing, it will be by the records that your case is judged;
4) If your records don't seem adequate, based on the principles in this chapter, show your doctor this chapter or consider looking for another doctor. Perhaps some doctors just aren't willing to put in the time and attention that Workers' Compensation requires.

N

CHAPTER 11

Medications, Physical Therapy And Other Treatment

"Doc, that Codeine you gave me must be no good--out of date or something. It doesn't take the pain away. Can't you prescribe something stronger?"

I find that patients who understand their treatment fully get the best results. For example, a patient who thinks Codeine should "take the pain away" doesn't understand how narcotics work, and he won't be comfortable until he does.

This chapter is a guide to the most common medications and treatments for work injuries, mostly musculoskeletal problems (treatment of occupational illness is covered more fully in special sections E to H.)

TREATMENT SUCCESS

Almost every treatment method in all of medicine follows two fundamental principles:
1) The correct diagnosis must be made. **Then** the correct treatment
   follows;
2) All treatment tries to let the injured part rest while the body's own
   recuperative powers do the healing.

We doctors can prescribe all sorts of pills, exercises and therapies but
the outcome really depends on the patient.

We can give you muscle relaxant pills so muscle spasm doesn't interfere with healing. But the actual healing will be your own body's job. We
can put you at bedrest and use traction for a herniated disc. But your own
spine tissues have to do the healing. We can inject medications to calm
down inflamed tissues. But then it's up to your muscle or tendon or joint
to make the repair. We can prescribe the right exercises for you. But it's
your body that responds with greater elasticity and strength. In every case,
it's the marvel of your own body's healing power that gets you well.

I like to emphasize to my patients that healing from an injury and returning to a normal life isn't something that happens **to** them. It's something they have to actively work for. The greatest asset any physician has
is his patient's desire to recover. I've found that patients who understand
these things heal more quickly, get more out of therapy, and even require
less medication in some cases.

Nevertheless, medications and other treatments each have specific
uses, and used correctly can speed healing considerably.

PAIN MEDICATIONS (ANALGESICS)

Analgesics (pain pills) don't **cure** any injury. But pain medications are
valuable after injury because relief from pain allows a patient to rest and
this helps the injured area heal. Analgesics decrease the pain > spasm >
more pain cycle: With less spasm irritated tissues settle down and this
also helps the healing process.

Codeine is the <u>narcotic</u> pain medication most commonly used for acute injuries. But don't expect it to "wipe out pain", because Codeine doesn't work that way. Here's how it does work: it changes your perception of pain. A couple of hours after you take some Codeine, someone might ask you how you're feeling. You might say, "Terrible--it still hurts something awful!" But they'll ask you something like, "Are you sure? You look pretty comfortable. In fact you've been kind of dozing off." And when you think about it, you'll realize: "My back does still hurt. But I just don't care so much."

This is why narcotics don't take pain away, they just make it so you don't care about the pain much.

Codeine is often combined with Tylenol. Codeine is to be taken every four to six hours as your pain makes it necessary. It can have side effects of constipation and stomach upset. And because Codeine is derived from Opium and Morphine, that good feeling can be addicting. I don't like to prescribe it for more than a couple of weeks or months in most injuries. Talwin is another analgesic, stronger than Codeine with similar effects.

Darvon is different kind of pain medication: A "non-narcotic" analgesic. It isn't nearly as habit-forming as Codeine. Some people find Darvon works well, some think it doesn't help much at all. Some people find it a "Cloud 9" drug and get high on it, but most don't.

Demerol is a powerful narcotic and should not be used for more than a few weeks. After that, some patients will have all sorts of reasons why "Demerol is the only thing that works for me, Doc", but the main reason is often that they're hooked. They like the way they feel with Demerol on board and they want more.

With all these analgesics, it's best to get off them as soon as possible. So I still like the original wonder drug, aspirin. It takes away a lot of pain, cuts down inflammation, it isn't addicting, and it's cheap. But too much aspirin can irritate your stomach and even cause intestinal bleeding, so you always have to swallow it with a full glass of water.

Tylenol is a less irritating alternative to aspirin. Many drugs are mixed with Tylenol and often their name changes: Darvon becomes Darvocet, Talwin becomes Talacen, etc.

ANTI-INFLAMMATORY DRUGS

Dolobid, Feldene, Naprosyn, Voltaren, Orudis, Clinoril, Motrin, and Advil are <u>not</u> pain pills. They're <u>not</u> muscle relaxants. <u>These are antiin-flammatory drugs</u>. They work by decreasing inflammation in injured tissues, muscles or joints.

> *"I don't want pills, Doc. All they do is cover things up. They don't treat the problem."*
> *This is a patient who had gotten bad advice from a well-meaning chiropractor. But I told him: "Some pills <u>do</u> treat the problem--these will cut down the inflammation." After I explained how they work, he took them. He got better.*

We prescribe these anti-inflammatories for bursitis, back or neck pain, muscle injuries, joint pain and arthritis, bone bruises and so on. Many times one of them will work when another does not, so do not give up if one or two don't help you. Ask your doctor if trying a third one is reasonable.

Because inflammation is painful and these pills attack it, they do function a bit as pain relievers. But they relieve the pain more by treating the problem than by changing your perception of pain as narcotics do. The original antiinflammatory drug was Cortisone, a steroid drug. The others are <u>not</u> steroids and they have different mechanisms of action. Therefore they're called "nonsteroidal" antiinflammatories or NSAI's.

> *"I was on that pill, Motrin I think it was. It helped my shoulder, but it sure bothered my stomach!*

NSAI's can have side effects of stomach irritation, so you have to take most of them with a full meal. You should not take these medications if you have ulcers. There usually are no other common side effects from NSAI's, though when I have a patient on them for a long time, I draw blood every three months to make sure he doesn't develop problems with his blood count or liver functions. It's rare but it can happen.

It is best to get off antiinflammatories as soon as possible, though you can take them for many months. I have had some patients on them for months or even a couple of years because they work so well. But while you're on NSAI's, make sure you take them exactly as your doctor prescribes. Patients that only take them once in a while when they hurt aren't getting much benefit because they don't keep up the blood levels of the medications.

MUSCLE RELAXANTS

When you have muscle spasm, your doctor will probably prescribe muscle relaxants. Typical muscle relaxants are Robaxin, Flexeril, Parafon Forte, and Norgesic. We use these to "soften up" injured and painful muscles. They reduce spasm so the muscles can heal.

Muscle relaxants are **not** pain pills. When you're taking some of these, you could feel drowsy or lazy (though most people don't react that way) and some might give you a dry mouth. These medications are not addicting.

Valium was and occasionally still is prescribed as a muscle relaxant. But it's really a tranquilizer. It is definitely habituating. In addition, many tranquilizers can destroy your ability to get deep healing sleep at night, and it takes several weeks for that effect to fade. I almost never prescribe Valium for muscle relaxation. I do occasionally give a patient three or four pills if he is too claustrophobic to go into a CT or MRI scanner.

Triavil can work as a muscle relaxant, but it's also an antidepressant. I often prescribe it for patients with chronic neck or back pain due to muscle spasm, and it works pretty well. But it does cause a dry mouth and/or a hangover-like sensation in the mornings, and many patients don't like Triavil for that reason.

MEDICATIONS FOR OCCUPATIONAL ILLNESSES

I will only briefly mention treatment of some occupational diseases here, because their treatment is covered in their respective sections.

For occupational skin problems and allergies dermatologists usually prescribe skin creams, lotions and ointments. These mostly contain some form of steroid to reduce the inflammatory skin reaction. Typical names are Topicort, TAC, Lidex, and Kenalog but there are probably a hundred more. They generally have few dangerous side effects but it is best to ask the dermatologist it if the medications could cause redness or other skin sensitivity.

For occupational lung injuries, the most useful medications are generally going to be bronchodilators to open up air passages. These might be Theo-Dur, Theolair, Theophylline, or Slo-Phyllin in pill form. Your doctor might also prescribe mists or inhaler sprays with names like Ventolin or Bronkometer. These can often cause a speedy or "hyper" feeling, often with a rapid heartbeat--as if you drank too much coffee. If you're bothered by this, ask your doctor to check and adjust the dosage.

You might also be given antibiotics if you have a simultaneous lung infection, but antibiotics are far too numerous to list here. If you have severe lung disease, you might be started on steroids to cut down the inflammatory reaction. Medications such as Cortisone, Prednisone, Medrol and others are typical. These can have side effects of mood swings and fluid retention. But over the short term (a few weeks) they should cause no serious side effects.

PHYSICAL THERAPY TREATMENTS

Many patients with musculoskeletal injuries need physical therapy. Your doctor might order therapy in the form of heat and massage for a neck or back injury, range of motion stretching for a muscle or joint injury, or perhaps instruction to build physical fitness.

> *"I want you to have hotpacks and traction for your low back, combined with some low back motion exercises. I'll write an order for daily treatments for the next three weeks, then we'll see how you're doing."* This was how I introduced a patient to the PT stage of treatment for her low back problem. But she seemed worried.
> She asked: *"Do I have to go into the hospital for the traction, Doctor? I don't think I can arrange that."*
> Fortunately going into the hospital as an inpatient isn't usually necessary. *"No, not at all. You'll just go every day to the outpatient therapy department at the hospital. Since you only live 10 minutes away it should be OK for you to make the drive."*

Physical therapy departments have traditionally been attached to hospitals but now in some states many are freestanding clinics. For PT treatments, the patient simply goes to the PT department, spends an hour or

two getting treatment, and then goes home. Registered Physical Therapists are generally very well trained to provide treatments to strained
muscles, ligaments, and injured and inflamed joints and in doing manual
muscle testing.

Doctors order physical therapy for both acute and chronic injuries. For
example, I might prescribe a short two-week course of daily ice packs, massage and gentle range of motion treatments for an acutely sprained hip or
thigh muscle, or similar treatment for a simple low back strain. I would
expect such injuries to be resolved by the end of that treatment period.

Or I might prescribe several weeks or even a couple of months of pas-
sive range of motion and then gentle physical exercise motion to start
freeing up a chronic frozen shoulder problem--something that's been
around for six months and is going to take a long time to resolve.

Does PT speed up healing? In general, I do find that many injuries
heal more quickly when I use PT. These are the severe strains of arms or
legs, some low back strains, most shoulder injuries, and knee strains. PT
also helps to get people moving safely after an operation, especially helpful with back, shoulder, knee and wrist operations.

As to whether PT actually shortens the healing time overall, I've
found that with many injuries the main value of PT is to keep a patient
regular in his exercises, to have him stretching the right amount, and to
keep him focused on the healing process. Obviously no patient can give
himself a back massage. But if a patient is completely motivated and able
to do all his exercises and other therapies correctly at home on a regular basis, he wouldn't need to go to therapy at all except for instructions,
and he'd probably recover just as soon.

Concerns About Therapy

With independent therapy clinics springing up all over, and physical
therapists starting to do manipulation like chiropractors (though they call
it manual medicine to distinguish it), I've seen therapists telling patients
the only reason to see a medical doctor is for surgery. Some of them will
either imply or tell you straight out that they don't need M.D.'s and neither do you, that they can diagnose and treat you just fine on their own.
Many people in Comp regard this as an unfortunate trend.

A high official in a state medical association in the Southwest told me: "You should see what the PT's in our state are doing. They do tests and procedures they were never trained to do, and I think they're starting to get unsuspecting patients into difficulties."

I know one doctor who puts it more bluntly: "PT's are getting dangerous. Now they treat without doctors' orders, but that's a gift they haven't earned. Even when I write specific instructions they alter them, and my patients are coming back with all sorts of oddball ideas about their injuries."

He went on: "Therapists are certainly smart enough to get into medical school and if they want to play doctor they should go. Then they'd learn more than PT--they'd go through medical school anatomy, pathology, biochemistry, physiology, pharmacology, medicine, surgery, and all the subspecialty training. But until they do that they don't have the training to diagnose and treat patients."

Of course there are two sides to this argument. There are doctors who say: "I just send my patients to therapists for treatment. I don't understand PT so I let them do the deciding for me. I don't have the time."

What should you do? I may be old-fashioned, but I've always found treatment most successful when I decide what therapy my patients need and modify it as I watch them respond. If you feel comfortable letting your own doctor give up this decision-making responsibility to let a therapist decide your treatment, it's up to you. I've seen therapists follow my treatment plans and help patients a lot. But I've also seen them exceed, change, and ignore my instructions and in those cases most of the time the patients don't get as good results.

Heat, Ice, Massage, Ultrasound

With most musculoskeletal injuries, I send patients to therapy to have various temperature or massage treatments on a daily basis. Typical PT modalities include heat, either in the form of hotpacks, infrared lamps called diathermy, melted paraffin baths, or ultrasound. There are also ice packs or ice massage for cold therapy, and alternating ice and hot soaks.

Ice and massage will relieve spasm and muscle pain and help to get a painful muscle moving. Then after a few days, hotpacks will start to do the same. Heat is also good for many joint pains. Massage in combination with temperature will help move old stagnant fluid out of injured muscles and tissues and get the circulation flowing. All this promotes healing, and it generally feels good, too.

I may recommend <u>ultrasound</u> in addition to massage. With this modality the therapist will run an ultrasound machine over your skin, causing ultrasonic waves to concentrate a few centimeters under the skin surface. It produces a kind of internal deep heat that surface hotpacks can't achieve. But this is safest only every other day, and ultrasound should never be used over a joint or a nerve. If you ever have pain during an ultrasound treatment, tell the therapist to stop. Talk to your doctor and change to a different type of treatment.

For some patients with acute low back injuries, I may prescribe the <u>Hubbard Tank</u>. This is a large whirlpool bath, about the size of a small pool. Patients float in the tank on a stretcher if they have too much discomfort to move around. In fact, we often hoist them into the pool with a small overhead crane so that they don't have to climb over the sides. I use this for once or twice a day therapy, particularly when I hospitalize patients with back problems. Virtually everyone finds it pleasant to float in the warm tank with whirlpool jets bubbling around them on all sides and it helps loosen them up.

I may also prescribe <u>muscle stimulation</u>. This is a type of electrical massage done with a tiny electrical current placed on your skin by a small metal pad or a pencil-like device. These treatments make a muscle contract rapidly, acting sort of like deep massage to move fluid in and out of the tissues. Muscle stimulation is helpful in treating strains and some sprains.

TRACTION

I usually include <u>traction</u> when I treat a simple cervical or lumbar disc herniation. Traction is another physical therapy procedure. It means a stretching in a lengthwise direction, usually of the spine. The theory behind traction is as follows: If pressure on the spine has caused a disc to bulge or rupture, then stretching the spine may reduce the pressure and treat the problem.

Traction can be manual or mechanical: Done with either a gentle pull by hand or by a traction machine which exerts a steady or intermittent pull at a certain force. Pelvic (low back) traction is done while the patient lies either face down or face up on a traction table. The force is provided by an intermittent mechanical pull.

Cervical (neck) traction can be performed by the therapist's own hand strength or by a machine. For home use, over-the-door traction units are available. With these you sit with your back to a door, your head in a harness, and an adjustable weight over a pulley at the top of the door.

Traction treatments are usually 15 to 20 minutes. Sometimes traction helps, but sometimes it doesn't. If it seems to help at first, then I'll pre-scribe it daily for three to six weeks or until there's no further improve-ment. If it hurts, I stop it. Some doctors might tell you that traction's old fashioned, but I still find it useful in many spine problems.

Exercise Therapy

The old days of putting people to bed or telling them not to move for weeks after an injury are long gone. Most physicians recognize the value of muscle motion after an injury.

Yes, it's true that we have to cast a fracture and keep it motionless un-til it heals, that we splint a muscle sprain or tendon inflammation while it settles down, and we often immobilize muscle or joint injuries. And we usually use a low back corset or brace to keep a patient's low back rigid to prevent re-straining it. Cervical collars are used for the same reason. These all go along with the fundamental treatment for all problems, which is to prescribe rest.

But muscle inactivity is the worst thing for a patient if it's prolonged. A patient put to bed for two weeks loses 20% of his body strength. His en-durance drops even more quickly. You know yourself that if you lie around for several days you'll get stiff, your muscles will ache and every little movement will start to bother you.

Jeffrey Saal, M.D., is a physiatrist and noted rehabilitation specialist in San Francisco. Dr. Saal has emphasized the role of exercise in treatment of injuries. He has said: "We need to treat our Workers' Compensation patients as if they're injured athletes". In other words, we can't turn them into inactive couch potatoes just because they were hurt.

There are two types of "exercise" treatment: specific range of motion for stretching of an injured part, and then general physical fitness exercise. I try to have my patients doing both of these from the very beginning.

Typical early treatment is a gentle stretching motion (range of motion) of the injured part as soon as you can easily tolerate it and it's safe. This will probably start with <u>passive</u> range of motion, where a physical therapist actually moves your healing arm, shoulder or leg for you through whatever motion is easy and within limits of comfort.

Then the stretching will progress through <u>assisted</u> range of motion, and eventually up to <u>active</u> motion. The value of these range of motion treatments is to decrease stiffness and get joints or muscles moving fluidly.

The next step is to begin building up the injured muscles by vigorous <u>physical fitness and conditioning exercise</u> to get your whole body tuned up and back in shape. I recommend swimming and walking, and then more heavy workouts--sometimes with weights and exercise equipment (see Chapter 16).

TENS

Some chronic muscle pain continues despite treatment. This is particularly true in the back or neck, with the myofascial pain syndrome I describe in section D, chronic pain from a compression fracture in the mid or low back, and with sacroiliac pain, joint pain and disc disease.

For these problems, I'll often order a trial of <u>TENS</u>. TENS stands for transcutaneous electronic nerve stimulation. A TENS unit is a small electronic box that you wear on your belt or in your pocket. You attach little wires from the box to the painful area with a stickum pad.

The TENS machine sends a tiny trickle of current into the painful area and "confuses" the local nerves. In about 40% of patients, this relieves the discomfort. You can wear a TENS an hour on and an hour off, or several hours at a time, though some people become allergic to the pads.

TENS does not really cure anything, but simply helps you tolerate the discomfort of an underlying injury and lets you get on more with your life. I think TENS units are great, and so do hundreds of patients. If TENS helps you, it certainly is a benefit. If not, you only lose about an hour of time to try it.

INJECTIONS

Some patients with long-lasting muscle spasm may have <u>trigger points</u>. A trigger point is a very tender small dot of pain in a painful muscle group. These often cause muscle spasm and pain over a larger area. Trigger points are particularly common in the upper back and shoulder girdle, but also frequently occur in the low back.

I've found that trigger point injections can often eliminate spasm and relieve muscle pain. If your doctor does an injection, he may use simple saline solution. He may use Novocain (just like the Novocain the dentist uses) alone, or mix Cortisone for an antiinflammation effect with the Novocain for the anesthetic effect. I find this combination works best most of the time, and often the trigger points don't return.

Injections also work well for many joint, ligament, or tendon problems. For example, a Cortisone and Novocain injection can relieve the pain of shoulder bursitis, tennis elbow, forearm tendinitis, a knee strain, and even some specific low back sprains. I often prescribe injections for sacroiliac joint and facet joint problems. The injections usually settle the inflammation down and allow the joint injury to heal.

When you have an injection, the Novocain initially stings but then numbs the area quickly and lasts for several hours. There may be a minor flare-up of discomfort in the area later the same day, a local icepack usually helps this.

Over the next several days the long-acting steroid takes effect, though you may have to wait up to two weeks for the full effect. With most trigger points and joint injections, you can expect your symptoms to usually be much improved within a few days.

"You want to put a needle in my elbow? With Cortisone in it? No way! That stuff's dangerous! I've heard you can't have more than one of those shots in your whole lifetime."

Patients are often concerned about a steroid injection because they've heard of steroid side effects. But in the tiny doses used for injections, this is not a concern. Injections can be repeated, but I recommend several weeks or even months between injections, just to avoid any difficulty.

Doctors do have to use caution with tendon or ligament injections. If these are done incorrectly or too frequently they <u>can</u> produce softening of tendon tissue, poor healing or even tendon degeneration. This is probably where the concern arose that injections should not be done too often.

BIOFEEDBACK THERAPY

If patients with chronic pain can learn to relax tense muscles, their pain will often diminish considerably and they can function better in their daily life. I often prescribe biofeedback therapy in such cases.

If you have biofeedback therapy treatment, the biofeedback therapist will hook you up to a computer monitor with small sensors placed on your skin over the tight muscles. You will be able to watch a computer screen, or listen to a tone, to monitor the tension in your muscles.

The biofeedback therapist will then teach you how to relax these muscles. Afterwards you'll practice the method on your own with the computer as a guide. Then at home you will continue the practice, often using audio tapes to remind you how to relax the muscle. Muscle biofeedback can be used as long as you have the underlying problem. There are no dangerous side effects of this type of muscle feedback.

OCCUPATIONAL THERAPY: O.T.

Patients with severe hand or arm injuries often require special care known as Occupational Therapy.

I saw a machinist whose left hand was crushed between a forklift and a wall, with three finger fractures and a wrist injury. After surgery *and casting, he had a very stiff hand and couldn't do his work. Unfortunately, he was a <u>left-handed</u> machinist.*

OT's can teach a patient with an injury such as this how to use the non-dominant hand for eating, toothbrushing, shaving, working and even writing. OT's will put a patient like this through hand, wrist, and finger exercises to increase specific flexibility. They can even make special splints to increase range of motion and teach specific dexterity techniques-- for example for fine manipulation at work tasks.

In some severe injuries, the OT department will manufacture or buy special adaptive devices for the patient. These will help him carry out out activities of daily living: For example, they may make a spoon, fork, or pen or screwdriver with a large fat grip that fits over the thumb or in the palm, to compensate for fingers that don't function well.

If you have a serious hand injury you will very likely benefit from the expertise of a good OT department. These are usually highly skilled individuals, and their whole lives are dedicated to making life easier for the patients.

QUESTIONS AND ANSWERS ABOUT TREATMENT

Q. "Do I have to take medications if I don't want to?"
A. It's a free country and you cannot be compelled to. But if they are the recommended treatment, you had better have a valid reason to refuse. Discuss it with your doctor--perhaps an alternative can be found.

Q. "The insurer has paid every bill but therapy. What's wrong?"
A. Ask them. Your doctor may have failed to write in his notes why he ordered it, or even that he did order it. If so, the insurer may not pay. Or, they may feel that the bill in question was for a non-work problem.

KNOWING WHEN TO STOP

What if you've gone through what you think is everything and you're still having trouble? Then it's time to sit down with your doctor and take stock.

Did you have a short period of bedrest, but not too long?   Have you been on at least two different antiinflammatories and muscle relaxants? Have you had heat and cold?   Have you had a corset or collar, PT for massage and traction, good range of motion and vigorous exercise fitness programs?   Was a TENS or biofeedback tried?   Has your doctor checked for other unsuspected problems, such as diabetes, gout, infections, or arthritis?   Has surgery been considered (see Chapter 13)?   Have you kept yourself generally healthy, lost weight, and stayed as active as you can?   (See Chapters 16 and 18).   Have all of the studies including X-rays and MRI's been done?   (See Chapter 8).

Sometimes all of these things have been tried, and a patient still isn't better.   Particularly with back and neck and some joint problems, sometimes a doctor has to gently let a patient know that there isn't anything else to do for the problem at least for now.   Whenever I have to tell a patient this my heart goes out to them.   But for many injuries we simply don't have all the answers yet.   Sometimes the biggest favor is to simply let a patient know this and let him get on with his life, pain or not (see Chapter 19).

However, this is only appropriate if it's really true that all possible treatment approaches have been exhausted.   Don't settle for less.

WRAP-UP

How to do yourself some favors with treatment:
1) Take your pills as prescribed, only for the purposes prescribed.   Learn what they do.   If you have any unusual or unpleasant side effects let your doctor know right away;
2) Ask your doctor to decide which physical therapy treatments you need;
3) Exercise as prescribed, as often as prescribed, for the reasons prescribed;
4) Give TENS, injections, and biofeedback a try if your doctor recommends them;
5) Take advantage of the specialized programs in an OT department if you have a hand injury or hand surgery.
6) Remember that treatment is a "tool", not a way of life.   Do your part, get as much out of it as possible, and then get on with things.

K

CHAPTER 12

Second Opinions
And Consultations

A woman with back pain says: "My doctor sent me here for consultation. He is wondering if you can recommend some more treatment that will help me improve faster."

* * *

A young fireman calls and tells my receptionist: "I've been seeing a doctor for three months, but I'm no different. When I ask him how I can get better all he does is give me pills and look to the sky for guidance. I want a second opinion."

If your Comp injury has any complexity at all, it's likely you'll see a doctor for a consultation or second opinion at least once. These evaluations can have a big effect on your case. They can change the course of your treatment, determine whether or not you have surgery, when or if you return to work, etc.

You can do several things to get the most from a consultation or second opinion. This chapter shows you how to prepare for these exams, how to give the consulting doctor the best information, and what to look for in the results.

Consultation: A Request For Assistance

Usually the reason for a consultation is fairly straightforward: Your own physician asks another physician, usually in a __different__ specialty, for advice. The purpose is to advance the understanding of your case, to modify the diagnosis, to suggest other treatment, etc. In other words, if your doctor decides that two heads might be better than one, he will arrange for a consultation.

A general practitioner might ask for an orthopedic consultation if a knee injury doesn't improve. A treating doctor might ask a neurosurgeon for consultation on a low back disc injury, or a dermatologist for advice on an occupational skin injury.

A family practitioner might request consultation from a neurologist on how to treat a complex nerve injury: "What can I do to help my patient recover arm strength?" An internist might ask a pulmonary specialist for assistance with diagnosis: "Is toxic inhalational exposure the correct diagnosis"?

How To Get The Best Consultation

There are several ways you can insure that you get the most benefits from a consultation. Some are simple common sense: First make sure your consultation is with a __doctor who likes to see your kind of problem__. You wouldn't want to get your hopes up that a consulting surgeon will help your knee problem if it turns out his expertise is mainly in shoulder and hand reconstructive surgery. You wouldn't want to see a consultant about your back injury if he doesn't enjoy treating back problems--and many doctors don't.

To find out if your problem is in the doctor's field of interest and expertise, simply call his secretary and ask. A good doctor's staff will almost always be able to tell you clearly where his specialized interests lie.

It's best to get to the appointment in plenty of time. This insures that you're not late and if you can sit for a few minutes to collect your thoughts you'll be more able to describe your problem clearly to the doctor.

I'd also recommend that you fill out your own forms in the doctor's office. I often see a man in my waiting room reading People Magazine or

Cycle World while his wife fills out the medical history or questionnaire. He lets her write down where he hurts, how long it's lasted, and so on and I wonder who's really going to be examined.

When you see the doctor, give your history clearly and accurately. Follow the guidelines in Chapter 7.

When you go for a consultation I recommend you carry with you all of your X-rays, scans, or lab results and give them to the doctor. Many times these critical items get lost in the mail and their absence really handicaps a consulting doctor. I would also recommend you hand-carry a summary letter and/or chart notes from your own doctor. Not all doctors will write such a summary letter (I have found that less than one in four do) but at least the records will be most helpful to the consulting doctor.

CAUTION: Don't expect that the consulting doctor will understand your whole history from glancing through the records. Be prepared to tell your history in your own words and in chronologic order. I've found that no matter how thorough chart notes might be, I always get a better feel for a problem when the patient tells me his history himself.

Use A Medical Timeline

One of the most valuable tools you can use to get a better consultation is a medical timeline. For even the simplest problem, I recommend you take a few minutes to literally draw out your history as in the examples on this page and next. Take your drawing with you and show it to the doctor. It can be as simple or as detailed as you want to make it.

This is a timeline for a simple, relatively uncomplicated low back injury:

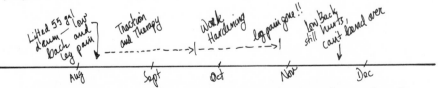

The next timeline is slightly more complicated; it shows that the patient had some improvement, then got worse and still has symptoms. It shows that he has had several different types of treatment, and makes it

clear that the treatment has not been successful yet. It shows clearly why
he needs the consultation:

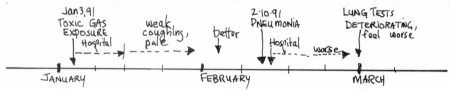

This timeline is for a different problem, even more complicated. The
patient eventually had surgery, but then had a re-injury with more and
different symptoms:

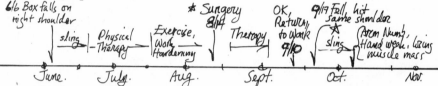

A timeline can save you and the consulting doctor a great deal of time.
Any doctor who's facing a tough evaluation will really appreciate having
information presented to him this clearly.

One thing I want to mention about writing down your history: Doctors have always looked a little askance at patients who come in with long
written lists of their symptoms and then recite them. There is even a
name for this, "la maladie du petit papiere" (the illness of the little paper).
Doctors consider such patients neurotic, thinking that the symptoms must
not be significant if the patient needs a paper to remember them. I've seen
people like this myself.

<u>But this does not apply to timelines</u> as I've shown them here. Such
timelines are plain and simple aids to give a doctor a handle on a complex
history. Presenting a timeline could be one of the most helpful things that
you can do, especially if your problem is complex.

To help you get a good consultation, I'd recommend that you confine
what you tell the doctor to the medical facts only. He's not a lawyer and
he's not really going to make it his business to find out who might have
done what wrong, who might have been at fault, or where the blame for
the injury lies. It's not appropriate for you to tell him something such as:
"The equipment was defective and I have three witnesses" or "The foreman wouldn't observe good safety practices". You simply need to tell him
what happened to you and how you feel.

Finally, consultations are often lengthy and you may get uncomfortable during a long time of sitting during the interview. If so, just stand up or ask to take a break, and tell the doctor why. It's a good idea to tell the consulting doctor what has made you uncomfortable--this can be helpful information for him.

THE CONSULTATION REPORT

At the completion of a consultation evaluation, ask the consulting doctor for his conclusions. Ask his diagnosis, suggestions for treatment, and prognosis. There is no reason to be shy about asking. You deserve to hear the answers. After all the consultation was requested by your doctor for your benefit.

The consulting doctor will also be putting his conclusions in a report. Just as with his verbal discussion with you, this report should provide clear direction for you and your doctor, if a clear conclusion is at all possible. Consultation reports that simply list diagnoses won't really advance your care much. The reason for a consultation is usually to get advice on what to do next, and if the visit doesn't provide that it has been a waste of time.

In reviewing consultations and doing them myself, I've found that the most successful ones are those that take all the available data into account, make firm recommendations when firm recommendations can be made, try to move the patient's case forward, and end by giving the patient some helpful information about his problem.

This means I tend to judge the quality of a consultation by how comprehensive the doctor's report is. A thorough and well-written report shows me what information the doctor reviewed and why he made the conclusions he did. On the other hand, a report doesn't carry much weight with me if the consulting doctor only writes a one-paragraph summary of a complex history, doesn't review records, and his exam is only three lines long.

You can get a copy of the consultation report by following the instructions in Chapter 10, You and Your Medical Records.

SECOND OPINIONS

A second opinion is considerably different from a consultation for several reasons. First of all, your doctor probably won't be the one asking for it. You or your rehab consultant or perhaps the insurer will request it. In fact, second opinions are often requested because patient or insurer or both are not satisfied with the progress of the case and want another doctor's opinion, perhaps even to consider changing physicians later.

A second difference is that a second opinion usually is to answer one specific question or to confirm whether your doctor has made the right recommendation.

> The "classic" second opinion is to answer the question, "Should this patient have surgery or not?" But I've also done second opinions when a patient just wanted the evaluation to confirm that his own doctor was on the right track. I once did a second opinion on a patient whose doctor had kept her off work six months and wouldn't commit himself as to how long she'd be off or if he'd let her even try light duty--ever! The insurer's question to me was simple: "What treatment is needed and what is the prognosis?"

Another difference between second opinions and consultations is that the doctor who does the second opinion will usually be in the <u>same specialty</u> as the doctor already treating you. This is because the evaluation's purpose is to either confirm that your doctor's treatment is correct, or reject it and suggest an alternative. This kind of evaluation will naturally be done by a doctor with similar professional training.

Other requests for second opinions might be from an employer who wonders if an injured worker will be able to do his old job when he returns, from a patient who doesn't think his doctor is listening to him, or from a patient who has been told he needs surgery but is frightened of it.

> One fascinating case where a second opinion was obviously needed was a refinery worker whose job required him to go up and down stairs all day, crouch and kneel, walk on slippery or wet surfaces, and climb 150 foot ladders up the side of towers. He had been off work two years, he'd had four knee operations and his doctor wrote a letter that he would <u>never return</u> to work.
> Then four months later the doctor wrote another note releasing him to work! At <u>full duty</u> with no restrictions at all! The employer took one look at the slip and requested a second opinion, asking: "Which of the

surgeon's recommendations should we listen to? What's different now that made him change his mind totally?"

Sometimes second opinions are needed when the patient's care is so fragmented that everyone needs the evaluation just to make some sense out of it. This was the case with Louie Barton, who worked in a mine pit.

Louie had a shoulder injury. His doctor took him off work and gave him pills, while the plant doctor recommended a shoulder sling and light duty. Then a specialist saw Louie and found the real problem, but his recommendation for surgery apparently was ignored or lost and he unfortunately didn't tell Louie his conclusions.

A year later the insurer obtained an independent medical examination but didn't send all the records or films to the IME doctor, so his report was incomplete. Finally Louie exercised his right to a second opinion, and I spent several tedious hours gathering all the information into one place. Once the history and symptoms were put together with the examination and the MRI, it was obvious that Louie still needed shoulder surgery. He went on to have it and he improved.

How To Get The Most From A Second Opinion

When you go for a second opinion you can get the most out of it if you follow all the suggestions I've given above for consultations: Be on time, fill out your own forms, give an accurate history (see Chapter 7), carry your X-rays and a summary letter or chart notes from your doctor (see above), etc.

Use the medical timeline I described earlier in this chapter. This is probably the single most valuable thing you can do when seeing any new doctor. Any doctor who tries to do a second opinion on a complex case will appreciate it immensely.

After any second opinion, ask the doctor what his conclusions are and what he recommends. You should expect a second opinion doctor to explain his conclusions to you. If he doesn't, don't hesitate to ask him.

The doctor will also usually write a report to the person who requested the second opinion, and it's customary for him to send a copy to your own doctor. Just as with consultations, a second opinion report should make it clear that the doctor evaluated all the information, did a thorough exam, and gave clear answers to the questions asked.

You can get a copy of the doctor's report by following the instructions in Chapter 10, just as with any other medical records. Evaluate the report just as I've already described for a consultation.

QUESTIONS I'M ASKED

Q: "What if my doctor sends me for a consultation? Will the Workers' Compensation insurance company pay for the visit and any testing he does?"

A: Yes. They should pay for both--as long as the evaluation is for the work injury or illness that they're already covering.

Q: "What if a consulting doctor wants to take X-rays? Do I have to let him take them?"

A: Not really, but if he wants them it's probably because they will help him make his opinion and that's what is important. If you've had recent X-rays and want to avoid more, bring the recent ones with you.

Q. "Will the second opinion or consulting doctor send a report to my doctor?"

A: Yes.

Q: "Can I get a copy of his report?"

A: Yes. Follow instructions in Chapter 10.

Q: "I don't think the doctor's consultation report was accurate. What do I do now?"

A: If the doctor got the history or facts wrong, follow the advice in Chapter 10 to correct them.

Q: "When my doctor sends me for a consultation, will I go back to my own doctor for treatment?"

A: Yes, unless he arranges otherwise. A consultation is just a one-time visit. Surgical consultations may be different if they lead to surgery, but this will be up to you and your doctor. (But don't forget, if a consulting doctor recommends surgery, you may then be required to get a second surgical opinion.)

A consultation is not just a referral for treatment. If your doctor refers you out to another doctor for treatment, he's more or less ending his care of you and sending you on to someone else.

Q: "Should I follow the advice of the second opinion doctor?"

A: If his reputation is good, if you had a good feeling about the visit, if you believe he did a thorough evaluation and had all the facts, then take his advice. Suppose the doctor says to you: "If you were my own mother or father I'd recommend this treatment, for this long, because I would expect this result". That's about the highest recommendation a doctor can give.

Q: "Can I transfer my care to the doctor I got a second opinion from?"

A: The ethical and courteous practice is that a second opinion doctor gives his opinion and sends a report to your own doctor, with whom you keep treating. In reality, changes of physician do happen but in most states you have to get permission from the insurer and you certainly ought to discuss it with your own doctor first.

Q: "I've been told that I have to go for an IME. Is that the same as a second opinion?"

A: No. An IME (Independent Medical Examination) is a special examination, usually set up by attorneys or insurers, and it has special rules: See Chapter 21.

WRAP-UP

How to do yourself some favors with consultations and second opinions:
1) Have a clear idea why you are going for the evaluation: At your doctor's request for assistance, at someone else's request (even your own), or to confirm the correctness of your own doctor's recommendations;
2) Hand-carry your X-rays, scans, lab tests, and records and give them to the consulting doctor;
3) Draw a medical timeline and bring it with you, give your history accurately and chronologically;
4) Ask the doctor to tell you his conclusions and recommendations.

M

CHAPTER 13

How To Decide About Surgery

"I saw a surgeon last week, but I didn't like what he said."

This man needs an operation to resolve his injury, but nothing has prepared him to face the idea of surgery. He's obviously frightened. "What did the surgeon tell you?" I ask him.

"Pretty much what you've just said, that I need the operation. But I'd still like to think it over. He didn't really guarantee me it would help, and I'm not sure I feel good about him being the one to do it anyway. How does a guy decide about this stuff?"

Patients have asked me so frequently about surgery that it became clear this book needed a chapter to help them wrestle with the question: "Should I have surgery or not?"

Injured workers facing an operation most often have back, neck, shoulder or knee injuries. But there are also wrist, elbow, ankle and foot injuries for which surgery is a possibility. A patient with these problems needs to know how to gauge whether he is truly a surgical candidate or not.

If you're having difficulty making up your mind whether or not to have surgery, deciding on a surgeon, or both, this chapter tells you how to proceed, how to locate and choose a surgeon, and how to prepare for the operation.

SOMETIMES THE DECISION IS OBVIOUS

Whether or not to have surgery is hardly a question with some injuries: Spinal cord injuries, severed arteries, severed digits or limbs, tendon lacerations, internal injuries or bleeding, certain skull fractures, severe fractures, etc. These will always require immediate emergency surgery as mandatory treatment to save life or limb.

If you have had one of these injuries then surgery was without question the correct treatment and it was probably performed long before you're reading this chapter. The choice was made for you by the nature of your injury. These problems are not the subject of this chapter. This chapter is about surgery for elective repair of less urgent injuries or other specific conditions.

ELECTIVE SURGERY: TRY CONSERVATIVE CARE FIRST

Suppose you have had a work injury, you have gone through initial care, now your doctor or someone else has told you that you should have an operation. What do you do next?

The first thing is to look at whether surgery is <u>at this time</u> the best approach for your injury. In other words, you need to determine if there are alternatives that you should try first.

Many injuries are in fact appropriate for "elective" surgery. Elective means the operation is voluntary, not mandatory, and scheduled at convenience. This is the opposite of the emergency situations I mentioned above where surgery is obligatory.

What kind of injuries could require elective surgery? Recurrent shoulder dislocations, carpal tunnel syndrome, knee injuries, some disc herniations, etc. are the most common ones. (The next section below gives a longer list that may include your specific injury.)

For these injuries, most doctors who treat Workers' Compensation problems will advise you that you should only consider an operation when conservative care has failed to resolve the problem.

This means that you should give exercises, medications, physical therapy, the simple passage of time and your body's own healing processes a chance. If after a reasonable trial of these you still cannot resume your normal life or consider returning to work, then the next step is to consider surgical intervention for your problem.

WHAT CAN SURGERY FIX?

There are several common injuries for which conservative care usually is not enough. Surgery can produce good resolution in many of these. Here is a partial list:
* Repeated shoulder dislocations, after a sling and shoulder exercises produce no improvement;
* Shoulder pain with inability to raise your arm despite exercise and medications and the passage of time;
* A fracture (such as the wrist navicular) that hasn't healed despite casting and several months of observation, assuming it interferes with your work;
* Carpal tunnel syndrome with numbness, tingling and inability to use your hand after night splints, medications, and injections have been tried;
* Severe knee pain, with locking and giving way despite injections, splint or brace, straight leg and quad exercises, assuming plain X-rays and MRI and thorough examinations have established a specific diagnosis;
* Tennis elbow if one year of treatment, immobilization, at least two injections, paraffin baths, and a tennis elbow band haven't helped;
* Ankle fracture with instability for a year or more and pain when you walk despite trials of a brace, extensive exercise, a special support shoe, injections and medications;
* Continued, severe, impossible-to-live-with radicular arm pain from a definite cervical disc after a full course of exercises, exercises and more exercises, posture training, biofeedback, medications and selective injections have not helped;

*   Continued sciatica from a lumbar disc that makes it absolutely impossible to live a normal life, constant leg pain, leg weakness, loss of sensation, definite diagnosis of the pain source, and after posture and body mechanics training, a full course of exercises and stabilization training, medications, traction, a back corset or brace and passage of time have not helped. (This applies unless you are losing control of bowel or bladder function--which may mean you need surgery urgently);
*   Low back instability from spondylolisthesis that is relieved by a corset, and after a full course of exercises, body mechanics training, weight loss, etc., and you understand exactly what the surgeon is going to fuse;
*   Dozens of other problems could be added to this list but are less common. For example, a wrist or finger fracture may need to be fused, a knee or ankle may need to be fused, an ankle or toe may need to be pinned, or a spur in a shoulder joint may need to be removed. These are all elective operations, performed after exercises and/or splints and other treatments have not helped.

Even though I can't describe all the elective operations possible, the general idea is that when there is no urgent need to operate you <u>always</u> try the non-surgical treatment first and give your body a chance to heal on its own.

The reason is that surgery doesn't "make you better". Some patients think surgery is some kind of a cure-all, kind of like changing a fuse or putting in new valves or rings. They assume that after surgery they'll be "good as new again".

But unfortunately it doesn't work this way. A post-op patient is <u>not</u> "good as new" again. Surgery merely removes an impediment to healing. Surgeons enter the body with a scalpel and amputate diseased, injured, broken, or degenerated tissue. It's still up to the body to heal from the operation as well as the injury. Surgery merely corrects the abnormality that prevented healing. This is why doctors consider surgery only the last resort in so many injuries.

So it's ironic, but you'll still have to go through conservative care after surgery to recover normal function. This will probably mean exercise, stretching to overcome stiffness, medications to decrease inflammation, rest, physical therapy, and the passage of time. It'll still be up to your own body's healing processes to recover.

How To Choose Your Surgeon

Suppose it's been determined that surgery could help your problem. What next? Find a surgeon you trust and have confidence in.

Patients ask me all the time: "How should I pick a surgeon?" I tell them exactly this: Before you get put to sleep for an operation you must feel completely comfortable with the surgeon you choose. You should feel that he has explained things to you and that you understand them. You should feel your surgeon is totally trustworthy and that he's given you direct and full answers to all the questions you've asked.

I tell them that if they have some little reservation deep inside that "maybe this surgeon isn't right," then I'll be happy to send them elsewhere. After all, a patient will be going to sleep under the surgeon's knife, trusting in his knowledge. There is no greater risk than a surgical patient who is afraid that his surgeon's skills aren't good enough.

I even tell my patients that they should like their surgeon. Does this sound corny? No-one has thought so and patients understand exactly why I say it. If a patient ever tells me: "That surgeon is so nice I wish he was my next door neighbor, I'd trust him with my life" then I tell them to go ahead, they've already chosen their surgeon.

But how do you actually find the surgeon in the first place? Any of several ways: Ask your doctor for his recommendation, ask family and friends and ask your minister, pastor, priest or rabbi. Spiritual counselors have seen lots of people go through surgery and can make recommendations to you. You can also ask your claim adjuster or rehabilitation consultant.

Then visit the surgeon, go through his examination, discuss his recommendations, and see what you think.

How To talk To The Surgeon

Suppose the surgeon's recommendation is, as you expected, to have the operation. He should assure you he knows the diagnosis and should fully explain what's wrong. You should also make sure he answers your questions about exactly what he will do and how it will help you, and that he addresses any other worries you have about having surgery.

The next thing I'd recommend is that you ask him to estimate the chances that surgery will improve your situation. If surgery had a 100% guarantee of "curing" a problem, few people would hesitate. But it usually doesn't. And most patients wouldn't accept a 50/50 chance.

Most surgery will be somewhere in between. If the operation you need has an 80% chance of producing improvement, only a 15% chance of producing no change, and a 5% chance of worsening, most people would consider this a fairly good risk. Ask your surgeon about your chances specifically and then ask him to tell you how to improve your chances (see below).

Next, simply ask the surgeon: "Is this surgery experimental?" If it is, any reputable surgeon should have told you already--but you should still ask just in case he forgot.

By experimental I don't mean only that it's a new type of procedure that's never been done before or is still being studied. I also mean that the procedure should not be new to your surgeon. Ask him if this is a frequently performed procedure for him. Ideally he should have done scores or hundreds. If he's done only one or two or three, he might be the best surgeon in town but I'd still recommend checking elsewhere before proceeding. The results could be unpredictable.

> *I saw a patient recently who had a specific procedure on his low back, even though he knew that the surgeon had* **never** *done it before nor had it ever been done at the hospital, in fact it was the first time it had been done in the state. Things might still have turned out well, but unfortunately for him they did not.*

The next thing to do is ask: "Is there anything open-ended about this surgery?" By open-ended I mean something that can't be predicted ahead of time. Sometimes you can't avoid open-endedness, for example if you're going to have arthroscopy of the knee. You will undoubtedly give the surgeon your permission to go ahead and open the knee further if he finds that you need a larger procedure. You will undoubtedly sign a consent for this.

But it should never be the case that you wake up after surgery to find that all sorts of things have been done that you had no idea about beforehand. Discuss with your surgeon what procedure he's planning to do and any limitations you might want to put on it.

You may still want to get another opinion if your state and insurer will allow it. If a second opinion is opposite to the first, you do have a problem and you should talk to your claim adjuster about perhaps getting a third opinion. One surgeon may have had different information, or perhaps there's not much agreement on the type of surgery for your problem. This is something you should go back to your own doctor to sort out.

On the other hand, if you get the second opinion and it agrees with the first, then proceed.

One thing to keep in mind: It's not your role to tell the surgeon how to work. I have one patient who required a shoulder operation, and he read somewhere that his particular surgery should be done with a plate rather than wires as the surgeon wished. Somehow he bullied the surgeon into going with the plate, now he has a poor result, and I certainly blame the surgeon for listening to him but I also blame him for trying to get involved where he had no business.

THE DECISION IS ULTIMATELY YOURS

A patient I'm seeing is reluctant to have an operation, despite a good chance of improvement. He calls me one day and asks: "On Comp they don't make you have surgery, do they?"

The next thing to do is: Think about it all. No-one can make a patient have surgery, least of all the insurer. Confer with trusted friends, family, doctor, rehabilitation consultant, even Dear Abby if you want. Even if surgery is fully indicated, it's still your decision. No-one can make you have an operation; America is a free country. Here is the most realistic way to take stock:

1. Has the surgeon been able to tell you exactly what's wrong?
2. Is there a good chance of correcting the problem with surgery?
3. Are you absolutely unable to go on as you are?
4. Have you tried all aspects of conservative care?
5. Do you have confidence in the surgeon?

If the answer is yes five times, you probably should go ahead and have the surgery and get it over with.

How To Prepare Yourself

The surgeon will do his part; what's your part? Is there anything you can do to stack the cards in your favor?

Definitely. Here's what I tell my patients: As many weeks as possible before surgery, start a good exercise program, lose weight if you need to, and stop smoking. Every doctor knows that the fitter, stronger, and healthier a patient is before surgery the faster he'll recover. There is nothing like a patient with firm abdominal muscles, strong leg and arm and chest muscles, clear lungs, and good body tone to make a surgeon's job easier.

Prepare yourself mentally to have discomfort. There's no question that a surgical incision will hurt and you'll probably be stiff and sore. If you're ready for this and follow the other recommendations in this chapter, you should get through the initial painful period quickly.

Being fit will also help you get over post-op pain. Start exercising now to reduce your post-op discomfort later. After surgery you'll undoubtedly have to do rehab exercises anyway and you might as well get in shape in advance.

As to weight loss, any surgeon will tell you he'd rather not have to operate through eight inches of fat. The main reason is for healing: Fatty tissue easily becomes infected, does not hold sutures well, and doesn't heal quickly.

As to smoking, any anesthesiologist will tell you that he'd rather put nonsmokers to sleep. It's safer. Any pulmonary doctor will tell you that nonsmokers have less post-op pneumonia. And every surgeon in the world will tell you that patients with healthy lungs recuperate more easily after surgery. Some studies have shown that smokers only have half as good results after back and disc surgeries, probably because their tissues get less oxygen and heal more slowly.

In addition, don't forget that now most hospitals will not allow smoking anywhere. So if you don't want to go cold turkey while you're also recovering from the operation, quit ahead of time.

Finally, just before the operation your surgeon will probably again explain things to you including the possible risks and possible complications. He'll ask you to sign an informed consent statement, in which you agree that you've heard and understood what he has said. The only advice I can give you about this standard procedure is that you should definitely ask all your questions and then if you're comfortable, sign the informed consent and close your eyes.

QUESTIONS AND ANSWERS ABOUT SURGERY AND WORKERS' COMPENSATION

Q. "What's the effect on my benefits if I have surgery? If I'm cured will my benefits go down?"

A. If your insurer has been covering you all along for the injury, coverage will continue while you have surgery and recuperate. If surgery "cures" you then your benefits will end just as they if you had healed without the operation. This shouldn't be a cause for concern if you really want to improve.

Q. "If I have surgery, will I be more or less likely to have a permanent disability?"

A. This depends on the state and is complicated. Most states' Workers' Compensation systems will base your permanent disability on how much function you have at the end of healing. For example, if you have limited range of motion of your shoulder it does not matter whether you have had surgery or not, your permanent disability rating will be based on your motion (see Chapter 22).

Q. "If I have surgery does it mean I'll end up disabled?

A. Usually not. Ask your surgeon this question before the operation. You should know what he expects your functional result to be.

There's often a good chance of improvement with surgery and patients do return to work afterward without difficulty. But other surgeries (such as placement of artificial knees or hips and some neck and back operations) do result in partial disability. Then whether or not you return to work will depend on the type of work you do and your surgical result. Heavy labor may be out, but different jobs will probably be possible.

Q. "If the doctors all recommend surgery but I refuse, will my benefits end?"

A. Probably--because if surgery is the best treatment and you don't have it, your progress will probably end.

WRAP-UP

How to do yourself some favors with surgery, the three guiding principles:
1) Conservative care should come first, give it a full try;
2) You should feel completely confident in your surgeon without any questions left unanswered;
3) Prepare yourself for surgery with exercises, good personal health, and the attitude that you've done all you can and are comfortable letting your surgeon do the rest.

K

CHAPTER 14

Rehabilitation Consultants (QRC's)

A patient is sitting at home, three months now he's been on Comp. The phone rings. "Hello, my name is Jennifer Adams. I'm a nurse, and I'm the Qualified Rehabilitation Consultant that's been assigned to work with you while you're on Workers' Compensation."

"You're what?"

"I'm a Rehabilitation Consultant. In this state, people like me are assigned when it looks like there could be a long period before return to work. I can explain my role to you if we could get together this week, then I can tell you the things we'll be working on."

"Well, I don't know about any of that. My doctor hasn't said anything about me going back to work. He says it'll be months before I could tolerate it."

"Yes, that's partly why I'm assigned. You see, your doctor probably doesn't know that your employer is able to provide a lighter job on a temporary basis while you recover. Now, how about us getting together tomorrow? I can explain all of this to you then."

"Mmmm--I suppose so. If it's something I'm supposed to do..."

At some point in your Workers' Compensation case you may pick up the telephone and discover that a Rehabilitation Consultant has been assigned to your case. This chapter tells you who these people are, what their job is, and how you can get the most assistance from them.

What's A Rehabilitation Consultant?

A Rehabilitation Consultant is a professional who is usually hired by your Workers' Compensation insurer, state, or sometimes by your employer. Sometimes they go by other names: Medical Managers, Rehabilitation Nurses, Rehab Specialists or Qualified Rehabilitation Consultants (QRC's) in some states. For this chapter I'll use the name QRC in most cases.

QRC's generally are professionals with a nursing background, though many come from other counseling, testing, training, vocational or social rehabilitation service professions. About 75% are female. In order to become a QRC these people have to study the field of rehabilitation, the state's Workers' Compensation laws, and then take qualifying examinations. They are licensed by the states in which they work.

A QRC is generally assigned to a case when an injury results in a slower than expected recovery, a prolonged period of treatment, or when their special expertise in job placement is needed. For example, in Minnesota if an injured employee is out of work 30 days due to a back injury or 60 days due to any other injury, a rehabilitation consultation is mandatory.

If you have a QRC assigned to you their purpose is to help you obtain as satisfactory a return to work as possible considering your injury and your skills and the job market in your area. The QRC will perform as an "objective, third party, neutral" individual. The QRC will talk with you, consult with your doctor, speak with your employer and send reports to the insurer about your progress. Their role is to work with all these people, not "taking sides" and not representing only one point of view.

One of the best QRC's I know said it this way: "Our job is to try and make a Comp case easier for everyone. We don't think of ourselves as emphasizing either the doctor's or the patient's or anyone else's interests over any other. Our goal is to help the patient get a successful return to work. We try to facilitate communication between everybody with this as the ultimate aim."

The QRC will attempt to coordinate your doctor's recommendations for return to work with your employer, so an appropriately modified job is waiting for you. A QRC can also advise you about Workers' Compensation procedures. A QRC may also help you obtain a second opinion (if one is needed, see Chapter 12) and in some states they can also assist you if there is a need to change doctors.

A QRC will test your vocational skills and aptitude if your injury prevents you from returning to your old job. A QRC will also help you in a job search or retraining.

However, QRC's will not act as doctors, therapists, or lawyers. QRC's will not treat you in any way, and they'll not institute, change, or interfere with your treatment program. They will not give legal advice. Their position is a neutral "uninvolved" rehabilitation specialist.

What Your QRC Can Do For You

I recommend that you start by meeting your QRC, who will probably offer to come to your house to meet. Otherwise you can meet at the QRC's office, some local coffee shop, etc.

Simply talk with your QRC, find out what his or her expertise is, and find out what he or she intends to do for you. If your QRC has already helped over 2,000 injured workers get back to work, chances are you can be helped too.

You're most likely to find that your QRC has a good perspective on your situation, your position under Workers' Compensation, and the outlook for getting back to work. He or she will probably have already studied your doctor's notes and will be able to help explain your medical problems to you.

Early in your case, your QRC will collect information from your doctor, relay it to your employer, and discuss the prognosis with them and with you. During this stage the QRC basically monitors your progress, keeps all parties informed, and keeps things flowing smoothly.

You can't imagine how helpful it is for an employer to receive a simple phone call such as: "Mr. Jones, Shirley is coming along well with her injury. The doctor expects her to be in therapy three or four more weeks and then he'll probably release her for work on a limited job for eight weeks." This is the kind of information employers love to get early.

Later, as your recovery progresses your QRC will ask your doctor for specific physical restrictions that will allow you to work safely. For example, your doctor may say you shouldn't lift over 10 pounds or be in a prolonged sitting position, or perhaps you won't be able to use foot controls or work with your neck flexed, or you shouldn't be exposed to dusts or gases, fumes or exhausts, etc.

The QRC takes these restrictions to the employer and analyzes potential jobs. Then she comes back with a job description for your doctor to inspect. These are things neither you or your doctor probably could do easily, and the QRC saves time for everybody.

> *I'm seeing a patient whose shoulder injury has healed enough that he could work but unfortunately he's an industrial electrician. His job was mainly overhead motions, and the employer says he has to come back to his full job or nothing at all. No work available.*
> *I give his QRC the safe limits: He can't work above shoulder height, he can't lift over 20 pounds, and he can't push or pull more than 150 pounds. She goes back to the employer with these restrictions to make him understand that they will be necessary for four to six more weeks.*
> *Lo and behold, they come up with a modified job that is safe, I okay it, and he works at the restricted duty until he recovers.*

It may happen that your employer either has no work available within your capacities, or is resisitant to the whole idea of light duty. Then the QRC has to work with him to literally create a new job for you.

Later on in the final stages of recovery, if you return to your old job the QRC will close his or her file: Mission accomplished. But if you don't recover fully, if you have long-term or permanent restrictions, or if you have some disability, the QRC will continue to work with you and help with the next steps.

I've seen hundreds of patients who can't return to their job: Laborers after back surgery, loggers who have lost a hand or arm, roofers with heel fractures, pipefitters with asbestosis, rubber or plastics workers with allergies, hairdressers with frozen shoulders, and so on.

If you end up with such a disability, the QRC could turn out to be your best friend. They'll find out from your doctor exactly what your capacities are, and then try to help find a job within them. But if you can't find a suitable job, and that's frequently the case, the QRC will put you through a series of vocational tests to determine what work might be appropriate. These tests will include aptitude and intelligence tests to pinpoint your strong points and skills, and interest tests to determine the areas you most likely will enjoy working in.

The final step will then be to help you find a job that matches your test scores. If your settlement (Chapter 23) includes retraining (Chapter 20) your QRC will probably help you get started in that also.

YOUR DOCTOR AND QRC'S

I know of doctors who refuse to talk to QRC's. Some have actually told me they regard the QRC as "an intrusion into the doctor-patient relationship, a drag on the Comp system". This is an unfortunate attitude, and usually wrong.

QRC's can be of vital assistance to doctors, especially in cases of chronic debilitating injuries or when there are complex Workers' Compensation issues.

The QRC can also be a conduit for information that your doctor might otherwise never get. She can get him information about your job, about the work environment that you will return to, etc. The QRC also makes it easy for a doctor to tell the employer about restrictions, delays in healing, etc. This saves busy doctors an enormous amount of time and any doctor who doesn't take advantage of it must just not realize how much it can help you, his patient.

The QRC can also help the doctor with followup, making appointments, etc. He or she can make things easy for him by alerting him to a patient's new symptoms, letting him know if the patient is going to physical therapy, if light duty has not worked out, etc. Sometimes the QRC gets this information much sooner than the doctor would.

The QRC also will usually have inside information about an employer's readiness to take an employee back. They can tell the doctor if the employer is dragging his feet. The QRC can run interference with the insurer to get approval for special tests or treatments or consultations. They work daily with insurers, they talk their language, and they can save any doctor hours of phone time.

One reason some doctors may shy away from QRC's is that they may feel pressured to make decisions that are not always easy. The QRC just by his or her presence will often stimulate a doctor to organize a treatment plan. It has to have this effect when the QRC arrives in the office and asks questions about the future.

This is necessary because Workers' Compensation is more than just casting a fracture or treating a lung injury: It's planning for treatment, progressive rehabilitation, and ultimate return to work. So when the QRC asks: "Doctor, when will it be safe for Shirley to do some light assembly work?", it has to cause that doctor to focus his thinking efforts on recovery, much more than if the question had never been asked.

It's true that some QRC's are in fact real pushy and hard to deal with. Some do sort of take over a patient's care, and a doctor will get fed up with that very quickly. I have even seen some QRC's try to institute care on their own. I don't blame the doctors for not liking to have these QRC's on the case.

I know one QRC that consistently looks at my restrictions, tells the patient she's going to find work within them, and then goes to the employer and puts the patient in a job that exceeds his capacities. Of course this is unsafe, of course patients have aggravations of their injuries, and then I have to start treatment all over again. I've seen her do this time after time, and I don't blame any doctor for not trusting her. I don't trust her either.

But I've worked with lots of QRC's and not many are like this, and at least half to three-fourths are quite professional and enormously helpful. Any doctor who treats Workers' Compensation patients should consider trying to work with QRC's.

Questions And Answers About QRC's

Q. "Do I have to cooperate with the QRC?"
A. In many states your cooperation with a QRC is mandatory, and if you don't cooperate your benefits will be cut off.

Q. "Can I change to a different QRC?"
A. If you have a good reason, in many states you are allowed one change.

If you have a QRC that just doesn't help you at all, misses appointments with you, doesn't contact your doctor or your employer, doesn't understand what your job involves, or is inconsistent, then you certainly should consider a change. In most states that have rehabilitation consultants there is a procedure for changing (state Workers' Compensation offices are listed in Chapter 24, How To Find Help).

Q. "My QRC is just trying to get me to work! I thought she was supposed to be helping me!

A. Well, of course: Return to work is the purpose of Workers' Compensation and expressly the goal of a QRC. Isn't that your purpose too? Believe me, down the road long after your doctor, your lawyer, and your Comp checks have disappeared if you don't have a job you won't have anything. The QRC is the one that can help you get that job.

WRAP-UP

How to do yourself some favors with QRC's:
1) If you're fortunate enough to have a QRC assigned to you, try to get as much out of his or her expertise as you can. The QRC can help make the whole Workers' Compensation system work for you;
2) Ask your doctor to work with both you and your QRC on followup visits and return to work;
3) When it comes time to return to work, the QRC will be most instumental in getting you your job.

K

CHAPTER 15

Chiropractic Treatment

"I won't take pills, Doctor. And I don't want exercises. The only thing that helps is an adjustment from my chiropractor. He puts the whole spine back in place every week."

"Doctor, do you believe in chiropractors?"

There's controversy about chiropractic treatment in most Workers' Comp systems throughout the country. There's controversy among insurers whether chiropractic should be covered, among medical doctors whether chiropractic is effective, and even among chiropractors about the care itself.

I've seen patients' claims denied because of what their chiropractor wrote, I've seen patients' benefits cut off because of a chiropractor's treatment methods, I've seen chiropractors' charts get patients into trouble down the road with later claims. I've also found that patients on Workers' Compensation don't realize that these things can happen.

In this chapter I'm not going to engage in chiropractor bashing and I'm not going to try to dissuade you from seeing chiropractors. I'm not going to attempt to explain chiropractic theory of treatment and how it differs from medical theory. This chapter is to show you, if you choose to see a chiropractor, several things to be aware of that could jeopardize your Workers' Compensation claim in the eyes of the insurer.

WORKERS' COMPENSATION AND CHIROPRACTIC

Virtually every state does include chiropractic treatment in Workers' Compensation coverage. But not without review and, sometimes, controversy. For example, as of July 1990 the state of Oregon no longer considers chiropractors to be attending physicians under Workers' Compensation laws. Oregon has ruled that chiropractors can see patients for 12 treatments or 30 days, whichever comes first. But after that chiropractic services are only compensable if they are ordered by an attending physician which means a Medical Doctor.

If your state allows you to choose chiropractic and you improve fairly quickly, there probably will be no difficulty with your claim. On the other hand, under Workers' Compensation all claims are reviewed. If the reviewer or claim adjuster concludes that your chiropractic treatment is excessive, he'll notify you that he won't cover it any longer. At that point you can either accept his decision or contest it following the procedure in your state. Depending on the facts a compensation judge will either uphold or reverse a claim adjuster's decision.

In any dispute a compensation judge might ask another chiropractor for an opinion. But there's controversy among chiropractors as to what is good, reasonable and effective care. Mark Sanders, D.C., is a private chiropractor, an instructor at a chiropractic college, and a utilization review consultant. He recently wrote in Medical Economics that "Some D.C.'s consider diagnosis unnecessary" and he also showed how chiropractic "treatments vary from accepted to absurd". He added, "There are many good chiropractors: They practice rationally, attend postgraduate courses, and read medical and chiropractic journals. But others don't, and that hurts the profession."

In a claim dispute a judge might also ask a medical doctor for his opinion on the reasonableness of care. If so, the M.D. will probably use standard criteria for reasonableness: Is there a diagnosis? Is there objective confirmation by studies such as X-rays or scans? Is there a clear treatment plan? Is there evidence the patient is getting better?

If your chiropractor has provided care that meets these tests, you'll have no problem.

But I've reviewed charts, evaluated injuries, and discussed cases with insurers and attorneys and chiropractors over the years and I've found that there are several problem areas that can get a patient's Comp claim into trouble. The following aspects of chiropractic treatment make insurers and medical consultants look askance at any claim:

1) Lengthy treatment;
2) Lack of results;
3) Poor records.
4) Inadequate diagnosis;
5) X-ray exposure;
6) Dangerous conditions.

The following sections show how each of these areas might lead an insurer to deny your claim or stop your benefits.

INSURERS' COMPLAINT #1: LENGTHY TREATMENT

The length of chiropractic treatment programs seems to be one area where chiropractors and insurers differ most often and most strenuously. I've spoken with chiropractors who tell me that a patient should show improvement in a few weeks or there's no reason to continue treatment. But others seem to feel the opposite, even that chiropractic treatment may need years to be effective. This is the source of insurers' objections.

Insurers seem to make complaints of prolonged treatment more often than about almost anything else about chiropractic. I've had hundreds of conversations similar to this one:

A Comp insurer wants me to review the chart of a patient with a three-year-old work injury: "He's still having treatment from a chiropractor, it's been three times a week for 136 weeks now. Is this reasonable?"

I ask, "What was the injury? What was the diagnosis? Has he been improving?"

They tell me: "That's just the problem, we can't find out. The patient says this is a back injury but when we request records all we get is a list of diagnoses and billing charges for all the times he's been seen. There are seven or eight diagnoses--subluxations and radiculalgia and so on-- but they don't make sense to us. Most of the notes say he's improving but then we wonder, why is he still going for treatment?"

I ask if there's any treatment plan. But the insurer says, "We wrote a letter asking just that and he said the patient is still having problems because he tried to decrease the frequency of visits. I guess that means he thinks lack of chiropractic care is a cause of injury! Now he says he's going to correct more spinal subluxations but implies it could take years more. The patient told us he plans to have treatments the rest of his life."

"Are you still covering treatment?".

"Are you kidding? We cut him off last week. We told him we won't pay for any more visits until we get a diagnosis, a treatment plan and some records. This whole thing is just ridiculous."

What's the objection to treatment for months or years? First, the cost: No insurer relishes the thought of an endless stream of chiropractic bills for as many years as a claimant should happen to live.

But it's more than that. Another objection is that no-one has convincingly demonstrated the value--in terms of objective clinical measurements--of such long-term treatment. I certainly don't know of any medical condition that requires two or three years of manipulation, mobilization, adjustment, or any other kind of manual therapy. Nor does any M.D. or physical therapist I've ever spoken to.

I asked a well-respected chiropractor with over 40 years of experience and treatment success. He told me: "No, no, no. That's way too long. There isn't any justification for three years of treatment--not for <u>anything</u>."

Another chiropractor that I occasionally work with says: "There should be measurable response to treatment in six weeks, usually after three or four. If treatment goes on for months it's only maintenance care, not true treatment.   Anything over one year would be extremely unusual."

Typical of M.D.'s comments about this are from a rehabilitation doctor: "I can't imagine a patient going to an M.D. three times a week for even two months without demanding improvement! What can these patients be thinking of, that they ignore the fact they haven't gotten one bit better in all that time? To me this isn't a doctor-patient relationship for treatment, this is dependency. The patient is dependent on seeing the chiropractor but he never gets any improvement to show for it."

To address these issues I just look at it simply: There's no such thing as lifetime treatment. The human body is not like a piece of fine wood furniture that improves the more coats of hand-rubbed lacquer it gets. Treatment, chiropractic or any other, should be given to correct a specific problem. Then the doctor should show the patient how to avoid the same problem in the future. That should be the end of it.

Insurers seem to look at it this way too. They'll pay for necessary chiropractic care, for a reasonable time, for a specific injury. But beyond that, they'll resist. So if you find that your treatment has lasted for months or years, and there's no clear plan for it to end, you can expect the Workers' Compensation insurer to start asking questions.

INSURERS' COMPLAINT #2: LACK OF RESULTS

Insurers, employers, rehabilitation consultants, and medical managers constantly evaluate the results of care. They ask: Is the patient improving? Is the treatment helping? Is there clear evidence he's getting better?

Insurers and medical managers are most comfortable when they see standard treatment that's based on verifiable principles. They have difficulty with treatment when there is no sign of it ever reaching completion or producing results. People in these positions see a lot of claims and with experience know what usually works. They like to see this kind of treatment on a claim.

Insurers know that medications often help, though they realize chiropractors can't prescribe medications except in a couple of exceptions. But insurers also know that physical therapy modalities, traction, exercise and other standard treatments (see Chapter 11) usually help patients with musculoskeletal injuries. They also know that diagnostic procedures such as good X-rays, CT's, scans, and MRI's are often crucial to the diagnosis. So when they don't see these things they begin to ask questions.

> *I'm seeing a patient who's had low back pain for 13 months and he's been under chiropractic "treatment" the whole time. He tells me his back is stiff and sore and he can't work. I ask him: "Have you had a trial of traction?"*
>
> *"No. Dr. Jim said traction wouldn't help me."*
>
> *"Has your chiropractor given you a back brace or a corset or a girdle?"*
>
> *"No, none of those things."*
>
> *"Have you ever had treatments with hot packs, ice, ultrasound, therapeutic massage? Have you had a TENS unit? Have you had any muscle relaxants or antiinflammatory pills?"*
>
> *"Well, he gave me some minerals."*
>
> *"Have you had instruction in body mechanics, lifting and pushing and pulling techniques, and so on? Have you been given specific back exercises to do?"*
>
> *"No. My chiropractor told me that cleaning my garage and walking around the house is enough."*
>
> *"Did he recommend any special tests, a CT scan or an MRI?"*
>
> *"No, but he said he might do some of those if I don't get better in a few more months. He told me my X-rays were okay."*
>
> *I ask the big question: "Tell me, are you feeling any better now than you were a year ago?"*
>
> *He pauses and thinks about it. He begins to look a little tense and he says: "Well, no, I guess not really." Then he brightens: "Dr. Jim says I am improving, though. I guess I must be."*

All the things I asked this patient about are routine treatments and procedures. Any patient with unexplained and unresolved back and leg pain should have these things done after only a few weeks, and certainly long before a year has passed.

Insurers aren't too accepting of treatment that provides no, or only temporary, relief. They want to see care that produces steady improvement. So if you've had nothing but chiropractic treatment daily or two to three times weekly, no medications or exercises or physical therapy and no sign of improvement, you can expect a problem with your claim. At the very least the insurer will ask your chiropractor some very tough questions. It's probable they'll ask you to see another doctor, one who will get your case moving forward. And it would be hard to fault their logic for doing so.

INSURER'S COMPLAINT #3: POOR CHIROPRACTIC RECORDS

Workers' Compensation depends on good documentation (see Chapter 10, You and Your Medical Records). Insurers need to see medical records that show the tracks of diagnosis, treatment, and progress, in fact they require these before they can pay benefits.

Possibly the biggest problem Comp insurers have with a patient's chiropractic treatment is that they can't get information about it. Insurers often tell me that chiropractic chart notes are inadequate or even nonexistent. One said: "All we get is a billing statement, and it just lists a collection of diagnoses. They can't all possibly be true, and there are no backup notes." A claim adjuster told me: "Some chiropractors' reports are so vague there's no way we can make useful conclusions from them."

To be sure, medical doctors also have poor records. But as I review charts from all over the country a far higher percentage of chiropractors' notes are truly inadequate for Workers' Comp purposes, I would say approximately 95%. Frequently these notes are just a page of scribbles with no patient's or doctor's name and with little or no information present.

Sometimes there's nothing but a series of dates, all with the word "same" or "muscle work" next to the date. I've seen page upon page of sequential records with every notation for two years saying "90% better" (logically this can't be true, because after only five treatments a patient like this would be 99.999% recovered).

I've included on the next page some examples of chiropractic records that I have found in charts, sometimes even comprising the entire chart. I see this kind of note every single day and I simply can't understand how any professional could have the nerve to provide these to insurers and call them medical records.

Insurers tell me that they consider notes like this to be non-medical, non-responsible, non-scientific, and non-useful. I've also had insurers tell

me that disclaimers often come with such chiropractic notes. They get a bundle of illegible records and a written statement that says: "These are office notes only and I warn against relying on them for any information about the patient".

One insurer told me: "None of us can make sense out of these notes. But if we ask the chiropractor a specific question the disclaimer means he's reserved the freedom to make up any answer he wants from memory. What he's really saying is that his notes are worthless... We agree!"

Another thing that makes it hard for a Workers' Compensation insurer to process a claim is the practice--which I've never seen in a medical office but which is apparently accepted in chiropractic offices--of keeping several charts for one patient. When a patient has a work injury, the chiropractor starts a new chart: One chart for each injury. This has the effect of making it appear that the patient was never in the office before, when in reality he could have been going there for years even for treatment to the same area of the body. Of course the result is that the insurer can't rely on any of the charts to be full or complete. Some insurers tell me that because of this they've decided they can never rely on <u>any</u> chiropractic records to be true.

On the subject of truth in records, I saw a patient recently who had a fairly complicated case, with chiropractic treatment off and on over the years. She had just run into her chiropractor in a store. He told her he'd gotten a letter from Workers' Compensation. This is how she related their conversation to me:

> *He didn't tell them anything, my chiropractor told me. He said he just doesn't keep all that paper work. He said: "I just told them about some popping in your neck. I just made something up."*
> *I got angry at him and told him it was my low back, not my neck. I told him he'd just wrecked my claim!*
> *You know what he said? He said he just makes it all up. He said he doesn't want to tell those people anything. Can you imagine that?-- and he's supposed to be a doctor!*

The bottom line is that in Workers' Compensation illegible or inaccurate records are a real liability for you. But this lack of objective record-keeping and reliance on treatment notations is so common that it damages a lot of patients' claims. It may be that some chiropractors feel this is all they need to care for their other patients, and if so that's fine. But it's not fine for a patient on Comp.

Perhaps chiropractors would defend this by saying their methods of treatment don't lend themselves to objective reporting or documentation of physical signs or patient progress. But if this is true, then this is another and perhaps more serious problem for chiropactors, because Workers' Compensation runs on objective and accurate documentation.   When they treat Workers' Compensation patients their records should include the diagnosis, treatment, and measurement of progress and be in a format that's useful. Any profession that can't provide this really doesn't have a viable place in Workers' Compensation.

So if you are seeing a chiropractor I would recommend you take a look at a copy of your records (see Chapter 10). The notes should be legible and not scribbled. They should document understandable diagnoses, plans, and treatment goals. Notes that simply say "much improved" every visit for three years won't help your case much. If these are the kind of notes you have, you'd be wise to prepare for a long delay in having your chiropractor's bills covered.

INSURERS' COMPLAINT #4: NONSTANDARD DIAGNOSIS AND INADEQUATE WORKUP

Insurers have difficulty processing a list of five, ten or more diagnoses for a patient who only had one simple injury. If a patient with a neck strain has a list of chiropractic diagnoses including "cervical brachial radiculalgia, disc herniation syndrome, subluxation of C1-C6, brachial plexopathy and occipital neuralgia" not only would this mean the patient probably should be almost dead, but the insurer simply won't accept them. The longer the list, the more difficult it is for the insurer to relate all the diagnoses to the injury.

If a chiropractor then adds five or six more simultaneous diagnoses for the low back, insurers often will simply not accept the claim at all.

One of the most frequently used diagnoses in chiropractic treatment is "subluxation". This especially causes problems. Medical doctors use the word subluxation to mean a bone or joint that has been slightly dislocated but then returns to near normal position; this can be documented on X-ray. But chiropractors have told me their use of the word subluxation means something different, and in fact by definition this diagnosis cannot be proven. This is a major problem for them, and for you if it's your case, because Workers' Compensation usually requires documentation of a diagnosis.

Another diagnostic problem can also get your claim into trouble. If your injury is to the neck, the list of diagnoses ought to be only about the neck: Neck strain or sprain, cervical disc injury, or whatever. But if your chiropractor's philosophy is to "adjust" not only your neck but also your low back, he'll note that he also did the low back treatment (in order to be paid for it). His billing will then list several more "diagnoses" related to your low back. This can be a real problem for two reasons: First the insurer will only pay for treatment to the area that's injured and will deny the bills for the low back. Secondly if you ever do have a low back injury later, an insurer may look to the earlier notes and conclude your problem was preexisting and they'll deny the second claim too.

Another problem with diagnosis as practiced by some chiropractors is that insurers sometimes don't see a standard diagnostic workup at all. If the claim is for a back injury and the chiropractor's diagnosis is a disc herniation, the insurer will likely want to see evidence the diagnosis was reached by objective testing such as a CT or MRI. They'll especially want to see this kind of backup if the chiropractor says there's a permanent disability (see Chapter 22).

But when the insurer sees no objective testing and all they have for backup is the chiropractor's clinical impression, they'll probably deny the claim. Insurers have said to me: "We don't pay for guesses, hunches, or feelings. We need to see proof. If the chiropractor can't provide it we'll have our claimant examined by a medical doctor."

PROBLEM AREA #5: X-RAY EXPOSURE

In my experience about three-fourths of chiropractic X-rays are of such poor quality that I can't make adequate diagnostic conclusions from them.

I usually have to obtain a new set of films to make the diagnosis. I always tell the patient why I have to do this, but once I received a phone call from a young hothead chiropractor threatening to sue me because I told his patient that the films weren't adequate for me to read.

So I asked chiropractors I work with about this lack of quality in the washed-out, poorly-aligned films I've seen. "Excessive exposure," one told me. Another said: "Too many films, taken too often, poorly-trained technicians. If he thinks his films are so great he should put them up side by side with some good ones and show us. If he can't produce better films than that we ought to shut him down. This man's work reflects poorly on us all."

I know that these days you're likely to get X-rayed in almost every office you go to, and that includes mine. But you should be aware of a few things for your own protection and benefit.

First of all, there should always be a lead shield for vital body areas and genitals. This means you should be wearing a lead apron on everything below the neck if your neck is being X-rayed, etc.

Second, medical doctors have concerns about the total spine X-rays from chiropractors' offices: The three-foot-long films that they hang on their viewboxes that cover you from neck to tailbone. The amount of radiation hitting your body when these films are taken is more X-ray than radiologists have told me should be used. A shielded film of either cervical, thoracic, or lumbar spine should be adequate.

Third, there's usually no need to take X-rays even every two or three months except to evaluate healing fractures, which chiropractors won't be treating. If an X-ray is adequate and shows the problem, then another X-ray a year later to look for changes should be sufficient.

Fourth, it's good practice to undress patients for X-rays. I've seen hundreds of chiropractic X-rays with bluejeans, bras, jewelry and belt buckles obscuring detail just where we want to see it the most. This isn't a big thing, though it is a sign of sloppy radiographic practice. If you see your own X-rays and your spine is obscured by a belt buckle or change in your pocket or a pants snap, you might consider a more professional clinic next time.

MISDIAGNOSED OR DANGEROUS CONDITIONS

> *A 55-year-old welder developed neck pain six months ago while working overhead. He saw a chiropractor for a while without relief. In my office now he says: "The chiropractor said I'd ruptured three discs in my neck. I went for a couple dozen treatments but then he said he couldn't help me. I've just been living with it."*

I've seen many patients like this man. When I look at their X-rays they have typical arthritic spurring. When I get an MRI there are <u>no</u> disc herniations at any level. With a few months of muscle relaxants, antiinflammatories and therapeutic exercises these people almost always improve. If they had listened to their chiropractor's diagnosis of disc herniations, they might have gone on for years thinking they were beyond help. This is one problem with a misdiagnosed condition.

But there are worse things that can happen:

> *A 35-year-old waitress fell at work and saw a chiropractor. "He's worked on me for three months now. He says I have subluxations. But my leg pain just keeps getting worse and worse and now I can barely walk. Can you help me?" she asked.*
>
> *She had an obvious lumbar disc herniation and I sent her to a neurosurgeon. After the operation I talked with him about what he'd found.*
>
> *"Biggest disc fragment I ever saw," he said. "She'll be lucky to get sensation back in that leg. She should never have had manipulation. I'm sure the chiropractor did some permanent damage, but I can never prove it."*

I've found that most chiropractors say that when there's any sign of a disc herniation and radiculopathy (see special sections C and D) they send the patient to an M.D. They know that adjustment in these cases and especially in the neck can cause severe damage.

So if you have neck pain with arm symptoms, low back pain with leg symptoms, and your chiropractor is treating you without special tests and doesn't refer you to an M.D., I recommend you discuss it with him and your claim adjuster as soon as possible. I would recommend a second opinion right away.

WRAP-UP

How to do yourself some favors with chiropractic:

1) If chiropractic treatment hasn't started to be obviously effective after eight to twelve weeks, it probably isn't going to;

2) Review your chiropractor's chart notes. You should be able to make sense out of them. They should include diagnosis, treatment, and prognosis (see Chapter 10);

3) A few X-rays may be adequate but certainly monthly and every other month X-rays are too much;

4) Your diagnosis should include only the area of injury. You could have a big problem down the road if your diagnosis lists areas that have not been injured;

5) Use chiropractic treatment like anything else: It's a tool to accomplish the goal of getting your injury resolved. It's not a life-long program to "keep you going".

L

CHAPTER 16

Exercise, Fitness
And Work Hardening

"Not less than two hours a day should be devoted to exercise."
....Thomas Jefferson

"Those who think they have not time for exercise will sooner or later have to find time for illness."
...Edward Stanley, Earl of Derby

Physical fitness and exercise may not be a cure-all for work injuries, but it comes close. The old days when we would put patients to bed and tell them not to move for weeks after an injury are, thankfully, long gone. I've found that after virtually every occupational injury or illness, the patients who start or maintain physical activity do the best. They feel better sooner, they don't suffer from the blahs, and they have safer returns to work.

So this chapter is really about getting well. It's about the best and safest exercises to do and when to do them, about pre-op and post-op exercises, and about the special treatment program called Work Hardening.

Taking The Mystery Out Of "Exercise Treatment"

The word "exercise" means different things at different times. **In the context of treating a work injury, exercise is either:**

A) **Stretching, flexibility and range of motion of an injured muscle or limb (see Chapter 11),**

B) **Physical fitness workouts, building-up of strength and endurance,**

C) **Or both at once.**

Stretching and flexibility motions come first, right after the injury. Then building fitness follows. It can be reasonable and often even preferable--to start <u>both kinds of exercises</u> simultaneously to have an integrated treatment program. The best situation is when a patient keep sup his fitness from the beginning without interruption.

Why Exercise When You're Injured?

Is there anything wrong with lying around, taking it easy, and getting soft after a work injury? Sure there is: You won't heal as fast, you'll feel worse, and you'll add a <u>second problem</u> to the original injury: Physical deconditioning, also known as being out of shape. Physical inactivity and the resultant muscle deconditioning is one of the biggest causes of delayed recovery in Workers' Compensation.

You don't have to be injured to find out how it feels to be out of shape. Just imagine doing nothing but lying on a sofa and watching TV for several days straight. After even two days, you would start to be stiff, muscles would be painful and every little task would start to be hard-even bending over to tie your shoes.

Muscles stay healthy and pain-free when they stay in motion. The simple truth is that even a little lack of activity causes muscles to shorten and stiffen. They lose strength and range of motion and the result is chronic muscle pain. This leads to less activity and more pain. Then a patient returns to the doctor and says, "Now everything hurts!"

The ultimate lack of activity is "bedrest treatment". Anyone on complete bedrest will start to lose muscle mass and strength within a couple of days and will lose 20% of total strength and tone every two weeks. This means 10 weeks of bedrest produces a weakling of only one third his original strength.

> *A young custodian had seen her own doctor because of upper back discomfort. He gave her muscle relaxants and pain medications and told her: "I want you at complete bedrest for six weeks."*
>
> *At six weeks she told him--big surprise--that she was sore and stiff. He told her she hadn't recovered and he put her at more rest.*
>
> *When I saw her 10 weeks later she complained of being out of breath even walking across the room! It turned out she had started with only a minor muscle strain, and the correct treatment should have been stretching and flexibility exercises: Just the opposite to the bedrest she got. Eventually she recovered from this, but what a waste of time!*

Inactivity causes not only stiffness. It also reinforces the idea of being an <u>invalid</u>: The worst thing that can happen to someone on Comp. A colleague put it this way: "The psychological impact of lying around is also significant. They start to focus on their discomfort rather than on getting well. They begin to consider themselves invalids. Then to treat them we have to treat their entire outlook and re-educate them into being active again. It's as if treatment for their injury has to stay on hold because their physical deconditioning is the major barrier to recovery."

EXERCISE: NATURE'S REPAIR KIT

No-one who understands how Mother Nature heals body tissue would ever let themselves get soft or stiff. It's true that some patients find it hard to believe that exercising an injured muscle or ligament could be good. After all, here they are hurting and stiff and we're telling them to move the part that hurts the most!

I recently listened to Jeffrey Saal, M.D., talk about tissue healing. Dr. Saal practices in San Francisco and is recognized internationally as an expert on rehabilitation. He said: "The first stage of injury is inflammation. In this phase tissues swell, fluid and pain-causing chemicals flood into the injured tissue, and blood vessels also ooze fluid that causes pain. Early in this stage we have to use antiinflammatories and pain medications, rest, and ice."

Dr. Saal was asked how long this treatment should last. He said: "No more than a week <u>at most</u>. That's because after seven days the tissues would start to form scars which cause tissue tightening and loss of mobility. But we get a patient to move the injured muscle at this stage, and it cuts down on the scarring and increases both strength and elasticity. We've found that we can actually get an <u>increase</u> in the strength of a tendon or ligament by moving it at this stage."

He said clearly: "The worst thing you can do at this stage is to not let them move. This is the stage to build muscle strength."

In other words, working inactive muscles--even ones that cause pain--may help resolve an injury more than anything else will. Even if a patient digs in his heels at the idea of exercise, if we can just get them to start the exercises, even gently, they will get the healing effects.

They'll feel better too. Exercise works because any muscle starts to feel good when it's used. Then when the patient uses another muscle it also starts to feel good, then another one, and so on. This muscle activity releases endorphins, the body's "feel-good" chemicals.

As a result, toning of muscles brings about some emotional well-being, which is a big plus for any patient who's been on Workers' Compensation a while. These patients need the satisfaction of starting a task--even exercising one or two muscles--and succeeding. (This is also the reason that some exercise is always part of chronic pain programs, see Chapter 19.)

WHEN TO START EXERCISE

It's never made sense to me to wait six weeks or more until an injury is "healed" and then try to get a patient back in shape. I try to get every one of my patients to see that activity and exercise are the right treatments from the very beginning.

What this means is that in my practice there is no artificial distinction between treatment and "rehabiliation". Rehab starts on day one of treatment.

As I was writing this chapter I saw Todd Mitchell who had a history of back strains off and on for seven years, temporary improvement, pain again, improvement, etc. He told me: "Eventually I figured there must be something permanently and seriously wrong so I got an attorney and put in a claim for disability."

But he also said that he got to a different doctor who put him through a structured exercise program. Todd learned to do daily back and abdominal exercises, completed a full fitness program, and at the end learned correct body mechanics for his job.

The result? This patient who thought he had a "permanent back injury" now happily says: "I have no pain, I'm back driving heavy equipment and I'm doing terrific. I have no symptoms at all and no limitations. They should have put me through that program five years ago."

It was a crime that Todd had been allowed to keep having back strains and to think he was disabled, when all he needed was the right exercise program. I told him so: "I guess you didn't <u>have</u> any disability. Your entire medical problem was just lack of exercise."

"You bet it was."

How To Start

I recommend my patients start with gentle range of motion of the injured part as soon as they can tolerate it and I feel it's safe. Even if a patient is severely injured, while he's in bed he can start doing some motion, even if it's moving only one hand. As soon as he's up and around he can start moving and stretching other muscles and then progress.

For many injuries, I may start with <u>passive</u>, then <u>assisted</u>, then <u>active range of motion</u> for flexibility and stretching therapy as I described in Chapter 11. I match the motions to the patient's specific injury and to their general level of muscle tone.

Fitness should always be part of anyone's routine. With a typical muscle sprain or uncomplicated fracture, I also recommend work-out or fitness exercises of the <u>non</u>-injured parts immediately. For example, even with a cast on one arm there's no reason to let the other arm and the legs become soft and weak. Patients like this could do general exercises such as walking, jogging, and even weight lifting with the other arm. These keep a patient toned up and fit--and feeling good despite having an injury.

For severe problems such as a disc herniation I recommend initial bedrest, then some exercises as soon as the patient can get out of bed. I recommend they start with some light walking as soon as possible, and at the earliest practical time I recommend gentle hot pool motion. This is not swimming, just moving around in the water to stay loose. In the water a patient is weightless so there are no gravity stresses or impacts.

Then as time passes and the patient makes progress I start him walking around in the pool, first backwards against the water and later forwards, perhaps paddling around with sidestroke, etc. After a few weeks of these gentle swimming and stretching exercises I recommend more kicking. Ultimately a patient can actually "jog in the deep end", which can be quite vigorous aerobic exercise but again without any impact.

> *"A patient's legs are his two best physicians."*
>
> *...Hippocrates*

I always recommend walking as one of the best all-around exercises. Sometimes patients look at me as if they think I'm crazy when I ask them to walk five miles a day. But I recommend they <u>start</u> at one mile a day and they can even break this down into three walks: Out of the house in the morning, go a few blocks and come back and repeat the same walk at noon and evening. It's surprising how easy it is to clock four or even five miles a day with this method.

WORK HARDENING PROGRAMS

If a musculoskeletal injury has not resolved with simple general stretching and fitness exercises, it's time to put a patient into a "Work Hardening" program. These are structured and supervised programs of strength, fitness, endurance, posture training and body mechanics practice. I've used Work Hardening for hundreds of patients, and it's effective.

These programs got their names from the idea of "hardening off" plant seedlings before putting them outside. The analogy is to "harden up" a patient's muscles after injury before putting him back to work. So they're really "patient hardening" programs--but for some reason no-one calls them that.

Work Hardening programs vary around the country, but in general a patient will attend them three or more times per week for two to four hours each day. Work Hardening is usually done in a rehabilitation or PT department under the watchful eyes of Work Hardening instructors or therapists.

Ken has basically recovered from a back injury. But he needs to strengthen specific muscles that he'll use on the job. "I'm writing a prescription for six weeks of Work Hardening, and I'll make it for three times a week. I'm going to start you out pushing and pulling about 50 pounds and working with some pulleys, and you can increase your weights later. You'll also be climbing stairs to increase endurance."

He says: "You know, my balance hasn't been so good since this injury."

I reassure him: "You'll also be learning better posture and balance with therapists supervising the whole time and watching your lifting skills too. In fact, when they start you in lifting training they may even attach a little buzzer to your back. If you bend too far forward it'll remind you to use better body mechanics."

"What are body mechanics?"

"The techniques of lifting, pushing, and pulling. Work Hardening includes a slide show to describe safe material handling skills for your job. You'll start next week--pick up some sweatsuits and gym shoes to do the workouts."

A good Work Hardening setup may look almost like a gym, with exercise equipment plus mock-ups of work areas for practice. The program that I've used the most has mock-up plumbing and electrical areas, construction sites, sand and gravel boxes for shoveling, wheelbarrows for pushing, chainsaws, etc.

If you go to a good program the exercises will be custom-designed for your injury and your situation. A good program will use stretching exercises to stabilize your trunk and spine muscles and will include flexibility and endurance exercises to help you stay resilient. This should develop exercises that are matched specifically to the tasks that you do at your job, not some other job or some "standard set" of exercise.

For example, if you are a delivery driver your Work Hardening program should emphasize the bending and lifting and stacking that you do every day. If you're a Nursing Assistant, your program should emphasize lifting and transferring patients, leaning over beds, squatting, etc. The best programs are job-specific like this, not just general fitness builders.

A Work Hardening program will also get you used to being back in a regular routine because you have to get up in the morning, get on your "work clothes", be at the program on time and use your muscles for "work". This helps you prepare emotionally as well as physically to eventually return to your job.

WHAT PATIENTS SAY ABOUT WORK HARDENING

I've found that patients like Work Hardening programs. Of the hundreds I've put into Work Hardening, only two or three have said it was boring or of little value to them. Virtually every other patient has said that it helped them, they felt stronger, less nervous about returning to work and so on.

> *"Everyone should go through this kind of program* before *they get hurt. It's the best thing that ever happened to me. I see how I did things unsafely before. And I sure wasn't in very good shape either--I found that out right away!"*

Some patients have told me how valuable it was to be with a couple of dozen other injured workers every day, all trying to get back to work, all learning to be fit, and all sharing some common discomfort and frustration. Patients tell me they develop camaraderie in such a situation.

> *One patient told me: "It helped emotionally to find out I'm not the only person in the world that has Workers' Compensation problems."*
>
> *Another patient with chronic myofascial pain in the upper back told me how she found that stretching, swimming and aerobics exercises were really the only thing that helped her. She said: "It was really hard to tell me that at first, wasn't it? I didn't want to hear it. And when I went to PT they'd show me some exercises but it didn't sink in."*

> *"Then when I got in the Y program and talked to other people who had the same thing and were getting better because of exercises, that helped me. Now I see it really did help. I wish you could tell people to get into exercise sooner."*

I can see it with my own eyes when a patient gets benefit form Work Hardening: They walk more upright, they move more briskly, and they have that "I'm in control of my life now" look. They tell me how much better they feel. They've been setting their own physical goals, controlling their symptoms, and I can see that they're starting to look ahead instead of backward.

A few patients complain of temporary stiffness or muscle pain after starting Work Hardening. This is almost always just a case of sore muscles, the kind that come with any new exercise. But if you are in a Work Hardening program and you begin to have more and more pain instead of less, get it checked out by your doctor right away. No Work Hardening program should ever make you worse.

WHAT COMES AFTER WORK HARDENING?

What happens when you finish a Work Hardening program? Simple: You go back to work (see Chapter 20) if there's a job waiting, or if your Rehabilitation Consultant can find one for you.

The way it goes is as follows: Your doctor reviews your Work Hardening capacities to see what you've been doing safely. For example, you may have been lifting 30 pounds from the floor or 45 pounds from waist level, pushing 150 pounds, climbing a ladder without difficulty, etc. He takes these into account and sets safe limits for you to start work again.

Then if a restricted duty job is available and it matches your capacities, your doctor will release you for a trial of work under the restrictions. There's quite a bit more to it than that, but that's in Chapter 20.

I have one caution for you: Make sure it's only your doctor that sets your work restrictions. I've seen it happen several times where Work Hardening therapists simply write down what they think is safe for a patient and he takes the slip to his employer who follows it exactly. In some cases the restrictions have been way off base. These patients were re-injured. Their doctors would have known better: They knew far more things about the patients than the Work Hardening staff could ever be aware of, and they would have set the restrictions at considerably lower levels that would have been safe. So don't get yourself in the same fix. Don't allow anyone but your doctor to set your restrictions or release you for work.

A LIFETIME OF FITNESS

Once you leave a supervised exercise program and return to work there's no such thing as "ending" your need for exercise. Flexibility and endurance are a lifelong requirement. This is why I try to put patients into independent exercise programs: Walking as often as possible, and swim.

"Exercise can preserve something of our early strength even in old age."

.....*Cicero*

I often recommend that patients work out on Nautilus two or three times a week. I've found that those who keep up with Nautilus stay fit, rarely come back to see me with re-injuries, and have few long-lasting symptoms. Over the years I've personally trained several hundred of my own patients on Nautilus machines and when I do I match their specific exercise routine to their injuries.

"Walking makes for a long life."

....*Hindu Proverb*

But no matter what kind of exercise is available, walking is still the best all around fitness-builder. It's free, it requires no special facilities, and you can do it anytime. Hippocrates described a patient's legs as being "the best physicians". A British walking expert recently echoed this when he said: "Whenever I'm not feeling good, I just consult my two doctors. I start walking and they tell my body how to heal." Regular walking probably does more to preserve health and foster peace of mind than almost any other exercise.

PRE-OP AND POST-OP EXERCISES

For patients who are about to have elective surgery, I recommend all the same exercise routines I discussed in this chapter: Start with the gentlest and then progress to more strenuous ones. If a patient can tolerate Work Hardening before surgery, that's the ideal pre-op program. If a patient has a severe injury, at the very least I recommend that before surgery they keep the uninjured areas moving as much as possible.

The surgical patients who follow these programs faithfully do the best at surgery, have the least pain afterwards, and recover the fastest.

After surgery I recommend the same treatment as if they had an acute injury (which, in fact, they technically have just had on the operating table). I start them on gentle range of motion, swimming, exercising the non-operated parts, walking, and so on. Then as soon as they can go into Work Hardening I recommend they start it. It's ideal post-op exercise.

WRAP-UP

How to do yourself some favors with exercises:

1) Start general range of motion and then fitness exercise as soon after any injury as your doctor says it's safe. There's nothing to be gained by lying around for weeks and while you're off work there's no reason to treat yourself as an invalid;

2) Exercise whatever you can: If your arm is injured then start walking, if your knee is injured start lifting, if your back is injured start swimming, if your ankle is injured exercise everything from the knees up;

3) Work Hardening is one of the most effective ways to prepare for a safe return to work;

4) Exercise and flexibility are lifetime needs for everyone. Walking is almost always the best exercise.

J

CHAPTER 17

The Psych Connection

"It's not in my head, Doc, it's in my back. You think I'm <u>imagining</u> this pain?"

"No. I know it's real and I know it's in your back. But I want you to have some counselling now. I think it will help you deal with the stresses of this injury and everything connected with it."

He leaned forward and looked at me square on. I could feel the intensity behind his words, as if he didn't know to be angry or worried. "You think I've gone nuts, Doc? Is that it?"

Almost every Workers' Compensation case can have an emotional component. Any injured person is naturally worried, but work injuries also carry built-in concerns about recovery, job security, self-esteem, peer pressure and isolation.

In this chapter I'll show you how psychological factors can impede healing and recovery, and how to beat stresses that come with Comp.

SOME HAVE IT, SOME DON'T

A person's psychological resilience often makes the difference between healing and not healing. Most medical and rehab professionals will agree that the patients who have "got it inside" are the ones who get better. We provide medical care and direction, but <u>it's the patient's makeup that makes the difference</u>.

I've had dozens of patients who threw in the towel, gave up their jobs and most of their life activities and crawled into a shell. But I've had dozens of others who literally "made themselves better". How did they do it?

What was it about Alice Quigley, for example? Alice had a severe wrist injury that became more painful no matter what anyone did for her including two surgeries, exercises, rehabilitation and a TENS. Over the years she developed so much pain that she couldn't use her hand. She couldn't even tolerate being touched. What was it about Alice that made her overcome all this and move ahead with her life and get back into the work she loves?

Or what was it about Tom Clinton, who had a neck injury in a rollover? Despite the best efforts of his chiropractor, myself, rehabilitation, therapy, biofeedback and so on he never did get free of pain. Then after two years he sat down in my exam room and told me he wouldn't have any more treatment. He said: "I'm tired of being on Comp, my adjuster is tired of me being on Comp, and I don't want to go through this any longer. I want to just get going with my life and I'm leaving the area to go to school at my own expense."

He had already researched the college, the courses, he had interviewed with an advisor and he was signed up. What was it about Tom that kept him from giving up?

Or take two 60-year-old semi drivers, both with severe shoulder injuries, both with surgery. Both vowed to get back on the road at the earliest possible date. But after recuperation and therapy and several months of sitting around, what happened? Jack told me, "I don't think I'll go back. That rocking chair is looking mighty good." But Lowell came to his followup visit and said: "Sure it still bothers me. I'll have to hire help for the loading, but I'm ready to go back if you'll let me. How about tomorrow?"

What makes this happen?   Why did Alice and Tom and Lowell change from "Comp patients" to people in control?   Unfortunately, nobody is too successful at identifying such people ahead of time.   But we are learning to recognize the stresses that can accompany injury and we do know some methods that patients can use to beat them.

WORKERS' COMPENSATION: STRESSES TO THE MAX

"I know you're not crazy.   But we know that just being a patient can alter someone's psychological status and cause emotional adjustment problems.   We know there is stress from having pain day in and day out.   And we know there's anxiety while being on Comp."
"You sure got that right, Doc."

I see patients who get hurt and think they are simply going to get Comp benefits, see the doctor and recover eventually.   They have no idea they can be subjected to a veritable barrage of psychological pressures by the situation.   I see and hear their reactions to their injuries, to their circumstances, and to imagined threats:

"It's just an injury, why so long to heal, why aren't I getting better--is there something wrong with me?"... loss of self-respect, being out of work ... little family frictions turning into big family frictions ... scrutiny, "I'm always in the spotlight, the Comp people are watching me, I can't even work in the garden or tune the car because someone will see me"... income drops, you feel like you're on the dole, it's a disability lifestyle and it seems to go on forever...

It hurts too much to do family activities,   "No, I hurt too much for that, maybe next week"..."My kids say 'Dad can't lift that, he's injured' and it's starting to get to me"... "My gut always hurts": Side effects from antiinflammatories and low energy from muscle relaxants... depres-sion ... isolation, no familiar co-worker faces and no daily routine ... fear of hurting the rest of your life, not getting your job, the money might run out, your spouse might leave ... anger at employers, resentment ... peer pressure: "My friends act like I'm a free-loader and they don't even come around anymore"...

Boredom on Comp and out of work ... loss of control--the biggest stress...an insensitive doctor tells a patient he's "disabled for life"...

uncertainty about the future ... the stress of constantly fighting with insurers ...

These are the stresses of a Comp case: They take their toll on everybody, they erode self-confidence, cause anxiety, lower self-esteem, inhibit restful sleep, interfere with decision making and go along with slow recovery.

Notice something? The injury causes only one of the stresses: Pain. All of the others, including the most paralyzing, are products of the situation.

The psychological stresses are even further aggravated by physical factors such as being out of shape and by bureaucratic factors such as delays in Comp claim processing, by medical delays in getting consultations or second opinions, by employers dragging their feet on light duty, etc.

Patients can't control any of these factors. Few of them would exist with a non-work injury. So it's being on Comp, not an injury, that can uncover psychological problems. Yes, some injuries are devastating enough in themselves: Loss of a limb or eye, a particularly gruesome industrial accident, etc. But usually it's the system itself that keeps the patient alienated, isolated, and uncertain.

Ten Ways To Keep Psychologically Cool

It is possible to remain resilient. You can absorb or duck the punches the Workers' Compensation system throws your way. You can win over the Comp stresses. All it takes is knowing how and then applying yourself.

KNOW THE PROBLEM. Knowing what you're up against is 3/4 of beating it. So know what the Comp system is, what you can expect from it and what it will demand from you. By learning the ins and outs of the system you regain some control over your own life. This is a confidence builder all by itself.

START SOME KIND OF WORK. Return to some daily work, even part time or light duty as soon as it's feasible (see Chapter 20). The psychological benefits of getting back into the mainstream of life are immeasurable.

EXERCISE. Some patients never get going again after spending a few months sitting around stiff and out of shape. These are the patients who succumb to Workers' Compensation stresses. Fitness exercise makes you feel good, it gives you a sense of instant accomplishment and it speeds healing (see Chapter 16). Simple and regular exercise is one of the best prescriptions for psychological stress.

KEEP A HEALTHY LIFESTYLE. You'll have the best recovery if you go to bed early, have a good diet, your home situation is good and your lifestyle is supportive and if you don't have a problem with alcohol or drug abuse (see Chapter 18).

SET A GOAL, MAKE THE GOAL, FEEL THE SUCCESS. When a patient is on Comp, achieving even one small thing can be a welcome change from frustration. Try a simple walking goal such as: "I will walk one mile today and tomorrow one and a half miles in two trips". Or try: "I will ask my Rehabilitation Consultant to do some testing to find out what jobs I am suited for since I can't go back to my heavy job. I will call her today." Or try a bigger goal such as: "I'll do everything I can to get back to my job in five weeks."

The best way to achieve a goal is to literally write it down on paper, re-read it every morning, then go out and do something each day to make it happen. By doing this you'll discover how exhilarating even one or two small wins can be.

ACCEPT DISCOMFORT. Many injuries do carry some long-lasting pain and discomfort. If you've had such an injury it's psychologically healthy to understand that and accept it as a fact of life.

KEEP MEDICATIONS TO A MINIMUM. Do take medications as your doctor prescribes them but try to avoid using unnecessary pills, particularly narcotics and tranquilizers. These drugs have side effects that can keep you feeling lethargic and some are addicting. Some tranquilizers have side effects that prevent you from getting refreshing rest (see Chapter 11).

LEARN STRESS MANAGEMENT. Learn to relax by learning a permanent and effective stress reduction technique. The literature and research that I've reviewed shows that the Transcendental Meditation technique is the most effective, easiest to learn, most appealing and worth its expense. Research shows that it reduces anxiety, improves concentration and is available at TM centers in most major cities. Your doctor may prescribe it as part of your treatment if he's familiar with it.

STAY AWAY FROM HYPNOSIS. I know that several pain clinics use hypnosis. But my opinion--which I reached after studying, teaching, and using hypnosis clinically--is that hypnosis should be avoided. I'd rather see patients paying attention to their own body's signals and perceptions than suppressing them. In some cases I've seen patients start to act a little neurotic as a result, and no-one on Comp needs to feel neurotic.

DON'T WASTE TIME ON "DISABILITY THINKING". I've seen some Comp patients fall into the trap of trying to "prove" they're disabled. They do this for either a legal reason or for secondary gain (see next pages) or out of anger. It cripples them emotionally: They change overnight from recovering employees to sad and emotionally unstable patients.

These patients waste their time and energy fighting to show everyone how disabled they are and that reduces their will to recover. This does not increase their disability ratings but it certainly does put a dark cloud over their whole existence. Avoid this trap.

COUNSELLING?

It may be appropriate for your doctor to refer you to a psychological clinic for some counselling, if stresses have overwhelmed you. I do this quite frequently and I always assure the patient that there's no disgrace in having a few visits to help sort things out.

I'm not talking about psychoanalysis or psychotherapy. I'm talking about three or four sessions to help a patient get a handle on whatever problem is getting in the way of recovery: Anger, resentment, frustration, alienation, concern over the future, etc.

I've found that a psychologist who is used to seeing the emotional difficulties of Comp patients can often show patients how to handle their problems remarkably well after only a few sessions. Ask your doctor if there's such a psychologist nearby. If your doctor sees much Workers' Compensation he'll probably know of a clinic with a good reputation and a good success rate.

Does Any Of This Stuff Really Work?

Answer: Well, yes and no. It all "works" if you do it. Fitness does make you feel better, but only if you do it right and regularly. Goal setting does work if you really set goals and work for them. TM does decrease anxiety if you meditate regularly. Counselling does work if you get to the right counselor.

But overall the success of all these measures is much less than it should be. Many things contribute to this failure: Too little treatment too late, inappropriate treatment, insufficient treatment, etc. But the main cause is that patients lack commitment and follow-through.

True Psychological Problems

Even after I explain all about psychological stress in the emotional roller coaster of Workers' Compensation some patients still ask: "Could it be I really am nuts?" The answer is: Probably not.

It's rare to see a truly severe mental illness that interferes with recovery from a work injury. It's even more rare for an injury to cause a mental illness. Just because a patient has continued pain and feels depressed or angry or confused does not mean that he has an emotional illness. It may just mean that he's reacted to multiple stresses.

However, we do occasionally see "symptom magnification" and "functional overlay". Both these terms mean that a patient reacts to his or her symptoms more strongly than is usual or "normal". They do not mean that a person is intentionally magnifying symptoms or that the symptoms are made up. Nor do they mean a person is crazy or lying or trying to magnify symptoms on purpose. These terms merely signify to us that these patients need more help in learning how to deal with symptoms and limitations.

Most people are not used to pain and a few can become so caught up in focusing on their symptoms that their troubles and the symptoms become worse. There are many causes of functional overlay including simple frustration, fatigue, and chronic pain. These factors simply make patients more susceptible to the psychological problems of their illness or injury. Short-term counselling usually helps these patients quickly.

SECONDARY GAIN

There's also something called "secondary gain" in Comp. This usually means that some patients have realized that the longer they stay disabled the longer they'll get the "free money" of Comp benefits. The result is that healing takes longer, complications are more frequent, and return to work is delayed. Simply put, secondary gain patients resist recovery.

There are other sources of secondary gain besides money: Some patients like the sympathy they get from their spouse. Some are angry at their employers and remain disabled as a way of getting back. Secondary gain is not always conscious. Most of these people are not intentionally faking their prolonged disability or "malingering". Most are probably unaware that they're dragging out recovery.

Doctors who treat Workers' Compensation injuries usually recognize secondary gain. They realize that the best treatment is to send the patient back to work. This is usually successful though patients often don't like it very much. I've had patients later tell me: "I was pretty mad at you when you made me go back to work. It worked out all right and it really was better for me to get back on the job. But I sure didn't think so at the time. I thought you were pretty mean."

DEPRESSION

Depression can be a very real problem in Comp, particularly when financial and family pressures are overwhelming. I had a patient recently, Sam Thompson, who was trying to get along with his chronic injury and was trying to put himself through school too. But he was irritable and worried about his future livelihood. His marriage started fraying at the edges. Simultaneously he had more pain, had more trouble at school, and came into my office in tears several times.

This is typical of a "situational depression" reaction to Workers' Compensation pressures. With medication and a few sessions of counselling, Sam did very well. He continued in school, he's looking towards graduation as a top student, and he'll be off Comp soon.

Depression in Comp is usually a short-term "adjustment" reaction. Doctors can usually treat such depression fairly easily with medications.

When depression truly gets in the way of treatment and daily activity I have recommended that some patients have short-term counselling. This is usually successful.

HYSTERIA

Hysteria or "conversion reaction" is one difficult psychological problem that we do see in Workers' Compensation injuries on a regular basis. Simply put, conversion reaction means that patients subconsciously convert anxiety or stress into physical symptoms.

The classic hysteria is a truck driver who runs over a child and "goes blind". There is no true physical blindness but nevertheless this man cannot see. Of course the underlying mechanism is as follows: The man is horrified at killing the child, his subconscious knows that if he can't see he won't be able to drive and if he can't drive he can't run over any more kids. His subconscious makes him "lose the ability to see". Sophisticated tests can demonstrate he in fact does see, but it doesn't matter whether the blindness is "real" or not. It's real to him and he doesn't see.

Other examples of hysteria are extreme symptoms of pain, unexplained limited use of an arm or hand or leg, etc. In hysteria the symptoms are usually far beyond what would be expected from the injury, which is often minor.

We always have to work up the symptoms assuming they are real, but in hysteria we can't find <u>medical</u> explanations. The psychological explanation is the conversion reaction.

Such problems are extremely difficult for doctors to deal with, because the patient is absolutely convinced that they have severe symptoms that prevent them from recovering.

When I see a patient with prolonged symptoms out of the ordinary, inexplicable findings, findings on examination that don't make sense or follow any known anatomic order I have to suspect hysteria. Then I will obtain a sophisticated evaluation from a psychologist. Even when the diagnosis of hysteria is established, these patients are very resistant to treatment. In fact they usually deny that the diagnosis is correct. These Comp cases usually have unsuccessful outcomes.

PSYCHOLOGICAL TESTS

How do doctors uncover the correct diagnosis when psychological problems exist? There are many methods including testing, but one test that has been proven useful is the world-famous Minnesota Multiphasic Personality Inventory.

> *"I want you to take this paper and pencil psychology test. It's called the MMPI-2 and it will give me a good idea how much your injury has been getting to you. It will show whether or not you are more depressed than I've suspected, how angry you might be about things, and so on."*
>
> *He's hesitant, obviously wondering if I'm telling him everything. "Does this mean you think I'm ready for the the booby hatch, Doc?"*
>
> *"No, this is just as much a diagnostic procedure as all the X-rays and scans I've already run. The results will help me formulate a treatment plan."*
>
> *"All right, Doc, I'll take it. But you'll tell me what it shows about me, won't you?"*

The MMPI is an approximately 500-item true or false personality test developed in Minnesota in the 1940's. This test has become the standard for psychological measurement world-wide, is more widely used than any other test in the world, has been translated into over 100 different languages and it's even in braille. It has recently been updated to the MMPI-2.

The MMPI is used in screening of astronauts, police, counsellors, athletes, etc. Medical students are trained how to use it and take the test at least once during school.

If your doctor asks you to take the MMPI, just go ahead and take it. It will help him get a much better read-out of your problems.

Don't be put off by some of the questions. Some of them are simple: "I like mechanics magazines: True or False?" is easy to answer. But there are others that are pretty unusual, having to do with areas of symptoms, feelings you might have, family affairs, etc.

Be honest when you take the MMPI. Even though these questions sound personal, be assured that the MMPI is scored by computer. No-one is going to look at your score sheet and think that your answers might be strange, or laugh at them. Mostly we're interested in the pattern of answers which the computer picks out easily.

The test also has many built-in checks on validity. In other words, it's easy to tell if someone has tried to fake it or present themselves in a falsely good light or bad light. It's simpler all around to just take the test forthrightly. The best recommendation is to take the test by going through each item and answering it as close to what is true for you as possible. Then go on to the next question. Don't take a lot of time with each question.

WRAP-UP

How to do yourself some favors when Comp stresses come up:
1) If you find yourself caught up in frustration, anger, indecision, anxiety or depression it's likely that the stresses of Workers' Compensation are catching up with you;
2) There are several methods of fighting the stresses of Comp including exercise, goal setting, relaxation and counselling, and all will work if you stick with them;
3) Your doctor orders psychological tests such as the MMPI to help you, not to trick you. Psychological tests are diagnostic tools that can help him set your treatment.

J

CHAPTER 18

Lifestyle And Family Influences On Recuperation

Health is the groundwork of all happiness.

...Leigh Hunt

Other men live to eat, while I eat to live.

...Socrates

Believe it or not, something as unremarkable as your lifestyle--how you live, eat and drink--could be a major factor in how quickly you re-cover from any injury, especially on Comp. The kind of support that you get at home from your spouse or others is almost as important.

Unfortunately these two things are often overlooked, perhaps because they are so mundane and non-glamorous. But it's a mistake because, quite simply, a patient's lifestyle and family matters could even make the difference between recovery and failure in Workers' Compensation cases.

> *One of the best outcomes after injury that I ever saw was a man who had three fractures of the spine and two fractures of the ankle. He sustained the injuries when he fell off a building and a heavy pipe fell on top of him. Despite the severity of his injuries he recovered quickly. Later he told me, "I'm surprised I did as well as I did".*
>
> *How did it happen that he recovered so well? It was hardly a mystery: He's optimum weight fits, a nonsmoker and nondrinker, his spouse was behind him every step of the way, and he maintained a positive attitude. I would have been surprised if he hadn't recovered quickly.*

When you're recovering from a work injury or illness it's <u>extremely</u> important to take good care of yourself. This chapter shows you how.

LIFESTYLE: DIET

The classic picture of the guy on Comp sitting in front of the TV all day-- with big boxes of donuts, huge bags of potato chips and popcorn plus a few cases of beer or Coke--is perhaps exaggerated. But for some, not too far from the truth. Don't let this happen to you.

Weight gain is a medical problem, and it's often a big problem with patients on Comp, because so many just lie around. Anyone who lies around will become obese, and any patient who is obese can't exercise. Even worse, weight gain gives a patient feelings of failure and lack of control. All this leads to anxiety and unhappiness, and these lead to-- more weight gain!

So, if you're thin now stay as thin as you can. If you've already gained weight, try to lose what you can. Do your best to stay at a stable and optimum weight while you're on Comp.

> *The Chinese do not make any distinction between food and medicine.*
>
> *...Lin Yutang, The Importance of Living*

A good kitchen is a good Apothecary shop.

...*William Bullein*

As to exactly what food to eat while you're recovering from an injury, it makes sense to follow the most healthy diet available. The food you eat is perhaps more important than anything else you do for your well-being.

There are lots of books around these days with food and diet recommendations. The best advice is to eat a wide variety of foods but eat with moderation. Also, it's easier on your system to have regular mealtimes and not snack in between them.

This is not a diet book, so it's probably simplest for me to recommend you obtain a copy of the "New American Diet". Several health and nutrition organizations have recently proposed this diet and a copy is probably at your library. It includes low amounts of fat, high amounts of carbohydrates and fiber, fruits and vegetables, and less red meat. The emphasis is on fresh foods and fewer pre-processed or refined foods.

A healthy diet that will help you recover does not consist of Coke and sweet rolls for breakfast, other junk food for lunch, and beer and pizza at night. I've always found that most people know deep inside what's most suitable for them to eat and what makes them feel best afterwards; follow that inner voice.

If someone truly wants to put his diet and nutrition in balance, he could look into the program described by Deepak Chopra, M.D., in his book <u>Perfect Health</u>. He describes a system of dividing people into three body types. His book shows each type how to use a holistic approach to balance his or her diet and activity and achieve optimum weight.

LIFESTYLE: EXERCISE

In several places I discuss the value of stretching and fitness exercise: In special sections B and C as part of treatment for strains, sprains and back injuries; in Chapter 11 as an important part of virtually every treatment; in Chapter 16 I explained how it works, and in Chapter 17 I showed that exercise is psychologically healthy. In the next chapter on chronic pain I also show how regular physical exercise helps reduce discomfort.

It's not only after injuries that physical activity is important. With any occupational illness, such as respiratory disease and others, it's also beneficial to stay as physically active as you can.

A daily walk of a half hour or so is pleasant, it's calming therapy, and it's a great time to be out with someone you're close to. Regular long walks are one of the ideal methods for weight loss and general fitness as well as stress reduction.

LIFESTYLE: REGULAR REST

Bed is a medicine.

...Italian Proverb

The way to the fastest recovery from an injury is to rest correctly: The right kind of rest, and the right amount, at the right time. This means-- even though the concept is old and hackneyed--it's healthiest to go to bed early, get a good night's sleep, and get up early. This is especially true while you're on Comp.

Rest, rest, perturbed spirit!

...Shakespeare

Everyone knows what it's like after too late a night: Tired, grumpy, everything seems hard. When a tired person meets a problem he sees no solutions.

Dr. William Dement, director of Stanford's Sleep Center, was recently quoted in Time Magazine as saying that "most Americans no longer know what it feels like to be fully alert" and they go through the day in a sort of twilight zone. Even one night of shorter sleep apparently causes more human error and more accidents, injuries, etc. Fatigue makes a person function at half efficiency or less.

To a person who's well-rested, problems aren't such problems. He sees the solution. He feels better. He is better. He enjoys a better mood all day, and if he's on Comp he finds it immensely easier to tackle his task of healing and recovering.

So I recommend you rest and bring more solutions to your Comp case. It's complicated and hard enough to be on Comp without feeling fatigued. A good rule of thumb is to remember that the quality of your day starts when you go to bed the night before.

FAMILY STRESSES

Mike's recovery had slowed down. His pain was worse. His attitude was taking a nose dive--he just wasn't putting much effort into his recovery anymore. And there were no medical or psychological explanations.

But I suspected the real problem--difficulty at home--and I asked him: "Michael, you've had this injury for six or seven months now. Pretty limited at home?" He was. "How about playing with your kids? Going out bowling? Dancing?" He couldn't do any of those.

"I gained some weight, too," he said.

I asked: "Do you think there's some family stress, some marital friction because of these limitations?"

He looked at me a few seconds. Then he looked away and said, "Yeah, maybe. I suppose so, in fact."

I waited and he went on: "I guess she doesn't understand or something. It is getting to her, I can tell that. It's like she's tired of me being around the house or something. And she's getting on me about the few beers I have, too."

There it was. Mike was showing what happens when a patient doesn't think he's getting support and sympathy at home. The next step would have to be a conference with both of them.

A Comp injury puts a lot of pressure on family dynamics, and most families are not prepared to deal with it. When I see treatment stalling, a patient's attitude changing for the worse, and the beginning of psychological stress effects I usually inquire about problems at home.

It's common with any prolonged Comp case to see this picture of home life. On the one side the patient is out of work, alienated from his peers, probably uncomfortable or in pain, and uncertain about the future. Then on the other side the spouse is putting up with him or her every day, has to adapt to unaccustomed limitations, and takes the brunt of his or her mood changes. In addition there is often a change in roles and a change in the financial situation. The common result is friction.

This family/spouse friction almost always interferes with the patient's recuperation. But it can also interfere with treatment itself.

But I've seen cases where a patient's spouse interferes with treatment by lack of support--the patient has no-one at home to turn to for support and sympathy, no-one has patience with him, and no-one understands what he's going through.

I've seen other cases where the spouse interferes by meddling with treatment--not getting prescriptions filled, not making it easy for the patient to get to PT, being hostile to doctors and claim adjusters, etc. I saw one man who always changed his wife's therapy schedules, changed her followup appointments with the doctor, and I believe even tried to change her medications. No treatment can be successful with this kind of interference.

I've also seen patients where the spouse sabotaged the recovery by undermining treatment and reinforcing feelings of disability to keep the patient home as long as possible. This was for various reasons--desire for continued Comp checks, desire to control a spouse or keep him at home, dislike and revenge aimed at an employer, resentment of the spouse's closest co-workers, etc.

SOLUTIONS TO FAMILY STRESSES

If stresses start to interfere with your recovery I recommend the following solutions:

1) First I recommend a conference between doctor, patient and spouse. It would be helpful for the spouse to read Chapter 18 on psychology beforehand. In the conference, the doctor should clearly explain your injury, why you have the discomfort you have, and why you have limitations. Your spouse should feel the freedom to ask any questions necessary. It would probably also help if your doctor gives some kind of prediction about how long before you get back to normal.

2) Second I recommend some short-term counselling for the patient, with the spouse in attendance at one or two sessions at least. These sessions should be with a psychologist or counsellor who understands the stresses and problems of Workers' Compensation. Three or four sessions will usually be enough to resolve the difficulties.

"You were right on, Doc, about that counselling", a patient recently told me. "I learned what I was doing, not to blame people, what happened and that kind of thing. My wife understood, we got back together. Now we help each other."

3) Third, the obvious best solution to family Comp stress is for the patient to return to work--even part time or light duty--as soon as safe. Merely returning to some work and normal life has psychological benefits of restoring confidence and self-esteem.

Alcohol Or Drug Problems

If you have a problem with chemical dependency, whether it's alcohol or any kind of drugs, then Workers' Compensation is only one of your difficulties--and perhaps the smaller one at that.

We drink to one another's health but in so doing we spoil our own.
...Jerome K. Jerome

Alcohol or drug use is far beyond the scope of this book. But you may be reading this chapter because someone close to you is on Comp and also on drugs or drinking. If so, try to get them some help if you can.

I know this is easier said than done, but it's still worth trying. I've seen alcoholism and drug dependency simply wreck recovery from a work injury. Patients with these problems start missing doctors' appointments, missing physical therapy, taking their medications erratically, and so on.

Drunkenness is simply voluntary insanity.
...Seneca

Usually in these cases the whole rehabilitation process becomes stalled and the patient has to go through a CD program before we can get on with treating their injury. If so, I can almost guarantee one thing: The insurer will stop benefits while the patient gets his CD under control. Afterward, when his life is more straightened around, the insurer will put him back on Comp to recover.

One other thing that you should know: Workers' Compensation benefits will probably be denied for any injury that resulted from use of alcohol or drugs at work. This is one of the few circumstances where an injury at work is not compensable. Drug-free workplaces are becoming a matter of law these days and it's likely no drug use on the job will be tolerated by employer after the patient returns to work.

WRAP-UP

How to do yourself some favors with lifestyle and family matters:
1) Remember that lifestyle is critical to well-being. You feel better and recover sooner with regular physical activity and a good diet;
2) Old-fashioned advice is still good: Go to bed early, get plenty of good rest, and give your best face to your Comp problems;
3) If your home situation is not conducive to recovery from injury, ask your doctor about it and request short-term counselling.
4) Chemical dependency can affect your Workers' Compensation benefits and your recovery. If it's a problem, get help early.

F

CHAPTER 19

Chronic Pain Management

"Doctor, is there a medical reason for me to keep having all this pain? Is it actually real?"

"Certainly it's real...It's real pain that you're experiencing."

"Oh, thank goodness you said that. It's been so long. I thought maybe it was all psychological."

Less than 1 out of 1000 Comp patients need this chapter. Very few injuries result in Chronic Pain Syndromes. Chronic pain can't be faked, but for those few people who do have it, chronic pain can be a persistent and potentially devastating problem.

This chapter describes how chronic pain usually develops, and what help is available if you have it.

CHRONIC PAIN

No-one fully agrees about the best definition of chronic pain.

The study of chronic pain is a relatively recent part of medicine--two or three decades at most and pain concepts are still rapidly changing. But we can describe in general the sequence of how a pain syndrome comes about.

If a patient has discomfort in some area of the body after an injury, it can make him anxious and discouraged. The result is that he cuts down on activity and gets stiff. The consequence of stiffness is more pain, and this makes him more anxious. If he also has muscle spasm, anxiety and pain will both increase. This produces a pain > spasm > pain and stress cycle that takes hold of the patient. This cycle becomes difficult to inter- rupt and becomes a "chronic pain" syndrome.

There are other ways that chronic pain takes hold. Sometimes pain can be so severe and so long-lasting that it causes emotional changes and wears down a patient. This is particularly true with long-lasting low back pain or neck pain.

Some patients are simply more disposed to brood excessively on pain as part of their personality. Pain begins to occupy their thinking, and soon chronic pain is the main feature of their life. The original injury may pretty much settle down, but they don't realize it and they remain focused on pain and limitations far beyond the normal recovery time.

Sri Vasudevan, M.D., is president of the American Academy of Pain Medicine. Dr. Vasudevan defines pain that lasts beyond the usual healing period--usually six months--as chronic or "persistent pain". In addition, he defines chronic pain as pain that causes significant changes in lifestyle, that "incapacitates" the patient, yet has relatively few physical or lab find- ings to explain the incapacitation. He says that chronic pain is often asso- ciated with drug or alcohol abuse, including abuse of prescription medica- tions. He notes that patients with a chronic pain syndrome usually demonstrate excessive preoccupation with their complaints.

Raymond Maciewicz, M.D., is the director of the Massachusetts Gen- eral Hospital Cancer Pain Center and the Spaulding Pain Rehabilitation Program. He says that patients with chronic pain syndromes often demonstrate "learned pain behavior" and activity avoidance, withdrawal, and significant psychosocial disruption due to their pain.

There's a distinction between chronic pain and other psychological problems. Patients with chronic pain are not making it up. They aren't "crazy". They aren't hypochondriacs or hysterics (see Chapter 17). I remember a professor in medical school saying that after only three days, even the most realistic person becomes partly convinced that his illness is both unknown to medical science and probably incurable. He said that after three months, most patients begin to think their symptoms are "in their head". It's no wonder that long-lasting pain can have an effect on a patient's moods and psychological status.

It is true that unrelenting 24-hour-a-day pain <u>could</u> make a person neurotic or hypochondriacal or depressed. But that's not the same as a chronic pain syndrome.

We don't regard chronic pain patients as neurotics. We treat them as injured people who have developed an understandable and sometimes predictable reaction to a long-term painful situation. We can help a lot of them with the right programs.

Someone asked me: "Couldn't a patient on Comp prolong his benefits by pretending he has a chronic pain syndrome?" The answer is: No, not easily. A sharp doctor would pick up on faking pretty quickly, as would a QRC. Claim adjusters are skilled at uncovering such behavior. And if there are no objective findings, there will be no permanent disability so the case would close anyway. There would be nothing to gain by pretending--and lots of hassles.

PAIN MANAGEMENT CLINICS

"I think you should have an evaluation at the Chronic Pain Clinic,"
I told Annabelle, a 50-year-old schoolbus driver whose work injury had
essentially healed but who seemed unusually incapacitated by pain.
"They can give you some help with this pain problem."
"Not a chance, Doctor. I'm not making this all up. I don't want
anybody brainwashing me. I don't need to go to any clinic."

> *"Well, Annabelle, just having persistent pain doesn't mean you're making it up. And it certainly doesn't mean you're crazy. But when a patient has pain as long as you have, it can wear you down and reduce your defenses. The pain clinic professionals won't try to tell you the pain is make-believe. They'll show you how to live around it a little easier."*
>
> *"I can do all that on my own. I don't need help."*
>
> *"Annabelle, I'd probably say the same thing myself. But they have skills at this. They'll show you techniques that you simply wouldn't be able to come up with on your own. It's not brainwashing and it's worth giving it a try if we can get the insurer to pay for it."*
>
> *Annabelle wasn't convinced, but she did agree to at least go for an evaluation.*

Most patients assume a pain management program will tell them to "wipe away the pain and tell me it's not there". But nothing could be farther from the truth. A pain clinic staff will tell you that the pain is there, and show you how to not only accept it but learn how to get along without being thrown for a loop.

A pain clinic is an interdisciplinary group of professionals. It often include psychologists, counsellors, rehabilitation consultants, nurses, doctors and exercise therapists. Such a staff is dedicated to showing patients how to re-approach normal life despite having chronic pain.

Dr. Ji Chia Liao is an anesthesiologist at the University of Minnesota who is involved in sophisticated treatment of chronic pain. He was recently quoted in a University publication as saying: "Chronic pain is so complex that to treat it effectively, there simply must be a multi-disciplinary effort."

Joel Seres, M.D., founded the Northwest Pain Center in Portland, Oregon. He says that key elements in the success of pain clinics are multi-professional staffs and educational programs to tell patients about the the effects of pain and emphasis on getting off addicting medications. Most pain programs include group and individual sessions to help patients learn how they've reacted to the loss of their former good health, how they're affected by uncertainty and frustration, and how to deal with lack of control. Pain clinics will also teach patients how to deal with anger, resentment, and feelings of alienation.

Most pain management programs last several weeks, the average being about a month. Many offer inpatient (five days a week) and outpatient programs. For the outpatient programs, patients often stay in motels on

Tuesday and Wednesday and Thursday nights and attend the clinic six to eight hours each day for three days. They then spend four-day weekends at home practicing what they've learned. Some people do fine with only the outpatient sessions, but a few with severe problems need a full four week inpatient program.

"Soft" Exercise, Biofeedback And Counselling

> *Annabelle changed into her swimsuit. She still limped, but was no longer so self-conscious about her injury or her limp. "After all," she thought, "all the other patients--clients I mean, I'm not supposed to think of myself as a patient--have things wrong with them too...Don't start without me, I'm coming!" she called to the pain clinic swim therapist who was already in the pool starting a stretching routine with the others.*
>
> *As Annabelle slipped into the water another lady said to her, "All this exercise, it's like going through boot camp or something. As if we're not busy enough with all the classes about pain and stress and independence."*
>
> *"No kidding. "But after these two weeks I do have to say I'm starting to feel better. How about you?"*
>
> *"Some, it's true. But it took a while. It took a couple of days to pick up that biofeedback."*

If you are in a typical chronic pain program you'll want to have some gym clothes and walking shoes. You'll be doing a lot of "soft exercise": Several sessions of walking each day, going through gentle range of motion exercises in a pool, and slowly increasing your tolerance for activities. You'll be going outdoors in good weather, and to walking malls or halls in bad.

Most pain programs will also include several group educational meetings and some individual counselling sessions to teach you about chronic pain and the value of physical activity.

They'll also probably include biofeedback training (see also Chapter 11). Biofeedback teaches patients how to relax muscle tension in various parts of the body. If you do start biofeedback, one of the pain clinic staff members will paste small computer sensors onto your skin over a muscle. On a monitor screen you'll be able to see whether muscle tension or spasm is present. Then the biofeedback therapist will show you how to re lax that specific muscle. When you do, you'll be able to watch the tension decrease by watching the monitor. Then you'll learn to do the same thing with other muscles in other areas of your body, including painful ones. Biofeedback is usually very effective with musculoskeletal pain problems.

A pain management program should generally include your spouse for at least a couple of sessions. I always tell my patients to take their spouse to at least the initial evaluation and one of two later sessions. Your spouse should also attend some of the group classes with you to learn a little about what you're going through. I've found that spouses can nearly always benefit from more information about what chronic pain does to a person on Comp.

Pain programs do emphasize getting off medications, particularly pain pills and tranquilizers. The reason is that one main goal of any pain management program is to show patients how to depend less on outside crutches.

One caution: A few patients have complained to me that more than half of the clients in their pain program were there to kick their drug habits. This was unfortunate: I don't feel that patients on Comp, trying to recover from work injury and chronic pain, should have to go through a program for drug addicts. The two problems are very different, and the clinical approaches are considerably different. So if your doctor has recommended a pain clinic, check it out first. Ask if it's primarily a drug treatment center. If so, you might ask your doctor to look for another program for you.

WHO HAS SUCCESS?

People that go into a pain management program with an open mind and positive attitude generally find that the program helps. These people attend in order to learn the skills of dealing with daily pain, just as they might with any other obstacle in life.

Pain management programs claim success rates of anywhere from one-thirds to two-thirds of their clients. "Success" means return to normal life and/or work, cessation of medication use, and no need to return to the program. Like any aspect of medical treatment--probably more so--some people will probably not get as much out of the program as others.

> *Annabelle has been stretching, kicking, and paddling for 20 minutes. She is worn out, but feeling some accomplishment. She says to a man kicking near her: "I can do twice as much as last week I think. How about you?"*
>
> *"Me too. But I wonder why someone else doesn't cooperate?" He glances sideways at a tough-looking, unsmiling man with long hair and 13 tattoos. He's just lolling at the corner of the pool and hasn't exercised at all.*
>
> *Annabelle says, "He never says anything in group meeting, does he?"*
>
> *"No--someone said he won't stop his drugs. He doesn't have much of an injury. I don't think his heart was in coming to the program. He doesn't seem to care much."*

The successful patients in pain programs are the ones who are actively involved in learning how to get over their discomfort as best they can and then get on with their life. These are people who already have some insight into the pain > spasm > stress cycle. These are people who have already taken an active role in their treatment and rehabilitation. With a patient such as this we can pretty well predict he will benefit from the program.

To get the most out of any pain management program, go into it with this attitude. Remember that the clinic is there to show you how to "live around" your discomfort as best you can. If you're on lot of medications, plan to get off them while you're in the program and stay off them afterward. Try to leave any anger at your employer or insurer at the door, and if you're still dwelling much on resentment make sure that you mention it to the clinic staff.

Lastly, don't go into a pain program expecting it to "wipe the pain away" because it may never do that. It's more realistic to expect the clinic to teach you "how to get along with a battle scar from life".

THE FAILURES

Are there any people who won't likely benefit from a pain clinic program? Yes: The defensive people, the ones who deny that chronic pain could cause them any psychological adjustment problems, the ones who believe they should "never have any pain again".

Others who will not benefit from a pain program are angry and resentful patients who say things like: "My company caused this problem and they're going to pay for it", those who cannot stop focusing on blame, who feel they've been forced into the pain program to be brainwashed, etc. Most pain clinics will not accept people such as this for treatment because they know they can seldom have success with such resistance or obstructiveness.

Other patients who may not get much from a pain program are those who have already given up. Some have bought into a disability lifestyle, some have secondary gain--but for either reason pain behavior for these people has become a permanent fixture of life. They say: "It's hurt for years and it's always going to hurt", "I'm disabled from work and things will never change", or "It's been this way ever since I got hurt 12 years ago".

Another group of patients who have poor results in pain management programs are those with hysteria or conversion reactions (see Chapter 17). These patients generally have little insight into the cause of most of their symptoms, they are not likely to accept any psychological counseling, and they usually fail to improve even after the best programs.

Lastly, I've found that patients with severe clinical depression who are on antidepressant medications frequently don't get much out of a pain program. These patients have too much difficulty just overcoming their depression to devote much time to classes, counselling or exercises.

I've found that it's much better to get serious depression under control first. Even so, the soft exercise portion of a pain program would be valuable for most depressed patients, because walking and exercise are two of the best treatments. So, if you have a depression problem as well as chronic pain, ask your physician to talk directly with the pain management staff about you.

Is it ever worth it for patients who fit the above description--angry, resentful, those who have given up, conversion reaction patients, and depressed patients--to go through a pain program? A few will get some benefit. But it's hard to predict which ones. It will probably depend on the combination of the patient's personality and his doctor's experience. It may not even be approved, depending on the claim adjuster's past experiences, and whether he has seen many good results or very few from other programs.

DO IT YOURSELF PROGRAMS?

The idea of do-it-yourself pain management was demonstrated by a patient of mine, Dan O'Neill (the only true patient's name I've used in this book). Dan had a severe low back problem, and unsuccessful back surgery which left him with continued pain for years. Not only that, in his case there was a great deal of difficulty with the insurer, bureaucracy, communication difficulties, and so on and it really got to Dan. It looked as if the insurer would not approve any more rehabilitation, but fortunately Dan had gone through a pain management program years earlier for an old neck injury.

So this time, after a year or more of frustration he was fed up with everything. He took matters into his own hands and did everything that he would have done in a formal rehabilitation pain program. He did all the exercises I recommended and more. Then he went farther. He bought an exercise bike and a mountain bike and took off 10 pounds. He got involved in volunteer work and and even ran for the City Council. He's just been elected for the second time, and now he's so busy with the Council it helps keep his mind off his back problems.

But even this wasn't enough for him. He also enrolled in college to learn a new line of work. He's in his 40's, he's in class with a definite goal, he made his professors aware of his back problems so they allow him to stand up during class and walk around, etc. He's focused on the classwork and was getting straight A's the last time I checked.

So here's this man with chronic severe pain. Yet he's going to school, doing his studies, working hard as a city councilman, and he exercises year round. He comes into the office with occasional flare-ups and we treat them. It's been tough for him sometimes but he's kept a vision of being master over his own life uppermost in mind. He has put all the basic principles of pain management into daily operation.

What Dan did, anyone could do.

WRAP-UP

How to do yourself some favors with chronic pain symptoms:
1) *Don't wait for your doctor to suggest a pain management program. If you've had six to twelve months of pain and things are not getting better, if you're frustrated and discouraged, you may have a chronic pain syndrome and need help with it;*
2) *Start a pain management program with an open mind. Expect the program to teach you about pain and how to minimize its effect on your life, and expect to cut down your medications. Leave anger and resentment at the door if you can.*
3) *You could do a lot for yourself to manage chronic pain, such as regular soft exercises, volunteer work, getting involved.*

H

CHAPTER 20

Return To Work,
Light Duty, Retraining

In one morning the town saw the worst construction accidents in 25 years. The volunteer ambulance crew even had to call out reinforcements.

First a 30-foot scaffolding collapsed with two carpenters on it and caught two laborers beneath. All four were injured, two seriously.

Across town 30 minutes later a young quarry worker was too close to a crusher, he became caught in the machinery and was pulled in. The machine swung him in circles, smashing arms, legs and head against the frame at least a dozen times before a co-worker could shut it down.

The emergency room staff felt as if they were in a disaster drill, press milling around, surgeons and IV's everywhere. These were heavy duty injuries.

It would be a long haul, but <u>eventually every single one of these five patients was able to return to work</u>.

There are only four ways to get back to work after an injury and each one is a big win for the patient. The four ways are: Return to full duty, early return to light or modified work during healing, alternative work, or retraining. This chapter describes the way each can go.

That means this chapter is about success. When a patient walks out of the doctor's office with a slip in his hand that says "OK for return to work", he's won.

FULL DUTY: THE BEST RETURN TO WORK

Kevin was one of the laborers caught under the scaffolding. He had a simple right elbow fracture, a broken nose, and back strain. The elbow fracture healed right on schedule with six weeks in a cast, and the broken nose was barely a problem. Kevin's back strain took about four weeks to heal with therapy, also right on schedule. He stayed active with swimming, workouts with his left arm, etc., throughout recovery. In fact Kevin started work the day the cast came off. His buddies gave him some help for a few days and that was that.

For Kevin, Workers' Compensation was a thing of the past.

This is the kind of outcome that everyone likes. 90% of Workers' Compensation injuries end this way. This kind of return to work is always an all-out success story. The work injury is relatively minor, it heals quickly, the employee stays in shape so there's no need for Work Hardening, and he goes back to his regular job as soon as the doctor says it's safe.

PROGRESSIVE WORK DURING HEALING

One of the carpenters on the scaffolding, Mark, had only a left wrist fracture and a lot of bruised and sore muscles. His break was not on his dominant side. He wore a fiberglass cast and took it easy for a couple of weeks to recover from his bruises.

One day he stopped by to see the foreman and told him he'd like to get back to work. The employer talked to the doctor: "We sure could use Mark back at the construction site. We're short so many men after all the injuries. We can have him do just the jobs that require one hand."

This was a well-respected builder in town, known for taking good care of his men. Would the doctor approve temporary light duty? This was the ideal situation; how could anyone say no?

Mark worked with his cast at light duty for about four weeks. On his next office visit the X-rays looked good and Mark walked out without a cast. Over the next month he gradually added more right-handed work, starting light and increasing until eventually he was doing his old job. The doctor discharged him from care, and for Mark Workers' Compensation was also a thing of the past.

Medical treatment under Workers' Compensation is always a balance between keeping the patient off work long enough for him to heal, and not letting him be off so long he gets rusty and out of shape.

When the injury doesn't interfere with work, or when some other temporary lighter work is available, in many cases it speeds recovery to return a patient to work during the healing process. All it takes is for the doctor to provide physical restrictions and the appropriate job to be available.

There are mental and physical benefits of this: It keeps the patient physically active, he doesn't lie around getting stiff and sore, and his job skills stay sharp. Early return to work lets an employee see himself as a functioning person rather than as an invalid or Comp claimant. He's off Comp, he's on the job.

Just as in professional sports when an injured player suits up and works out with the team because he's part of the team, any employee who works during recovery feels he's part of the "team" too. This makes early return to work one of the best forms of "treatment".

In addition, early return to work is usually better financially for the employee. Not only is he earning money, but there's a built in guarantee that he has his job. Sometimes the best emotional treatment--even cure-- is to simply get him back to the job where he can feel "normal" again.

The ideal return to work during treatment can only happen when the injury won't affect the employee's ability to do the job in any way. For example, an employee with a knee injury could work at a desk job with few limitations. A patient with an injury to the non-dominant hand or arm can often do their job quite easily, as for example could a person such as myself if I had a left arm injury.

The only caution about early return to work is that both patient and doctor must be certain the work will not interfere with healing or be dangerous. For example, if you are recovering from a back injury, a shoveling or truck driving job would be risky. So if your doctor is considering an early return to work for you, make sure he understands exactly what your job requires.

> *The other laborer had been trying to get away when the falling scaffolding caught and pinned him. He had an ankle fracture and a twisted knee with torn cartilage.*
>
> *His recovery took longer than the other men: One operation to screw and plate the ankle, another to remove the cartilage, eight weeks in casts, two months of therapy to regain joint motion, then a third surgery to remove the hardware and finally Work Hardening for eight weeks.*
>
> *He wasn't ready for his old labor job but there was no reason to stay off work at that point. He started back part-time at light duty as a parts runner, and he gradually got back into climbing stairs, lifting, hauling and shoveling, etc.*
>
> *Eventually the doctor decided his capacities were enough to try full duty. He did all right and he's still going strong. His ankle is still stiff but he does his job and he's off Workers' Compensation--another win. It took eleven months in all.*

The transition from "injured worker" to working employee by way of light duty is probably the most common method of return to work. It eases the employee back into the job without trauma or danger.

"Light work" could be either reduced physical work such as lifting only a few pounds instead of heavy weights and sitting down rather than working at a standup job, or it could be working part-time such as half days rather than full days.

Usually light duty is only a temporary accommodation by the employer, with the expectation that the employee will recover enough to tolerate his full duty work. In fact, I've found that most employers will provide light duty only if I firmly assure them that the employee will be back at full duty within a few weeks. Very few employers will provide a permanent light duty job.

If you do return to light duty, you should follow your doctor's restrictions and stay within them. If you exceed them and have a recurrent injury, it could likely set you back considerably and it may not be as easy to treat as the first time.

ALTERNATE EMPLOYMENT

Occasionally it will be obvious from a patient's injuries that they will clearly prohibit him from ever going back to his old job. The reason could be any of several: Incomplete healing of a fracture, a stiff joint, lack of endurance due to respiratory injury, loss of strength after a spine injury, high risk of recurrent disc injury, loss of limb, loss of vision or hearing or balance, intolerance for heat or cold, etc.

Sometimes it's possible to modify a job to suit a patient's limitations. But if no amount of modification will make the job suitable, then something else has to be done.

> The young quarry worker, Angelo, was taken to surgery immediately. The surgeons did their best, but he lost his right arm above the elbow and his left leg below the knee. He had a long rehab: PT for months, then two prostheses and practice walking and using a hook, and treatment for depression. He had lots of support from family and friends and even got married during rehab, but at the end he was still a 22-year-old man with no job, no education beyond high school, and there weren't many jobs around for someone like him with an artificial arm and leg.
> One day his claim adjuster was visiting Angelo and happened to glance into the spare room. It was crammed to the ceiling with stereo gear, ham radios, electronic equipment and video screens. When he asked about it Angelo's face lit up. He talked non-stop for an hour about his main love: Electronics.
> Angelo's claim adjuster and rehabilitation consultant took him down to see the manager of a local TV and audio store. It was the stuff of fairy tales: He saw that Angelo was more knowledgeable than most of his sales people, there was a vacancy within two weeks and Angelo tried it. He fit right in, loved the work and now three years later he's assistant manager.

If you aren't going to be able to handle your old work, the next step would be to look for alternative work in the same plant. Your doctor will discuss your restrictions with the employer, and if you have a Rehabilitation Consultant he or she will try to find a suitable position for you. There may be similar work within your capacities.

But if the employer simply can't provide any alternate work then you'll have to look elsewhere. You can start looking for a job in your area that utilizes the skills you already possess. If it's not obvious what your skills are, and you are fortunate enough to have a Rehabilitation Consultant or QRC, he or she can help with vocational and aptitude testing to point you to the type of work you'll be most successful doing. Rehabilitation Consultants often have books, files, networks and computer programs to help locate available jobs.

Depending on the region you live in the job search might pay off. In a major metropolitan area the chances are you'll find a suitable job quickly. But on the other hand if you live 60 miles from the nearest small town and have significant physical restrictions it will probably be extremely difficult.

If it is difficult to find a job at first, don't lose heart. Just as it did for Angelo, the right job can turn up in unexpected places at the most unexpected times.

RETRAINING

> *The rescue squad pulled Roberto, the other construction carpenter, from the heaviest of the wreckage after two hours. He had a hip fracture, two lumbar disc herniations, and a thoracic spine compression fracture.*
>
> *Despite hip pinning, lumbar disc surgery, a back brace and extensive therapy Roberto still had lots of pain. He started Work Hardening. Though it helped him regain strength, he still couldn't bend or lift more than a few pounds.*
>
> *The employer was small and didn't have an alternative job. They couldn't create a new light duty job for Roberto. He tried looking for other related jobs, but in a slow economy there just weren't any. Roberto didn't need testing--it was clear that he knew construction. The problem was finding a job in that field.*
>
> *But when 6 months passed and nothing at all showed up, they tested Roberto to see what other skills and aptitudes he had, and what else might interest him.*

Then everyone conferred: Insurer, Roberto, the doctor, and the Rehabilitation Consultant. It was obvious he would have to learn some new field, or a new area in the construction field.

But there was a problem: He hadn't completed enough school. So the insurer ultimately authorized limited schooling and retraining. First, classes to bring up his basic math and language skills. Then vocational training as a construction estimator.

Roberto does estimating now, though he does continue to have lots of back pain. He's getting around, he's making better money than he did before, and he's still in the field he likes.

Retraining into a different type of work may be an answer in the most severe injuries, or in a few cases where no job of any kind is likely to turn up in the foreseeable future.

Retraining is handled differently in every state. In some states all retraining is coordinated by a Department of Vocational Rehabilitation (DVR) or an agency with a similar title. In others retraining is conducted privately by agreement between insurer, employee, and training facilities such as vocational or technical schools or colleges.

In all cases the optimum program will test the employee for aptitude, skills and interests first. Then the program will bring the employee's basic skills up to par as needed and then start him in school to learn the new trade or occupation.

If you think that your situation is going to require retraining, you have to follow these steps to achieve it: First, determine whether or not the insurer will consider retraining you (see Chapter 23). Second, have your skills and aptitudes tested. Third, locate the training program. Fourth, attend.

A word to the wise: If you are going through retraining, the insurer will expect you to keep your nose to the grindstone. It's neither uncommon nor unreasonable for an insurer who pays for retraining to require updates on your attendance at school and reports on your grades. If you skip school, don't hit the books, and generally goof off it will probably jeopardize your retraining benefits.

INSURER'S ATTITUDES ABOUT RETRAINING

Every severely injured employee seems to want to be retrained these days. "I think I'd like to be a brain surgeon," they say, "and the insurer ought to pay me to learn it."

But the reality is that insurers are generally not eager to even discuss retraining unless all other possibilities have been considered, and even then only in the most severe injuries.

"It's absolutely the last resort," a claim adjuster told me. "We never consider retraining when there's a possibility of returning to light duty, even permanent light duty, or alternative employment of some type. Retraining is costly and often goes far beyond our obligations."

Another insurer has said: "Yes, retraining is often a possibility. But only in cases when the injury is so severe that any other return to work is improbable. Even then, in some cases of older employees or those with few basic skills, it's still often more realistic to look at permanent disability payments rather than a retraining program. Schooling doesn't always make the most sense."

So whatever your specific situation, I recommend you focus on your recovery from injury, your physical capacities now, and what likely return to work you can find within your present situation. Retraining is something that may happen if it's needed, but it's needed in only a small percentage of work injuries.

EMPLOYER'S ATTITUDES ABOUT LIGHT DUTY

"We hate it," the personnel director of a large manufacturing company told me. "Light duty is nothing but trouble for us. It throws off our work schedules, other employees resent seeing a co-worker "loafing", our union resists it, and we don't really find that it accomplishes much anyway."

"We love it," the benefits manager of a large utility told me. "Whenever we have an injury the first thing we do is contact the patient and his or her doctor. We tell them that we'll provide the employee with benefits no matter what, and that we'll bend over backwards to provide him with a job within his capacities as soon as he's able to come back. We value every single one of our people and want them back. We've found that light duty has significantly reduced our Comp problems and costs and it seems to be good for employee morale."

Nevertheless, some employers will not have light duty available. Some have just never had to consider it, some would find it impossible to provide, and some have rules against it. "Don't come back until you're 100%" is a refrain heard throughout this country.

I realize that many employers think light duty is a pain and I've heard most of the arguments against it. But it's often the only way that some injured employees will return to work.

The employers who resist light duty should listen to one of my patients, Dale Herman.

> *Dale is a machinist at a Fortune 500 subsidiary which has a categoric rule against light duty. Dale had back surgery and was doing well, but the employer wouldn't take him back while he healed.*
> *"This is stupid!" Dale always told me on followup visits. "They really ought to have light duty--I know I could be working at something. This is costing them a fortune and I know their Comp rates are going sky high!"*
> *"Besides," he said, "it would be better for me to get in the habit of getting up in the morning, because all I'm doing now is sitting around and getting lazy. I'm bored. They don't seem to realize I'm taking money from Comp, I have a disability policy, I don't have to buy gas and they even pay me mileage to come see you. They should be putting some of that money into having me at work. It would be better for me and better for them."*

Or employers who resist light duty could listen to Rosa Horlick. Her injury was essentially healed but she was still stiff and deconditioned. After I put her through Work Hardening her employer did make a light duty job available.

> *Rosa told me, "It was scary going into that warehouse job. I'd been out of circulation and I was getting depressed, I had to learn new things, I had to use a computer and I didn't know any of the people. But overall it was a lot better than being home biting my nails."*
> *"Getting back at light duty got me out of the house like I needed, it got me back into things and it was good."*

ATTENDING PHYSICIAN'S **RETURN TO WORK RECOMMENDATIONS RECORD**	Company Name	
Patient's Name (Last) (First)	(Middle Initial)	Date of Injury/Illness

TO BE COMPLETED BY ATTENDING PHYSICIAN—PLEASE CHECK

DIAGNOSIS/CONDITION (Brief Explanation)

I saw and treated this patient on _____ and based on the above description of the patient's current medical problem:
Date

1. ☐ Recommend his/her return to work with no limitations on _____.
Date

2. ☐ He/She may return to work on_____with the following limitations:
Date

CHECK ONLY AS RELATES TO ABOVE CONDITIONS

☐ **Sedentary Work.** Lifting 10 pounds maximum and occasionally lifting and/or carrying such articles as dockets, ledgers, and small tools. Although a sedentary job is defined as one which involves sitting, a certain amount of walking and standing is often necessary in carrying out job duties. Jobs are sedentary if walking and standing are required only occasionally and other sedentary criteria are met.

☐ **Light Work.** Lifting 20 pounds maximum with frequent lifting and/or carrying of objects weighing up to 10 pounds. Even though the weight lifted may be only a negligible amount, a job is in this category when it requires walking or standing to a significant degree or when it involves sitting most of the time with a degree of pushing and pulling of arm and/or leg controls.

☐ **Light Medium Work.** Lifting 30 pounds maximum with frequent lifting and/or carrying of objects weighing up to 20 pounds.

☐ **Medium Work.** Lifting 50 pounds maximum with frequent lifting and/or carrying of objects weighing up to 25 pounds.

☐ **Light Heavy Work.** Lifting 75 pounds maximum with frequent lifting and/or carrying of objects weighing up to 40 pounds.

☐ **Heavy Work.** Lifting 100 pounds maximum with frequent lifting and/or carrying of objects weighing up to 50 pounds.

1. In an 8 hour work day patient may:
   a. Stand/Walk
   ☐ None   ☐ 4-6 Hours
   ☐ 1-4 Hours   ☐ 6-8 Hours
   b. Sit
   ☐ 1-3 Hours   ☐ 3-5 Hours   ☐ 5-8 Hours
   c. Drive
   ☐ 1-3 Hours   ☐ 3-5 Hours   ☐ 5-8 Hours
2. Patient may use hand(s) for repetitive:
   ☐ Single Grasping   ☐ Pushing & Pulling
   ☐ Fine Manipulation
3. Patient may use foot/feet for repetitive movement as in operating foot controls: ☐ Yes   ☐ No

4. Patient may:

	Not At All	Occasionally	Frequently
a. Bend	☐	☐	☐
b. Twist	☐	☐	☐
c. Squat	☐	☐	☐
d. Climb	☐	☐	☐
e. Reach	☐	☐	☐

OTHER INSTRUCTIONS AND/OR LIMITATIONS INCLUDING PRESCRIBED MEDICATIONS

3. ☐ These restrictions are in effect until _____ or until patient is reevaluated on _____
Date   Date

4. He/she is totally incapacitated at this time. Patient will be reevaluated on _____.
Date

5. Referred To: ☐ None   ☐ Private physician _____
Doctor

      ☐ Return Here_____ ☐ A Consultant _____
Date & Time   Doctor, Date & Time

Physician's Signature	Date

AUTHORIZATION TO RELEASE INFORMATION

I hereby authorize my attending physician and/or hospital to release any information or copies thereof acquired in the course of my examination or treatment for the injury identified above to my employer or his representative.

Patient's Signature	Date

How To Return At Light Duty

When your doctor does send you back to work he should state your specific capacities in writing so there's no miscommunication about what you can tolerate.

Most states have a form covering physical restrictions for return to work. An example of a standard form is shown on the previous page. Some physicians have their own customized forms. But whatever the method used, your doctor should write your lifting capacities clearly on such a form and make recommendations such as: "Lifting no more than 20 pounds from table height or 15 pounds from floor", "able to push 150 pounds", "no work overhead", "no work above shoulder level", "no bending at waist", "no exposure to gases or exhausts", "no exposure to cutting oils", etc., depending on your particular problem.

Take the work slip to your employer when you leave the doctor's office.

A scribbled prescription slip that says "Light work for three weeks" is worthless. It could even be dangerous because anyone could interpret it whatever way they want. If your doctor writes such a slip, make sure you tell him just what your job requires and ask him to set specific restrictions so that you don't have a risk of re-injury.

If you're seeing a specialist in Occupational Medicine, such doctors usually have knowledge about every type of work requirements. But if you're seeing another type of doctor and you suspect he doesn't fully understand just how and where you have to work and with what materials and in what positions, then tell him about your job in detail. Even better, show him a photo of a job or bring him a videotape. Most doctors will be most happy to review a video and make more informed recommendations. It's a must for your doctor to be familiar with the job you do and without such familiarity I'm not sure he could make a truly safe release to work.

Later, as time goes by your doctor will reevaluate your progress and capacities again. If you recover further he'll probably lower your restrictions until eventually he'll release you for full duty. Then you too can say goodbye to the world of Workers' Compensation.

Questions About Returning To Work

Q. "After I return to work am I at more risk of injury?"

A. Whether you're at high, average or low risk depends on your injury, your degree of recovery, and your job. For example, suppose a patient has disc surgery and then returns to driving a bulldozer or over-the-road trucking bouncing along for 12 hours a day, or to construction welding. Back patients in these jobs are at high risk for re-injury.

On the other hand, if a patient has a shoulder, knee or ankle injury and then returns to clerical or managerial work that patient would be at low risk of injury. So the risk depends on the problem and the best thing to do would be to ask your doctor.

Q. "What if I'm sent back to work part time? Will I lose my benefits?"

A. Workers' Compensation will pay for the hours you're not working.

Q. "What if I start back at part time but then I get laid off?"

A. Your benefits will continue.

Q. "What if I'm on light duty and my employer asks me to do more than my doctor's restrictions? I'm afraid I'll hurt myself."

A. Show your restricted duty slip to your supervisor. If that doesn't work show it to the personnel department. If that doesn't work go right to a phone and call your doctor so he can call your employer to straighten it out immediately. Don't leave the job in a huff, don't get fired for insubordination or for refusing work. Call the doctor instead.

Q. "What if my family doctor and the company doctor disagree? My own doctor wants to keep me off work several more months but the other doctor says I can do some kind of work now. Can the company choose whatever opinion they want?"

A. Possibly, but the "company" doctor should have objective justification for his conclusions. If you disagree, ask your claim adjuster or the state Workers' Compensation office for a conference to sort it out.

Q. "Light duty was too hard but rather than make a fuss I just quit. Was that all right?"

A. No. If you have difficulty tolerating light duty, tell your doctor and he may wish to change the restrictions. If you quit and don't make it known that it was because you couldn't tolerate the work, your benefits will probably stop.

Q. "Can I exceed my restrictions and try to work up to full duty?"

A. Some patients do this on their own but I don't recommend it. It's risky to try it without doctor's advice and monitoring.

Q. "The doctor told me I could go back to work but said I should use my discretion when I lift. My employer says this means I can do any job they have, but I don't think so. Who's right?

A. Your doctor was wrong. There's no place in Workers' Compensation for a vague duty slip--either you have restrictions or you don't. Ask your doctor to write down exactly what you can do at work or ask to see another doctor that will.

Q. "I'm on light duty but I think my co-workers resent it. They think I'm sitting down on the job or faking. And one of my friends is on light duty too but he thinks it's beneath his dignity. What can we do about these things?"

A. There are no simple methods. Try to pay no attention to your co-workers, remember that they're only human, and remember that light duty is only temporary. Concentrate on getting well and returning to full duty and perhaps that will help. And reassure your friend that light duty is certainly not beneath anyone's dignity, it's far healthier than just sitting around at home.

Q. "I'm worried that my doctor could release me to full duty and my employer could let me go the next day."

A. I don't have any good answers for this. It does happen. The best thing I can recommend is to finish a full exercise and Work Hardening program and then go through light duty so you are sure you can handle full duty. Then ask your doctor to put you through a formal Functional Capacity Testing before you officially start full work. Then if you get laid off you will have few or no restrictions and you can look for another job with a clean slate and with confidence.

Q. "I still have pain even though I've been at light duty for a year. Does that mean I should just stop working for good?"

A.   There's nothing inherently wrong or dangerous about having some discomfort. It's not usually the same thing as causing damage or re-injury. Check it out with your doctor to make sure. But after all some injuries do cause permanent disability and pain may accompany it. Unfortunately, no one in Workers' Compensation can guarantee you a pain-free life after injury.

Q.   "I was given a permanent disability. How come I'm not at light duty?"

A.   Permanent disabilities are often more legal definitions than medical, and a disability doesn't always mean a patient needs light work. I sort out disabilities and what they really mean in Chapter 22.

WRAP-UP

How to do yourself some favors with return to work:
1) Take advantage of an early return to work if your doctor says it's safe and if you're lucky enough to have an employer that offers light duty;
2) Stay within your light duty job restrictions until they're changed by your doctor;
3) Make sure your doctor understands your job and its physical requirements when he sends you back to work.
4) Retraining is a last resort, available in only a few cases.

G

CHAPTER 21

IME's (Independent Medical Examinations)

Dear Claimant:

We have scheduled you for an Independent Medical Examination by John Jones, M.D. on March 14th. We are entitled to this examination by law and your attendance is mandatory. You have the right to have your own physician or other person present for the examination, but at your own expense.

We are enclosing a check for your mileage expenses. If for some reason you will be unable to keep this appointment please notify us as soon as possible.

Workers' Comp Insurance Co.

You might be sent for an Independent Medical Examination (an IME) at any time in the course of your injury, especially if your case is complex, unusually prolonged, or if there is some dispute.

IME's are a fairly routine part of Workers' Compensation in most states. If scheduled, they are mandatory: You have to go. <u>An IME report can have a profound medical and legal impact on your case</u>. For instance, the outcome of an IME can determine whether or not your claim is accepted, which doctor you can see, and whether you receive a disability payment. This chapter shows you how to get the most accurate IME.

THE NATURE OF AN IME

IME's go by various names: Med-Legal exams, Neutral Medical Evaluations (NME's), Agreed Medical Examinations (AME's) and Disability Claims Examinations (DCE's).

If you are going for an IME it will most likely be at the request of the Workers' Compensation insurer or their representative: they set up 90 to 95% of IME's. They often need a thorough medical appraisal by an objective physician and an IME is often the only way they can get it.

"Doctor, they sent me here for an evaluation. But I have no idea why--you're not my regular doctor. Can you explain it to me?"

An IME is usually requested to answer one or more important, complex, difficult, or controversial questions about a case. Examples are: Has a patient reached maximum healing? What's a patient's disability rating? What's the contribution of several different injuries to disability? How to sort out complex issues of causation? What are a patient's capacities for work? What is the need for rehabilitation? Sometimes an IME is to determine all of these at the same time.

IME's are also used when there is a dispute: For example when one doctor says a patient cannot work but another says he can, when an insurer thinks a disability claim is too high, or when two or more insurers have to determine which is responsible for paying benefits.

Insurers will commonly order an IME whenever an employee retains an attorney and makes a claim: The insurer then needs a neutral and objective evaluation of the employee's status.

An IME will be performed by a physician who has expertise in areas specifically relevant to your case: For example expertise in back or neck problems, lung injuries, work capacities; for determination of a disability rating, etc.

IME's are expensive, not many physicians will do them. This is for several reasons. An IME is time-consuming, an IME often demands special knowledge of disability ratings systems, and to do an IME often puts a physician in the middle of a controversy or dispute.

By the very nature of IME's they are usually complex--far more than a second opinion or medical consultation. An IME is not a consultation. IME's take longer--up to two or three hours. The exam is more detailed--it addresses more and tougher questions. The doctor doing an IME will send his report to whomever requested the exam, but is not allowed to communicate with your doctor.

The conclusions of the IME doctor will be reviewed by the requesting source and then used to make decisions. Their decisions can be of great significance to you. For example if an insurer requested the IME they may use the report as a basis for accepting or denying your claim, for paying or cutting off your benefits. If your attorney requested the exam, he may use the doctor's conclusions to decide whether or not to pursue legal action, or to calculate how much disability to claim for you.

IME's: Neutral Or Biased?

I only know how to do one kind of IME: A neutral and independent exam with a report that contains my objective findings and logical conclusions.

It might be there is an argument going on about the case--with complex IME's there usually is--but it doesn't matter to me how it eventually comes out. When I do an IME evaluation, my emphasis is on a factual report based on the information I have. I write it so I can back up my conclusions with logic and medical fact if I ever have to testify about it.

I think the marks of any IME should be thoroughness, professionalism, and objectivity. This is the kind of examination and report that two national organizations, the American College of Occupational Medicine (ACOM) and the American Academy of Disability Evaluating Physicians (AADEP), train doctors to perform.

I've found that most insurers--at least 75%--do want a fair and unbiased IME. They use such IME's to objectively determine the status of their claims. It's as if they engage the doctor as a consultant to them.

Insurers want the true story from an IME, just as anyone would if he were paying a consultant. They want to know where they stand with respect to the injured patient's condition. They want the doctor to call a spade a spade: If it looks like there's not much of an injury they expect him to say that, and if there's a severe injury they expect him to say that.

One common criticism of IME's is that they are biased. But the best-- the only--policy for an IME doctor should be neutrality. In being neutral I certainly know that I have written IME reports that didn't make the insurer who requested them very happy. But I believe they went by these reports because they knew the conclusions were as factual as possible.

No reputable insurer or reputable attorney would want a doctor to bias his report for or against a patient.

Mark Battista, M.D., is Chief Medical Director of UNUM Corporation and past president of Insurance Medical Group, New England. He said to me: "We would never want to see a doctor bias his reports. We want an objective evaluation of our claimants' status: That helps us the most. If we ever saw a doctor slanting his reports we would certainly never use him again." I think this is how it should be, and I'd like to think every IME doctor does fair exams.

However, I've read thousands of IME reports and I find that one of the biggest problems in this area of Workers' Compensation is IME's that are in fact biased. Half or more seem to be written mainly to please the person who requested them.

I've seen IME doctors leave out significant facts or records, emphasize certain tests instead of others, and make obviously slanted conclusions that have no basis in the facts of the case.

Why does this happen? Probably for at least three reasons. First, a few insurers, and a few attorneys, do seem to actually want slanted opinions: Reports that will help them win cases, cut off benefits or deny disability despite the facts of the case. They want "adverse" exams, not independent exams, and they find doctors that will do them.

Second, some doctors seem to mistakenly feel they have to write a report that will please the requesting source or they won't be paid for the exam.

Third, some doctors of "the old school" just feel that an IME doctor should "take sides". One of these doctors told me exactly this at one of our national meetings on disability. We were arguing about bias and he said: "Come on now, of course I bias my reports to favor one side. Everyone does. That's how the game is played."

I replied to him: "That's not honest. It's not ethical. And this isn't a game to the patient. If you take sides it's as much as saying that your medical opinion is really worthless because it's just up for purchase." But he never did hear me. I occasionally see his reports and it is obvious that he still biases them.

CHECKING OUT THE DOCTOR

How can you be sure you can get an objective and unbiased exam? Unfortunately, you have no way of choosing the doctor you'll see; it's the insurer's prerogative to schedule an IME with anyone they want. Some insurers and attorneys have the definite reputation of always choosing IME doctors with reputations for skill and professionalism who write their findings as neutral reports and tell it like it is. Others have a more spotty reputation. You could check with the Workers' Compensation office in your state about the insurer's reputation, and about the doctor's also.

You might also ask the IME doctor if he's a fellow in AADEP (the American Academy of Disability Evaluating Physicians). AADEP is establishing subspecialty status for the field of disability evaluation, and there are currently a thousand or so physicians who have completed rigorous postgraduate education in evaluation of disability. From these doctors you at least have a better chance of getting a true and unbiased report.

If it does turn out the doctor's IME report seems biased, you won't be able to change it but you can write a letter to him and the insurer clearly stating what you object to. And if the report contains factual errors (wrong history, wrong X-ray reports, etc.) you should write a similar letter (see section on The IME Report later in this chapter). Of course you should keep copies of your letters.

If the insurer later makes a decision unfavorable to you based on what you think is an incorrect report, you could request a conference to dispute it. If that doesn't help, and you still believe the IME was wrong, you will probably have to consult an attorney.

I believe that over time bias in IME's will be less common. As AADEP and ACOM and other organizations conduct further training and set more standards in this field, IME's will become more and more objective over the years. Perhaps the ideal someday would be to have physicians appointed by both sides of a dispute, or by a Workers' Compensation judge. Both sides could agree ahead of time to accept the doctor's opinion as to the diagnosis and medical conclusions.

How To Get The Most From An IME

The doctor doing an IME gets one shot at it. He can only see you one time under the rules of Workers' Compensation. And he cannot contact your own doctor for information. That means he will form his opinion about your condition, work capacity, and disability from what you tell him and what he finds on exam. But he will also review all your medical records. In fact he'll rely heavily on them for facts. If your history is inaccurate or your exam is not valid, his conclusions won't match the facts and may damage your claim.

So for an IME, tell your history accurately. Present your symptoms as best you can. Use the specific instructions I gave in Chapter 7 on how to use the right terms and a diagram of your problem. Draw a medical timeline of your history just as I showed in Chapter 12--this can help an IME doctor immensely.

Give your history in chronological order. Be factual, logical, and clear. Tell the doctor: "This happened, this is how I felt, this is how I was treated, this is how the treatment worked, this is what happened next, here's how I feel now, here's what I hope happens in the future," etc.

Start with the <u>first</u> injury, not just a work injury that happened a year after a motorcycle accident, and <u>not just the injury that this present insurance company is covering</u>.

When you go for the exam, be straightforward and be yourself. Arrive on time or slightly early. Doctors who do IME's are usually pretty well organized and the time of your exam will have been set aside specifically for you. If you arrive late and there is not enough time for him to do an unhurried exam, you may be rescheduled for another day.

Allow plenty of time for the exam. These are not quickie evaluations, and you should expect to spend some time with a detailed interview, a full examination and possibly tests such as X-rays afterwards.

What <u>Not</u> To Do On An IME

There's no need to embellish your history with blame and criticism of employers or insurers.

> *"Yes, I fell at work. But did they tell you how it happened? Did they tell you there was a leak they wouldn't fix? Did they tell you we'd complained about the floor for years? You know, it's common knowledge the supervisors don't follow safety practices. They're going to get a big fine someday, I'm sure of it."*

The IME doctor won't be concerned with who was at fault, why you fell, why the toxic gas was released, etc. Don't bother trying to establish that someone else caused the accident, that some employer treated you badly, etc. There may be a time and place for that, but it's not during an IME.

There's no need for dramatic language to make your injury seem worse. If you have a serious problem, it will be readily apparent to the doctor.

I've had patients tell me all of the following: "I hurt my shoulder and I couldn't walk for five weeks"; "The doctors didn't dare examine me because they knew I'd kick the bucket if they did"; "I'm totally disabled and I'll never be able to do anything again"; "I'm incurable". All that patients accomplish by dramatizations like these is to make the doctor skeptical of their whole history.

When he had come in for an IME, he sat with arms crossed, chin jutting forward, tight-lipped. "I dare you to ask me a question," his body language fairly shouted.

Don't arrive hostile, suspicious, or with a chip on your shoulder.

I asked, "When did you first have back trouble?" He looked at me, then looked away, and said: "When I fell on the job."

Now, I had all his records in front of me. I could see that he'd had back problems for years. In fact he'd been seeing a chiropractor right up to just before the fall. So I asked again: "No previous difficulties with your back?"

"No. Never a thing."

Don't try to evade questions, conceal important facts, or fool the doctor. The medical records usually show the facts and when the doctor finds that you've concealed significant information he will wonder what else you're concealing. And it will be embarassing to you.

Be simple, honest and direct when he asks if this or that hurts, when you had this or that symptom, etc.

I tested his leg strength. But every time I asked him to move the left one, he showed the motion we call cogwheeling or give-away. This is an attempt to look weak, though the muscles have normal strength.

I asked him to bend forward and backward at the waist. He grunted and gasped, though he moved no more than 10 degrees. But I saw he was tightening up his low back muscles, voluntarily keeping his motion limited.

I touched his leg with a vibrating tuning fork. "Can you feel that?" I asked. He looked away, seemed to think about it, and finally said: "No, not a thing". But I knew there could be no reason for numbness in that location.

Don't try to outguess the doctor or fool him during the exam. Medical exams are far too sophisticated these days for symptoms to be easily faked; a good doctor can usually pick that up in a minute. For example, if the doctor does a neurological exam and tests your perception of pinprick sensation he'll ask if a pin feels sharp. Just answer yes or no. When a patient looks as if he's calculating every answer and every move, the doctor suspects he's hiding something. Doctors look extremely carefully at any attempt to appear weak or to fake a response.

You may find that your attorney will tell you there's no such thing as a neutral or fair exam--I know quite a few that do say this. I've seen the "instruction sheets" that this kind of attorney gives their clients: "Tell this doctor nothing, volunteer no information, don't cooperate with him. Remember he's working against you".

One patient came in to see me for an IME and started out by saying: "My attorney told me what this was all about and I only have to tell you yes or no. I'm not going to help you with anything else."

If you are argumentative, if you're rude to the IME doctor, if you don't cooperate there's absolutely no way it can help you. Nine times out of ten it will damage your case in some way later. Even if you're seeing one of the biased IME doctors, it's all the more reason to be as cooperative and polite as possible. Believe me, you have nothing to gain by hostility during an IME. If your attorney tells you different, he's living in some other world.

Lastly, don't arrive for an IME drunk or hungover.

THE IME REPORT

After an Independent Medical Examination the doctor will put his conclusions into a report. He's not at liberty to discuss his findings with you at the end of the exam. IME reports are usually lengthy and should clearly state the doctor's reasons for his answers to the questions he was asked.

> *"Doctor, you've asked my husband all these questions. Now can we find out what you think? We'd like you to send us a copy of your report."*

The IME report belongs only to the requesting source. It does not belong to you, nor to your doctor, nor to your attorney unless he was the one who requested the IME. Some insurers do routinely send a copy of the report to the Examinee but others do not. You have no access to IME reports because they are different from common medical records. An IME is not for advice, consultation or treatment. The IME doctor is strictly an independent party and not your treating physician. Therefore the visit does not establish a doctor-patient relationship.

In a few states you can make a written request for the report, pay a retrieval and copy fee, and get the copy mailed to you. But if not, your state
Workers' Compensation office might be able to get a copy for you. An attorney will know how to get a copy of the report; whether he shows it to
you is up to him.

> *"Doc, they sent me for an IME. I didn't like it much, and I'm not
> sure he listened to me very carefully. I got a copy of his report, but he
> got a lot of things wrong. Anything I can do about it? I called him,
> but he won't talk to me.*

What if you disagree with the IME report? I recommend complaining. If you find some inaccuracy, you could call the doctor's office to tell
him about it. The IME doctor may not want to discuss his report with
you--very few will--but he certainly will read a letter if you send it to him.
If there are facts in it that make him change his opinion, he'll write an
amended report.

Make sure you keep a copy of your letter--you may need it later.

But if you dislike his report simply because it doesn't support your
case, that's a different story. IME's are the place for accurate medical diagnosis and firm conclusions about tough questions. But being accurate
could also mean that the report points out where the facts disagree with
your claim as well as where they agree. Merely "not liking the report" is a
lot different than finding inaccuracies.

One last thing: an IME report takes time to prepare. Don't expect it to
be mailed the day after you see the doctor. It may take weeks, especially
if he didn't have all the X-rays or records on time.

QUESTIONS AND ANSWERS ABOUT IME'S

Q. "I'm supposed to go for an IME but I have no idea why. I don't
think there's any dispute about my claim."
A. IME's can be requested for many reasons, some of them quite in-
nocuous. For example, I've done IME's to answer such questions as: Has
this patient reached the end of healing? Does he have any disability for
this injury? Did he have any disability before this injury? These are simply questions that the insurance company needs to know the answer to,
there's no dispute.

Of course I've also done IME's to answer questions such as "This patient's attorney claims a disability that is far higher than we think is justified, what is the true disability?"; "We know there's an injury here, but we want to know how much of the disability is related to an old injury and covered by another insurer"; "We think this man is faking and we need an examination to see if there's really anything wrong with him".

Q. "I was sent for an IME a month ago. Now they've terminated my benefits without explanation. What can I do?"

A. Talk to your claim adjuster as soon as possible. If you get no satisfactory explanation, contact your state Workers' Compensation office. If you get nowhere there--though you probably will you will have to see an attorney.

Q. "Do I have to appear for an IME?"

A. Yes. If you don't show up you'd better have a terrific excuse or the insurer will probably cancel your benefits.

Q. "Can I ask for an IME myself?"

A. No. This would usually be done by your attorney.

Q. "Will I get paid for the trip?"

A. Yes. It's not uncommon to travel a distance for an IME because doctors who do them are not available in many locations. The insurer should pay for mileage at the current rate, parking at the doctor's office, and sometimes meals and lodging if the distance requires it. You will probably **not** be reimbursed for a spouse's or friend's meals or lodging.

Q. "Can I have someone with me during an IME?"

A. Yes, that's your legal right in most cases. Most people bring their spouse, but many states allow you to have your own medical doctor or chiropractor present. You should realize that the IME doctor can and probably will insist that the person with you remains totally silent; it is the doctor's right to do so. If your friend violates that request he or she will probably be asked to leave.

Q. "Can I bring a tape recorder?"

A. That's up to the doctor doing the IME. Most won't allow it, nor will I, and courts have upheld my policy. I don't recommend you try to conceal a tape recorder. It has been tried, but patients become quite embarrassed when it is discovered.

Q. "Do I have to bring my own X-rays for an IME?"

A. It's usually the requesting source's obligation to provide the IME doctor with records and X-rays. But if they don't arrive in time the examination will suffer for it. So if you've been asked to bring them you can insure a more accurate exam by doing so. This certainly is an added bother, but believe me it will pay off when the doctor has all the facts at hand. Missing X-rays or records invariably turn out to be the most important ones.

Q. "Do I have to have new X-rays taken if an IME doctor wants to take them?"

A. If he has a valid reason you probably will have to have them. And that goes for any other tests he wants to do that do not involve invasive procedures (tests that puncture the skin) or dangerous materials. He has the <u>right</u> to do any other tests that he can medically justify including psychological tests.

Q. "As soon as I retained an attorney and made a claim the insurer sent me for an IME. Why?"

A. Whenever a patient gets an attorney and files a legal action the insurer is probably going to order an IME. This is because a patient's attorney could make a claim for anything he likes: A million dollars in benefits, loss of job for a hundred years, anything he likes and he doesn't need more than one scribbled note from a family doctor to do it. It costs him absolutely nothing to file the claim. Then the insurer or their attorney has to get an IME to figure out what the claim is all about and to see it it has any merit, let alone to decide whether or not to pay. This is why 90% of IME's are done at the request of insurers or their attorneys.

Q. "Can I ask the IME doctor some questions about what he thinks?"

A. You can ask, but most doctors doing an IME will not answer them because they aren't supposed to be giving advice. There is one exception: I feel it is every doctor's obligation to alert an examinee to a dangerous condition if he finds one during an IME. I usually do this in a letter to the examinee with a copy to his doctor.

Q. "I had an IME and the doctor said I couldn't do heavy work. Now how can I get him to fill out my monthly disability insurance forms? He says he won't do it."

A. If the doctor performed the IME, he's not the appropriate person to complete those forms because you're not his patient. Your treating doctor should do them.

Q. "Can I go back to an IME doctor for treatment if I liked him?"

A. Not without permission in most cases. It does happen, usually when the IME doctor a) made firm recommendations for treatment that could help; b) moved the case along in some way; c) was obviously fair; d) seemed to be more thorough than any other doctor was. To go back for treatment you will need approval from the insurer. If you have an attorney you will need his permission also. If there's some dispute, he may not want to let you do it.

WRAP-UP

How to do yourself some favors with IME's. Remember that:
1) IME's are standard components of the Workers' Compensation process and if scheduled, your attendance is mandatory;
2) IME's are often for very ordinary reasons and not always because of disputes;
3) The best policy is to be cooperative and straightforward when you go for an IME, and to tell your history as accurately as you can;
4) The report of an IME belongs to the party who requested the evaluation;
5) The healthiest way to look at an IME is as you would everything else about Comp: It might produce information that you can use to get better or move your case along. The IME doctor may find some problem that was overlooked, or suggest some treatment that hasn't been tried yet and that might be the one thing that gets you better.

L

CHAPTER 22

Maximum Healing
&
Disability Ratings

"Doctor, how can I be at Maximum Healing? I'm nowhere near as good as before I was hurt. I still have pain. I certainly can't be healed to maximum yet!"

* * *

"Doc, they tell me I've got a disability rating of 10%. Does that mean I can do 90% of my old job?"

Two Workers' Compensation terms seem to throw a lot of people for a loop--patients <u>and</u> doctors. These terms are "Maximum Healing" and "Permanent Disability".

Yet every single Workers' Compensation case has to address these two concepts at the end. Both of them have a major impact on a patient's case. This chapter explains them.

What Happens At The End Of A Case

Your case will have to come to some resolution sometime. Your treatment will progress up to a point, you'll either recover or you won't, you'll either be left with some residual effects or you won't.

When the insurer sees that this time is approaching they'll write your doctor and ask him to formally determine whether treatment has reached an end and whether you have any permanent injury. Your doctor--or another--**must** make a decision on these matters. He'll review the whole chart and respond to the insurer in writing.

If your doctor is unable or unwilling to make these decisions, the insurer will ask him when he thinks it will be possible to decide. Then they'll wait and ask him again. If he doesn't know or will not give the insurer an answer, the insurer will probably arrange an IME (see Chapter 21) to get the determinations. They will ask the IME doctor: Has this patient reached his Maximum Healing? Is there any Permanent Disability?

Maximum Healing

When the insurer asks your doctor if you have reached Maximum Healing, they are asking a question that has both medical and legal meanings. Medical because they're asking if you have recovered as much as you're going to; legal because if you've reached Maximum Healing your Comp case is nearly over.

Maximum Healing may be known as Maximum Medical Improvement (MMI), plateau of healing, maximum recovery, End Of Healing (EOH), Permanent and Stationary (P&S), Stable Medical State (SMS), etc., depending on the Workers' Compensation system of your state. They all mean the same thing.

Maximum Healing means that <u>you have gotten about as much better as you're likely to get</u>. The official definition in most states is something like this:

The point of recovery beyond which further medical treatment is not reasonably expected to produce improvement.

Maximum Healing means one thing only: That you are stable and unlikely to improve further. Maximum Healing does <u>not</u> imply or require that you be as good as you were before your injury. It does <u>not</u> imply that you are pain-free. It only means there is no more active treatment planned, that you have either recovered or reached the point where you are no longer improving. Nine times out of ten the insurer will know from your doctor's medical records if you have likely reached Maximum Healing. In fact for the most minor injuries--strains, bruises, etc.--Maximum Healing will be reached after only a few days. When the insurer sees this, they'll ask your doctor to declare Maximum Healing or a healing plateau.

If your doctor says you have not reached a plateau, he is saying that more treatment will change your condition for the better. The insurer will accept his opinion only if he backs it up with good reason.

Once Maximum Healing has been declared the insurer will begin taking steps to settle and close your claim. In some states there is no Maximum Healing: Patients remain on Comp forever until they either recover or until the employer provides an alternate job. But in most states the insurer will notify you that your benefits will soon be ending.

IF YOU DISAGREE WITH MAXIMUM HEALING

I often see patients who feel they have not come anywhere near Maximum Healing, though a doctor has declared that they have. "There must be some mistake," they say. "I'm nowhere near maximum. I can't even do my old job." Usually, they dispute the Maximum Healing declaration because no-one explained what it really means.

If you disagree with the doctor's reasons for Maximum Healing declaration, first write down your arguments so they are extremely clear. Then your first recourse is to discuss them with your doctor. Show him why you think you haven't reached Maximum Healing and ask if more treatment would help.

If you don't get anywhere with your doctor, discuss it with your rehabilitation consultant if you have one and then with your claim adjuster. If the claim adjuster agrees with you, the insurer will continue your benefits while you get more treatment.

A 45-year-old waitress fell six months ago. She still has neck and upper back and arm pain. She's a little upset and tells me: "The insurance company is going to cut off my benefits because my doctor says I've reached Maximum Healing. But he hasn't really done anything. He just gave me lots of pills and it just doesn't seem right that they're closing my case."

I look through the file and tell her, "It seems you haven't had any physical therapy yet or a TENS unit, or injections to trigger points, or a general exercise program. Is that right?" She hasn't had any of them.

I write the insurer that this patient has not reached Maximum Healing. I estimate another three months of active treatment will be needed and I give my reasons. It's very likely they will reinstate her benefits and authorize further treatment.

If a dispute remains after discussing it, you may have to ask for a second opinion or ask for a Workers' Compensation conference. If you have a conference and still disagree with the decision, ask an attorney for advice.

But eventually everyone does reach a stable point, a plateau of healing. You will too. At that point your doctor will have to determine if you have a disability rating or not.

DISABILITY RATINGS

Every Workers' Compensation injury has to be "rated" as to whether it has caused a "permanent disability". This means is there some physical damage, limitation, or other medical condition that is permanent.

The insurer will probably ask your doctor to make this determination at the same time they ask him about Maximum Healing.

The doctor will first have to decide whether your injury produced any <u>physical impairment</u> (a physical limitation or loss of some function) that will be permanent. Examples would be loss of motion of a shoulder, hand, knee or foot, limited lifting capacity, loss of sight, loss of a hand, etc.

Impairment is a strictly medical judgement, based on objective findings, standard medical criteria and the doctor's experience. The impairment rating will then be translated into a "disability rating". Doctors may use a guide published by the American Medical Association to determine impairment, or guides put out by the state in which you live.

The simplest injuries--bumps, abrasions, strains, etc.--will cause no permanent damage and have no impairment. Most fractures won't either, though a few will if they result in loss of motion. Many neck and back injuries will cause impairment, particularly if they lead to surgery.

> *I am examining a man to determine his disability rating. I find he's been confused by conflicting opinions. He says, "I can't do my old job anymore. The company hasn't found a new one for me. My doctor told me I'm 50% disabled, whatever that means, but my lawyer told me that I should claim I'm 100% disabled. Does this mean I'm all washed up?"*
>
> *I review his problem. Because of a shoulder and elbow injury he doesn't have much motion. After measuring his motion, I see he has a partial disability of about 30% of the arm or 18% of the whole body according to the tables for his state. I tell him this and show him it's nowhere near a permanent total disability.*
>
> *"That's what I figured too," he says. "After all, I can work and do almost what I did before. I thought 50% disability was way too much, and I certainly wasn't ready to pack it in and retire."*

Your doctor will have to translate the degree of medical impairment into a <u>rating of permanent disability</u>. Disability is a part-legal, part-medical term and is interpreted slightly differently by each state's Workers' Compensation laws.

Your doctor will use guides from the American Medical Association or from your state's laws to come up with a percent of your disability. This may be anywhere from zero to 100% "of the whole body", or from zero to 100% of a hand, arm, leg, etc. States differ on use of "whole body" or "body parts" for rating--I don't know if anyone understands why, other than that's the way the laws were written.

The actual ratings can vary widely depending on what state you are in. For example in Minnesota an injured employee who has average or poor results from back surgery will probably have a "whole body rating" of 11% or 13%. But five miles away in Wisconsin the same patient would be rated at about 5%. In another state that accepts the AMA guidelines the injury would be approximately 10%.

Disability ratings and the systems to calculate them usually defy easy understanding. There are thousands of different injuries, many different rating methods, and 50 states each with their own laws. I would recommend you not try to figure a disability rating out, and especially don't

compare yours with friends or acquaintances. There are too many vari-
ables and the percent of disability often has little to do with the severity of
the injury and less to do with the ability to work.

For example, suppose a pipefitter has a 13% rating for poor results
from back surgery. He may be totally unable to do his job, yet a right-
handed salesman could lose his left thumb on the job and have a rating of
21.5%--even though he could work without difficulty!

As a general rule, the main impact of a disability rating is on your final settlement. The insurer or state will take your doctor's disability rating
percentage and covert it to a financial figure that they will eventually pay
you. Each state has different formulas for this, based on your weekly
salary at the time of injury or on a schedule that matches disability to dollars or on some other method. Basically, the higher the rating the greater
the dollar distribution to you, the lower the rating the lower the dollars.

In closing, when trying to understand disability, these are the terms
you'll probably hear the most:
PPD (Permanent Partial Disability): A disability rating expressed as
a percent, such as 10% of the body. This is the most common kind
of rating.
PTD (Permanent Total Disability): Permanently unable to work
after Maximum Healing is reached. This is uncommon these days,
because usually some job is possible.

If You Disagree With Your Disability Rating

Your doctor or an IME doctor should determine your disability based on
the facts of your case as closely as they can be determined. The rating
should be calculated according to logical principles and a standard method.
Theoretically two patients with identical injuries would have the same
permanency, all things being equal.

But of course all things--especially patients, injuries, and recoveries--
never are equal. And doctors bring to bear varying amounts of judgement
and thoroughness when they do disability ratings. Some doctors don't
like doing them, others are very skilled with the rating process. Two doctors might measure range of motion differently, interpret an MRI differently, or make different judgements as to how severe a problem is. And

some doctors simply make mistakes: I've seen ratings that were simply in error because the doctor used the wrong page.

Some treating doctors even bias their ratings. I know of one orthopedic surgeon who told me he always slants his reports and permanency ratings so that his patients, or the clients of attorneys that send patients to him, will receive extra money in their settlement. Some doctors bias their reports to please whomever requested the report. Both unethical practices--also disgusting.

For any of these reasons there could be disagreement on the amount of permanency you have been given. If the insurer thinks the permanency is wrong they will arrange an IME. But if you think the rating is incorrect, try to discuss it with the doctor that did the rating. If it was your own doctor he'll probably talk it over with you. If it was an IME doctor he probably will not, but he would probably read a letter to him that explains your objections and sets out your reasons. If it shows him facts he didn't have, he may revise his rating.

You can also discuss your complaints with your claim adjuster. If that doesn't get you anywhere you can ask the state Workers' Compensation office for help (see Chapter 24).

Before you start any of these discussions, first write out on paper something like the following:

"I think my permanent disability rating is incorrect for the following reasons: ..."

You should be able to back up your arguments with facts. Merely not liking a rating is not an adequate reason for disputing it. If you speak with the state office and have a conference and still get nowhere, and you are still sure that your rating is wrong, you will probably have to contact an attorney for advice.

DISABILITY RATINGS AND PAIN

Many patients are surprised to find that Workers' Compensation usually doesn't pay much attention to discomfort or pain, at least when it comes to making disability ratings.

Pain is not, by itself, a criteria of permanent injury or disability. You may say "It still hurts" or "I can't breathe easily" but if your tests show that your injury has resolved, the discomfort won't affect your permanent disability rating very much. You might say "I can't do any work", but without measurements to document it, permanency won't be affected.

This is because compensation laws about disability ratings usually demand concrete evidence of injury and limitation: A burn scar, loss of a limb, a disc herniation that was documented on MRI, a specific operation, loss of lung function, a measurably shorter leg after a fracture, etc. These are hard evidence or <u>objective</u> findings. Workers' Compensation usually requires them to be present for there to be a permanent disability. Subjective complaints can't be proven; in the world of Workers' Compensation they don't much count.

Q. "Does everyone have a disability rating?"
A. Every work injury has to be <u>rated</u>. 95% of them have a disability rating of zero because they heal fully.

Q. "What if two doctors disagree about my permanency rating?"
A. You may have to go through a Workers' Compensation conference to resolve the difference.

Q. "Are permanent disability ratings forever?
A. That's the definition of "permanent". See Chapter 26.

WRAP-UP

How to do yourself some favors with Maximum Healing and disability ratings:
1) At the end of an injury, a doctor will have to declare whether or not you've reached Maximum Healing--whether you're as good as you're going to get;
2) He'll also have to rate your injury as either permanently "disabling", partially or completely disabling, or not disabling at all;
3) There are ways to dispute a doctor's declaration of either;
4) Remember: Maximum Healing does not mean you are "good as new", and a disability rating does not always correlate with how much you can work, with your degree of impairment, or with pain.

K

CHAPTER 23

Closing Your Claim

"Well, Doc, the insurance company tells me they're gonna close up my case. They said I'll be getting a lump sum payment for a disability rating.

"But this is all new to me. If I get this disability payment, does that mean I can't see any more doctors? Am I supposed to be better now?"

There's a time when every Workers' Compensation case formally comes to an end. Depending on the case, this could be merely a formality or a negotiated "settlement". For the vast majority of claims, closure requires no specific action by the patient.

Therefore this chapter applies to only a few people, probably less than 5% of all Workers' Compensation cases. These will be cases of a "permanent injury" with some form of disability rating. Even some of these patients may not need this chapter.

But if there is some dispute about your disability, about how much work you can do, or about some other complicating factor, you could have to go through a settlement process. This chapter shows you what it is and how to do it.

CLAIM CLOSURE

Statistically almost all Workers' Compensation injuries--more than 95%--
lead to no more than two weeks of lost time. These injuries heal quickly
and the patients have no residuals. These cases are simply closed as soon
as the patient's doctor declares he has reached maximum healing (see
Chapter 22). No "settlement" is necessary because there's nothing that
needs settling. That's the end of the story.

Of the remaining few cases, there may be some degree of permanent
residual impairment. If you have such an injury your doctor will rate the
amount of permanent disability (see Chapter 22) and notify the insurer.
The insurer will initiate claim closure, usually by mail. You will be noti-
fied by mail, and if you have a disability payment coming you'll receive a
check. That will be that: No "settlement" negotiations necessary.

Only a tiny percent of injuries are left that will require that some
things be "settled".

CLAIM SETTLEMENT

If you have a severe injury, significant limitations, a complex case or there
is some dispute about your case, you might have to go through a claim settlement process to determine your final benefits before you and the insurer go separate ways. In other words, the extent of your disability payments and/or injury benefits might to some extent be negotiable.

The procedures for claim closure and case settlement vary so widely by
insurer and by state that my guidelines and recommendations here will
have to be somewhat general.

If you have a permanent disability rating, payment to you (oddly
called an "award") is calculated by the insurer.

Each state has its own rules for converting your doctor's disability rating, which he expresses in the form of a percent, into a dollar figure. This
is done by formula and might take into account your previous wage, the
number of weeks you have been off, factors about your employability, and
other factors unique to each state. The state legislature sets the formula in
almost every case.

You might be able to request how you receive your payment: All in a lump sum now, spread out over time, or in an annuity. You'll have to work out these matters with your claim adjuster.

The method of payment could significantly affect the total amount that you ultimately receive. If financial matters like this are new to you, your state's Workers' Compensation office can advise you (see next chapter for addresses and phone numbers) or you could get advice from an attorney (see Chapter 25).

NEGOTIATIONS

To establish the contents and structure of your case settlement, you could simply work out an agreement with your claim adjuster, especially if it's not complicated. However, you may have to actually negotiate the settlement, perhaps with advice from and/or representation by an attorney. If so, the attorney will actually do the negotiating; I do recommend you stay in close touch during the whole process.

You may have to attend a settlement conference at a state Workers' Compensation office to finalize your agreement. If you do, I recommend you take copies of all your Workers' Compensation notes (see Chapter 4). Write down on a piece of paper the things that are most important to you so that they are clear when you are in the conference. Also write down your reasons for each. You will feel much more confident in a conference if you have all of this in front of you.

If you have retained an attorney he will be making the request and giving the reasons, but you need to tell <u>him</u> what you want beforehand. Use the same method: Write it all down.

How should you act in a conference? Be yourself. Simply tell your story as it happened with your backup notes in front of you. Make it clear to everyone, including your attorney, exactly what it is you want.

You might be negotiating any of the following matters in your settlement discussions:
-Payment of outstanding medical bills including medications, hospitals, therapy, Work Hardening, etc.;
-Back pay or benefits owed to you;

-Mileage payments;

-Future medical care. Ask your doctor if he expects you to need more medical care specifically for your work injury, and how long you will need it. Then get this included in your settlement if possible (also see the discussion in Chapter 26);

-Settlements might also include more rehabilitation, agreement that your employer will provide light duty for a certain period of time, agreement to help you with a job search for a specific number of months, schooling for an alternative job (see Chapter 20), help in setting up a new trade or business, etc. I've seen patients given a start in gunsmithing, bait shop ownership, candy-making, gift shops, even sausage-making as a part of settlement. But this only occurs with the most severe injuries when no other job is available.

FACTORS THAT COMPLICATE SETTLEMENT

Some case closures are straightforward. There's impairment, a disability rating, the employee is paid, life goes on. But in a few cases complicating factors decrease the amount of the Workers' Compensation insurer's financial responsibility at time of closure. These are cases where the issue is what exactly caused lasting disability. There are three common complicating factors:

1) Predisposing conditions;
2) Preexisting problems;
3) Non-work injuries to the same area as the work injury.

1) PREDISPOSING CONDITIONS: A personal health problem or condition may make it more likely that a person has a work injury. These are called predisposing conditions. Examples are congenital anomalies or degenerative disease in the neck or low back, lung disease, obesity, etc. As an example, an employee with asthma is more likely to have an allergic lung injury at work; part of his disability is due to the asthma.

2) PREEXISTING PROBLEMS: An employee might have a disease or medical problem in a particular area of the body and then have a work injury to the same area. The preexisting problem causes the work injury to be more severe than it ordinarily would have been and/or to heal poorly. This type of complicating factor is similar to a predisposing condition. Examples of preexisting problems are wrist tendinitis before developing

carpal tunnel syndrome, bursitis before a shoulder injury occurs, a long string of prior back or neck problems, previous surgery, liver disease that preexisted a toxic exposure, etc. The eventual disability is partly due to the preexisting problem.

3) PRIOR NON-WORK INJURIES: If an employee has had one or more at-home or recreational injuries and then injures the same area at work, the Workers' Compensation claim for disability is muddled by the previous injuries. The insurer will perhaps suspect that the previous injuries actually caused some or all of the current disability. These injuries make it very hard for an employee to prove that the work injury has caused his current and lasting impairment. As a most simple example, if a person had a severe burn scar but then also gets burned at work, how could he claim a disabling scar from the work injury?

Disputes over any of these complicating factors can drag on for years. When there is more than one injury, there can also be more than one insurer involved. If so, the insurers will want to split up payment of eventual disability benefits. In cases such as this, each insurer will probably send the patient for an Independent Medical Examination (see Chapter 21) in an attempt to sort out responsibility.

After Settlement

Once your claim is settled and you've received payment for permanent impairment, there's only one thing to do: Get on with things.

> *Paul Tanner had run a resort alone but his shoulder injury put a stop to that. He didn't know what he would do.*
> *After claim settlement he received a lump sum check for partial disability. "I used that money to change things around for me," he says now. "I bought a different mower, a trimmer, automatic kitchen aids like power can openers and mixers, I got a different delivery truck and I started hiring help for all the things I can't do any more.*
> *My shoulder is no better--it never will be I guess. But now I can at least keep my resort going, thanks to that payment."*

Disability payments are meant to help you along with your life, to in some way compensate you for a permanent injury or impairment.

Disability payments don't "treat the injury". Nor do they put patients on easy street.

I've known a few patients who think a permanency award is going to solve all their problems and make them rich, but I try to point them towards reality. I tell them, "If you have a disability from a work injury you'll get a payment because that's the system. But it isn't the lottery. I've never seen it sufficient to retire to the Bahamas. It's most practical to keep your mind focused on your future work."

QUESTIONS AND ANSWERS

Q. "Once I've settled my claim, am I just cut free? Is that the end of it?"

A. It depends entirely upon your settlement. If you're completely healed from your injury you probably are "cut free" and that will be the end of it. But with a severe injury you might need future medical care, therapy, surgery, etc.

Q. "How do I make sure I get future medical benefits?"

A. You build it into your settlement.

Q. "What if I have another injury after settlement?"

A. If it's a new injury you file a new claim. If it's only an "aggravation" of your old injury the insurer will probably pay benefits. However, if your employer has changed Workers' Compensation insurers, the new insurer may deny the injury saying it's due to a preexisting problem.

Q. "What if my settlement includes part-time work and my plant shuts down?"

A. You may be able to continue getting partial Workers' Compensation benefits just as you were before. Check with your state office.

Q. "What if my settlement includes light duty and my plant is sold?"

A. You might be out of luck. In many states the new owner might not have to hire you. There are laws that let a new owner start with a brand new workforce.

Q. "What if I've been off a long time, then I settle my case and return to work but I'm fired?"

A. You'll have to either find a new job or go on unemployment. But you could have a serious problem if you were off work so long that you don't have enough hours to qualify for unemployment. Find out first.

Q. "If I ever apply for another job do I have to tell them I settled a Workers' Compensation claim with a disability rating?"

A. Yes. If you conceal it, most states' laws allow a new employer to dismiss you when they find out. If you ever have another injury, the new employer may not have any responsibility to provide you with Workers' Compensation benefits if you concealed a prior injury to the same area (also see Chapter 26).

Q. "Are there any disadvantages to a large disability award?"

A. There might be. You may find that future job interviews don't turn out well. When a potential employer hears of your "permanent work injury" job leads may suddenly dry up (see Chapter 26).

The bigger the award, the more skittish a potential employer might become. I've seen some patients feel they should have focused more on having a future job than getting a one-time payment.

WRAP-UP

How to do yourself some favors with claim settlement:
1) Only a small portion of Workers' Compensation claims need any kind of "settlement" negotiations;
2) If you do go through a settlement process make sure you have all your Workers' Compensation files and notes, and prepare your goals ahead of time in writing;
3) Consider future medical care, outstanding medical bills, future jobs, and other special items;
4) If you have preexisting or predisposing medical conditions, they will probably affect your settlement considerably;
5) Use claim settlement money to help you get along in your job--it's not a windfall.

G

CHAPTER 24

How To Find Help

"Doc, I'm not getting my Comp checks on time. And when they do come the amount doesn't seem right. Got any ideas what I can do? I have no idea who to ask about this."

If you have a problem with Workers' Compensation, help is available. Help can come from any of several sources, but you have to know how and where to look. This chapter shows how to find it. The six steps in this chapter will probably take care of 99% of Workers' Compensation glitches. Follow them in order.

Begin By Knowing What You Need

Write down your question, complaint, or problem on a piece of paper. If you can put it in black and white, it assures that you understand the real nature of the difficulty and will be able to express it clearly.

Make sure that you actually have a problem, not just a vague complaint. For example, "I don't like being on Comp" isn't really a problem, it's just a feeling. But, "My checks are always two weeks late" is a real problem, something you can ask about and get help with. Others: "I got hurt at work and I filled out a report but they claim it didn't happen on the job;" "My prescriptions aren't getting paid for;" "No-one will tell me what my benefits are."

These are all specific complaints, easy to understand and easy to address. If you can state your complaints in clear terms like this you are ready to ask someone to solve them for you.

Assemble your notes with your claim number, date of injury, etc., from your Workers' Compensation file (see Chapter 4). This documentation will help you back up your complaint.

Then put on your paper a few more sentences stating exactly what you want to happen and your reasons for wanting it. Examples would be: "I want to receive my Comp checks on time and in the right amount"; "I want my employer to accept my claim as a work injury"; "I want to know just what my benefits are"; and so on.

Once you have all this on paper, you're ready for Step #1.

Step #1: Start With Your Doctor

The easiest place to begin, and perhaps all you will have to do, is to tell your doctor about your difficulty. You might reply: "My doctor? He can't solve a Workers' Compensation problem--he's a doctor!".

But it might be that you don't even have a true Workers' Compensation problem. You might have a problem related only to medical records and don't realize it. If so, your doctor could solve it easily.

For example, insurers will often suspend benefits when a doctor doesn't provide them with medical records. If this is behind your problem, your doctor can solve it by sending his records. In fact he probably will, once he realizes that you're having a hardship because of him.

Or, the insurer might have misunderstood something your doctor wrote. This happens all the time: I saw a case where the insurer wouldn't pay for medical care because the doctor didn't make it clear what he was treating. One phone call reinstated the patient's benefits.

The problem might be due to miscommunication between doctor and employer or insurer. If so, your doctor can help by calling them. The problem might be due to uncertainty, for example the employer might not have gotten information about whether you will ever return to work. Your doctor could certainly help with this.

Even if your Workers' Compensation difficulty is not something your doctor can clear up, it's at least better that he be aware of it. Then, should he receive a call or letter from the insurer, he'll be prepared and in a better position to help you.

Step #2: Next, Ask Your QRC

If your Workers' Compensation problem is nothing your doctor can solve, and you have a rehabilitation consultant or QRC, call him/her next to ask about it. It's absolutely amazing what a good QRC can do to resolve communication problems, bypass red tape, and disentangle bureaucratic difficulties.

If you haven't read Chapter 14 about what QRC's do and how they can help, read it now and then ask yours if he/she can help you. They speak the three languages of medicine, insurance, and Workers' Compensation and might be able to solve your problem with only a phone call or two.

Step #3: Contact Your Employer

If your doctor and QRC are unable to straighten things out or resolve your problem, it might help to call your employer directly. Perhaps they aren't forwarding bills to the insurer, perhaps they've mistakenly denied your claim, perhaps there was a clerical error, perhaps they don't have some essential information that only you can provide.

Employers often feel they are in the dark in a Workers' Compensation case. They don't hear from the doctor, they don't see the injured employee, they don't know how to plan for the future. Sometimes an employer will suspend benefits simply for lack of this information.

STEP #4: TALK TO YOUR CLAIM ADJUSTER

If neither doctor nor QRC nor employer can solve your problem, the next step is to go over it with your claim adjuster.

You should have stayed in close touch with your claim adjuster throughout your whole case (see Chapter 6). But if you haven't, now is the time. Get your written material in front of you and call up the claim adjuster. Ask him/her to help you solve your problem.

Claim adjusters really manage your entire file, so they can usually resolve delays, get you a second opinion, sort out mixups, move balky computers, explain permanent disability or financial benefits, etc. By the time you get through this step, it's most likely your problem will be gone.

STEP #5: CALL YOUR STATE WORKERS' COMPENSATION OFFICE

If you've talked with doctor, QRC, employer and claim adjuster and   you still   have   a   problem,   contact   the Workers' Compensation office in your state. Their telephone numbers and addresses are at the end of this chapter.

I've spoken to these offices and virtually everyone I've spoken to has been helpful. These are friendly people, knowledgeable about Workers' Compensation, and they've probably heard at least once every problem that can happen. They're ready to help: That's their job.

When you call, have your claim number, date of injury and insurer's name and your questions all written out. Be ready to tell them exactly what you need. Give them something specific to act on such as: "I need my check by next Friday"; "I need to see a specialist because I'm not improving"; etc.

And remember, every state has some sort of publication for employees on Comp. Some are easy to read, some aren't, but they will all help you learn more about your specific benefits under your state's laws.

STEP #6: GET LEGAL ADVICE

You have a rare Workers' Compensation case if you still have problems after talking to your doctor, employer, QRC, claim adjuster and state office. But if you do, then you probably need legal help. In fact, I've seen a few cases where the state office has recommended that a patient get advice from and retain an attorney.

Contacting and working with an attorney is covered in the next chapter, which you should read before going ahead with this step.

THE LAST RESORT

In more than 20 years of practice I have only had one patient who didn't get things settled by going through all the above steps. That patient finally wrote his congressman, and he did get results. If all else fails, this might work for you too.

WRAP-UP

How to do yourself some favors when you need to find help:
1) Write your problem down in clear form;
2) Talk to your doctor first because he may be able to eliminate the problem;
3) Next, talk with your rehabilitation consultant and employer if you still have a problem;
4) Then talk to your claim adjuster if the problem isn't resolved;
5) If nothing has helped call the state Workers' Compensation office;
6) If none of the above works, you will need legal advice.

H

ALABAMA

Workmen's Compensation Division
Department of Industrial Relations
Industrial Relations Building
Montgomery, Alabama 36130
(205) 261-2868

ALASKA

Workers' Compensation Division
Department of Labor
P.O. Box 25512
Juneau, Alaska 99802-5512
(907) 465-2790

ARIZONA

Industrial Commission
800 West Washington
P.O. Box 19070
Phoenix, Arizona 85005-9070
(602) 542-4661

ARKANSAS

Workers' Compensation Commission
Justice Building
625 Marshall Street
Little Rock, Arkansas 72201
(501) 682-3930

CALIFORNIA

Division of Industrial Accidents
P.O. Box 603, Room 103
San Francisco, California 94102
(415) 737-2618

COLORADO

Workers' Compensation Section
Division of Labor
Chancry Building
1120 Lincoln Street, 14th Floor
Denver, Colorado 80203
(303) 764-2913

CONNECTICUT

Workers' Compensation Commission
1890 Dixwell Avenue
Hamden, Connecticut 06514
(203) 789-7783

DELAWARE

Industrial Accident Board
State Office Building, 6th Floor
820 North French Street
Wilmington, Delaware 19801
(302) 571-2885

DISTRICT OF COLUMBIA

Dept. of Employment Services
Office of Workers' Compensation
P.O. Box 56098
Washington, D.C. 20011
(202) 576-6265

FLORIDA

Div. of Workers' Compensation
Dept. of Labor and Employment Security
301 Forrest Building
2728 Centerview Drive
Tallahassee, Florida 32399-0680
(904) 488-2548

GEORGIA

Board of Workers' Compensation
South Tower, Suite 1000
One CNN Center
Atlanta, Georgia 30303-2788
(404) 656-3875

HAWAII

Disability Compensation Division
Dept. of Labor and Industrial Relations
830 Punchbowl Street, Room 209
Honolulu, Hawaii 96813
(808) 548-4131

IDAHO

Industrial Commission
317 Main Street
Boise, Idaho 83720
(208) 334-6000

ILLINOIS

Industrial Commission
100 West Randolph Street, Ste. 8-200
Chicago, Illinois 60602
(312) 814-6500

INDIANA

Workers' Comp. Industrial Board
601 State Office Building
100 North Senate Avenue
Indianapolis, Indiana 46204
(317) 232-3808

IOWA

Division of Industrial Services
Department of Employment Services
1000 East Grand Avenue
Des Moines, Iowa 50319
(515) 281-5934

KANSAS

Division of Workers' Compensation
Department of Human Resources
600 Merchant Bank Tower
800 SW Jackson
Topeka, Kansas 66612-1227
(913) 296-3441

KENTUCKY

Workers' Compensation Board
Perimeter Park West, Bldg. C
1270 Louisville Road, Building C
Frankfort, Kentucky 40601
(502) 564-5550

LOUISIANA

Dept. of Employment and Training
Office of Workers' Comp. Admin.
P.O. Box 94040
Baton Rouge, Louisiana 70804-9040
(504) 342-7555

MAINE

Workers' Compensation Commission
State House Station 27
Augusta, Maine 04333
(207) 289-3751

MARYLAND

Workers' Compensation Commission
6 North Liberty Street
Baltimore, Maryland 21201
(303) 333-4700

MASSACHUSETTS

Department of Industrial Accidents
600 Washington Street, 7th Floor
Boston, Massachusetts 02111
(617) 727-4300

MICHIGAN

Bureau of Workers' Disability Comp.
Department of Labor
P.O. Box 30016
309 North Washington Square
Lansing, Michigan 48909
(517) 373-3480

MINNESOTA

Workers' Compensation Division
Department of Labor and Industry
443 Lafayette Road North
St. Paul, Minnesota 55155
(612) 296-6107

MISSISSIPPI

Workers' Compensation Commission
1428 Lakeland Drive
P.O. Box 5300
Jackson, Mississippi 39296-5300
(601) 987-4200

MISSOURI

Division of Workers' Compensation
Dept. of Labor and Industrial Relations
P.O. Box 58
Jefferson City, Missouri 65102
(314) 751-4231

MONTANA

State Comp. Mutual Insurance Fund
5 South Last Chance Gulch
Helena, Montana 59601
(406) 444-6518

NEBRASKA

Workers' Compensation Court
State House, 13th Floor
P.O. Box 98908
Lincoln, Nebraska 68509-8908
(402) 471-2568

NEVADA

State Industrial Insurance System
515 East Musser Street
Carson City, Nevada 89714
(702) 687-5220

NEW HAMPSHIRE

Department of Labor
19 Pillsbury Street
Concord, New Hampshire 03301
(603) 271-3171

NEW JERSEY

Division of Workers' Compensation
Department of Labor
Call Number 381
Trenton, New Jersey 08625-0399
(609) 292-2414

NEW MEXICO

Workers' Compensation Admin.
P.O. Box 27198
Albuquerque, New Mexico
87125-7198
(505) 841-8787

NEW YORK

Workers' Compensation Board
180 Livingston Street
Brooklyn, New York 11248
(718) 802-6600

NORTH CAROLINA

Industrial Commission
Dobbs Building
430 North Salisbury Street
Raleigh, North Carolina 27611
(919) 733-4820

NORTH DAKOTA

Workers' Compensation Bureau
Russell Building-Hwy. 83 North
4007 N. State Street
Bismark, North Dakota 58501
(701) 224-2700

OHIO

Bureau of Workers' Compensation
246 North High Street
Columbus, Ohio 43215
(614) 466-2950

OKLAHOMA

Oklahoma Workers' Comp. Court
1915 North Stiles
Oklahoma City, Oklahoma
73105-4904
(405) 557-7600

OREGON

Department of Insurance & Finance
Labor and Industries Building
Salem, Oregon 97310
(503) 378-4100

PENNSYLVANIA

Bureau of Workers' Compensation
Department of Labor and Industry
1171 South Cameron Street, Rm. 103
Harrisburg, Pennsylvania 17104-2511
(717) 783-5421

RHODE ISLAND

Dept. of Workers' Compensation
610 Manton Avenue
Providence, Rhode Island 02909
(401) 272-0700

SOUTH CAROLINA

Workers' Compensation Commission
1612 Manon Street
P.O. Box 1715
Columbia, South Carolina 29202-5700
(803) 737-5700

SOUTH DAKOTA

Division of Labor and Management
Department of Labor
Kneip Building, Third Floor
700 Governors Drive
Pierre, South Dakota 57501
(605) 773-3681

TENNESSEE

Workers' Compensation Division
Department of Labor
501 Union Building, Second Floor
Nashville, Tennessee 37243-0661
(615) 741-2395

TEXAS

Workers' Compensation Commission
200 East Riverside Drive, 1st Floor
Austin, Texas 78704
(512) 448-7900

UTAH

Industrial Commission
160 East 300 South
Salt Lake City, Utah 84111
(801) 530-6800

VERMONT

Department of Labor and Industry
State Office Building
120 State Street
Montpelier, Vermont 05602
(802) 828-2286

VIRGINIA

Industrial Commission
1000 DMV Building
P.O. Box 1794
Richmond, Virginia 23220
(804) 367-8600

WASHINGTON

Department of Labor and Industries
General Administration Building
HC101
Olympia, Washington 98506
(206) 753-6307

WEST VIRGINIA

Workers' Compensation Commission
P.O. Box 3151
Charleston, West Virginia 25332
(304) 348-2580

WISCONSIN

Workers' Compensation Division
Department of Industry, Labor, and
Human Relations
P.O. Box 7901
201 East Washington Avenue, Room 161
Madison, Wisconsin 53707
(608) 266-1340

WYOMING

Workers' Compensation Division
122 West 25th Street, 2nd Floor
East Wing, Herschler Building
Cheyenne, Wyoming 82002
(307) 777-7441

CHAPTER 25

Getting Legal Advice

"The priest sees men at their best, the lawyer sees them at their worst, the doctor sees them as they are."

...Anonymous

Do you need an attorney? Yes, if you have some Workers' Compensation problem that can't be solved any other way (see last chapter). But there are some things you should know first.

You might want to merely consult with an attorney at any stage of your case, and this will not lead to any problems. But <u>retaining</u> an attorney can affect virtually every aspect of your life as a Comp claimant-- not always for the better. This chapter tells you what to be aware of before seeking an attorney's advice.

The Value Of An Attorney

The odds are that you'll never require legal representation for a Workers' Compensation claim--only a few percent of claimants do. Unfortunately, more patients probably hurry to sign up with an attorney at the first sign of difficulty than need to.

In this chapter I'm not going to run down attorneys--that's already done too much and not helpful.

If a person finds he has a legal problem, an attorney is indispensable. The few times it's happened to me I've been on the phone with an attorney inside two minutes flat. And it's helped hundreds of Comp patients, too.

I've been taking care of patients whose benefits have been suspended and I've seen how a good attorney, with a few hours paperwork, can get their benefits going again. I've seen cases where insurers refused to authorize certain testing or surgery. After the patients' lawyers intervened, the tests were done and the surgeries performed and the patients recovered and returned to work.

I've seen cases where patients' attorneys went to bat for them and got insurers to stop stonewalling them, to accept their claims, and to give them the disability settlements that the facts justified. I know attorneys have gotten stalled cases unstalled, and I've seen them get difficult claim adjusters to be more helpful.

I've seen several patients whose claim adjusters even recommended they get legal representation. Their adjusters told them specifically: "I can't do anything more because of our companys' policies. You'd better get an attorney to help you now."

Even so you may not need an attorney even if you think you do.

> A patient was terribly upset over what he thought was a dastardly move by the insurer to ruin his life. "I'm going to find an attorney to help me," he said. He calmed down once he talked to the state Workers' Compensation office. They showed him that what had happened was a normal part of every Comp case and it had little or no effect on his benefits.

Get adequate information about your problem first. If the answer isn't in this book, follow the first five steps in Chapter 24 and get all the free advice you can before taking the step of hiring an attorney. If you've exhausted all those steps and still haven't gotten what you think you need, perhaps you do need an attorney to help you.

A Few Things To Think About Before You Go

But, there are several things that should make you think twice before having an attorney take over your Comp claim. Most importantly you must understand that when you have an attorney it can change everything. It's not the same as, say, just seeing another doctor or getting a second opinion. Retaining an attorney throws you into an entirely different mode of operation, a different posture so to speak, possibly into a life of argument rather than treatment, sometimes of disability rather than recovery.

As soon as you are represented by an attorney it can be like drawing a battle line. A Workers' Compensation professional said to me, "Doctors operate as facilitators of treatment, as healers. But attorneys operate as adversaries. Patients don't understand that when they jump into a legal mode, it's as if the forces all line up and unfortunately it may be the patient on one side versus everyone else on the other." This is why everyone involved in your case may regard you in a different light once you get an attorney--whether this is justified or not it can happen and does.

YOUR DOCTOR'S REACTION

Be prepared: Your doctor could react negatively. "What's an attorney going to do for you?" a doctor might say. "Is your attorney going to make you feel better? Is he going to help you get back to work faster?" Many doctors say they are suspicious of patients' motivation for lawsuits: "Perhaps he's not trying to get better after all" certainly runs through the doctor's mind. Doctors also tend to dislike answering attorneys' questions, fear of having the answers misquoted or manipulated is a common reason--and doctors are darned unhappy about having to testify in court.

YOUR EMPLOYER'S REACTION

Many employers react negatively when they find out an employee on Comp has engaged an attorney. This is especially so if they feel they've met the employee at least halfway, provided the employee benefits, held a job open, etc.

> *The employer says to the claim adjuster: "He's got a lawyer now, does he? Well, then he can talk to our lawyer. I'm going to waste any more of my time if that's the thanks I get. Maybe we just won't keep that job open after all. If he wants a fight, he'll find out we can fight too!"*

I've found that patients seldom realize ahead of time how adversarial a legal action seems to an employer. "It changes how we regard an employee, that's for sure," a large employer told me. "We figure it's the end of cooperation, the end of us trying to help him heal. We always want our injured employees back as soon as possible, but when one gets an attorney we start looking for a replacement." So, before you risk alienating your employer by legal action, it makes sense to consider the future. Do you plan to return to work at the same company? Do you expect to have a good relationship there? How would it feel to go back after a court battle--especially if you aren't the winner?

THE INSURER'S REACTION

Are you aware that after you are represented by an attorney your claim adjuster cannot talk to you? In almost every case the insurer will only be able to communicate with you through your attorney. And an insurer's reaction is similar to an employer's: They prepare for a fight. After all, 99% of the time the reason for retaining an attorney has to do with benefits problems, and that usually relates to the insurer.

"As soon as we get notification they've hired an attorney, we send the file to our legal staff," a claim adjuster told me. "We have to assume the claim will deteriorate. We prepare for a noticable slowdown in recovery. When the suit is filed, the primary goal of Workers' Compensation--recovery and return to work--is lost. We naturally begin to wonder whether we have a motivated employee anymore, or a claimant with secondary gain now. I don't think Comp claimants always understand the ramifications of filing a suit." (This does not apply to simply <u>consulting</u> with an attorney).

YOUR CREDIBILITY

Whether it's justified or not, when you retain an attorney your credibility can take a nosedive. While you were in only the medical system, your doctor and QRC and claim adjuster and employer could assume your goal was to recover and return to work. When you told the doctor your symptoms he could take them at face value as guideposts to the diagnosis.

But these assumptions change once legal action starts. A doctor said to me: "Once patients have an attorney, I don't know whether to believe their complaints or not. I can't tell anymore if they're really trying to get well or trying to stay off work. And I almost always see their progress come to a standstill." A QRC said it similarly: "After they get an attorney, patients start to act as if they have to prove they are disabled every day. They say they want to get back to work, but they aren't convincing to me."

The bottom line is simple. You should weigh all these things--doctors', insurers', and employers' reactions--before you make the decision to retain an attorney. If you still need one, if it's going to be worth it, proceed.

FINDING AN ATTORNEY

Probably the best way to find a Workers' Compensation attorney is to ask your present attorney, if you have one, for a referral to someone in his firm or a cooperating firm.

You could ask your doctor. Any physician who sees many Workers' Compensation injuries has seen the local Comp attorneys in action. He can tell you which are helpful and realistic, which are more argumentive or obstructive. You might ask your QRC, or the state Workers' Compensation office. Each would probably give you a list of three attorneys from which to choose. Ask your claim adjuster? Usually not.

How about choosing an attorney from Yellow Page ads? These will probably give you insight into which are aggressive and flamboyant, but not necessarily which attorneys are most skilled, reasonable, even-tempered, and effective. I would opt for a Workers' Compensation attorney with a reputation for quiet competence, one who gets things done on time and on target.

WORKING WITH AN ATTORNEY

Like everything else in Comp--and in life--if you know exactly what you want in a legal case you stand a better chance of getting it. Write down your goals, the reasons you want legal representation and what you want to accomplish. These are the things you'll tell the attorney when you first meet him. For example: "I want my job back because I like it and I have a lot of seniority"; or "I want rehab service because I can't work around those substances anymore and I need some help to work elsewhere"; or "I need training into a new job because I can't do heavy work anymore"; etc.

Obtain your medical records if you can and bring them with you when you see the attorney. It will save him time and you money. Bring your Comp notes, claim number, and date of injury (see Chapter 4). If your attorney requires an updated medical report he will ask a doctor for one. If he needs an IME (see Chapter 21) he will arrange one.

Ask for realistic advice. Does he think you can get what you want? Is your case strong or weak? Have you been doing the right things to strengthen your case, cooperating with doctors, etc.? Follow your attorney's advice on legal matters. He will be your legal advisor (not your medical advisor, I hope) and it's most efficient to do what he says.

But not blindly. Legal advice should make some sense to you, even if you don't know law. If it doesn't, ask for explanations. His advice should always move something forward, either your legal or medical or rehab status. If it doesn't, there's something wrong.

A claim adjuster told me: "A certain attorney always delays things for his clients. As soon as he gets the case he demands a change of doctors and a change of QRC's. He always changes to these do-nothing QRC's and to doctors who keep patients off work for years. He must think he's accomplishing something, but he does his clients a tremendous disservice."

I saw one of this attorney's clients once, in fact I treated him for a couple of years. One day the attorney called me to request a disability rating. He was mad at his own client just then and said to me: "You know what that S.O.B. did? He went out and got a job! It's ruined my claim!" So if you are satisfied with something but your attorney tries to change it, I would recommend that you ask why and don't get caught up in unproductive delaying tactics.

3 Things To Watch Out For

When a patient retains an attorney or starts legal action a few things could happen that inhibit his medical progress. They don't help his legal case or his future life after settlement either. These don't always happen, of course, rather they occur when attorneys are argumentative, obstructive, or use delaying tactics. If you see any of these things happening to you, consider making a fundamental change.

PROMOTING DISABILITY

I've seen a few patients change from outgoing, motivated injured workers into secretive, suspicious, resentful patients who think they'll win bigger if they can show how bad off they are. Probably attorneys do not cause this change; it may be part of the patient's personality. These patients start "proving disability". They begin to view the insurer as a capricious enemy and QRC's as untrustworthy. They accept treatment reluctantly. They seem afraid to act on any advice that might make them better. A few of these patients probably do manage to get a slightly higher disability payment at the end of their case than they might have otherwise. But not much higher, and it's a hollow "victory". They're left with the legacy of a long battle with the insurer, alienation from their former employer, the self-perception of being disabled, and a bitter taste. If you find you are working with one of the few attorneys that promote this style, I would recommend you think twice.

INTERFERENCE WITH MEDICAL CARE

I've seen a couple of attorneys get more involved in medical decision-making than seems good for their clients. This is a rare problem but it happens.

> I had a patient who obviously had a lumbar disc herniation from his work injury. I needed some X-rays and a CT. "My attorney won't allow it", he told me. I called the attorney. "No, I won't allow X-rays to be taken", he said. I couldn't understand it: The studies would have clinched his case for him, let alone helped his client medically.

I've seen a few attorneys refuse to allow special tests, refuse second opinions with surgeons that could help their clients, and I've even seen them cancel operations. Unless these attorneys have a license to practice medicine, they are being obstructive, short-sighted, and hurting their clients. Don't let it happen to you unless there's an extremely logical reason.

EXAGGERATED REPORTS

I once saw a letter from a patient's attorney to a chiropractor, requesting a disability rating. It basically said: "The higher you rate this man's permanent disability, the more you'll get paid." I've heard of other attorneys who tell their clients to act as injured as possible every time they see any doctor, especially on an IME, to get a falsely written medical report. But these things don't work. "We can always pick these reports apart", a claim adjuster told me, "and all it does is hurt their case in the end." If you receive such advice, you might want to think again before acting on it.

Going To Court

At some point you may have to testify in your case, either by giving testimony in front of a hearing examiner or judge or by deposition. Handle both the same.

First one attorney will ask you questions about yourself, your injury, your claim, etc.: "Direct examination". Then the other will ask his own questions: "Cross examination". Then they'll take turns, until they're both done.

My advice to patients who are testifying is the same advice I gave in Chapter 23 on claim settlement: Lay out your problem, tell what happened to you, and give the facts clearly. Tell what effect your injury had, what your symptoms are, and how the injury has changed your ability to tolerate activities of daily living and whether or not you can work.

Then lay out what you want: A job, retraining, your own hot dog stand, just to be left alone, whatever it is. Be yourself, be honest. If the system works the way it should, you'll get what the law allows:

Don't expect a quick answer. In many cases court dates are postponed, there are unexpected delays, and court decisions can take time to generate. Though in some Workers' Compensation conferences you can get a decision immediately, in other situations you might have to wait weeks or months to hear the verdict.

WHEN YOUR DOCTOR TESTIFIES

You might have the opportunity to observe a doctor's testimony, either in person or by transcript. You may notice several things. First, the attorneys will ask the doctor many short questions and it's not likely the doctor will be able to simply present your medical problem, the course of treatment, and what he concludes. He may try to describe this logically and factually, but I find that often one or the other attorney does not want it laid out this way and takes steps to thwart his attempts.

You might also see that one or the other attorney will question the doctor by skipping around, back and forth out of chronological order, from this report to that one, with questions in no logical sequence. "All they did was try to make me uncomfortable so I got flustered", one doctor said. "They didn't seem to want the facts", another told me, "just to get me to say things they could twist around. They never did let me give my full opinion."

You might also notice that one or the other attorney will try to imply that the doctor has inadequate expertise to testify in your case--certainly if he doesn't like what the doctor's saying. "When we have a strong case we can attack on the facts", an attorney confided in me. "But when we have a weak case, we can attack the doctor. We study his past testimony so we can try to catch him in little inconsistencies--this is how we weaken his credibility."

You'll almost always hear a new term: The doctor will be asked to give his answers "to a reasonable medical certainty". You may be surprised at his conclusions, perhaps thinking to yourself "How can he say yes or no to that question? No one can know that for sure." But "reasonable medical certainty" or "reasonable medical probability" means that the conclusion is more likely than not. In other words, it's at least 51% likely. It's not 100% sure. Knowing this might help you make sense out of what your doctor, or an IME doctor, concludes in his testimony.

You want to know what it feels like to be a doctor giving testimony? It's often frustrating: We often feel we cannot say what should be said. It's commonly disillusioning: We often feel that we see tricks instead of logic win a case. It's occasionally disgusting: We watch our words get twisted and used out of context and we can't prevent it. This is from a transcript of a deposition:

"Doctor, you were hired to do this exam on behalf of the insurance company to help them win, weren't you?"

"No, Sir, I wasn't hired, the attorney engaged my services for an Independent Medical Examination. It doesn't matter to me whose behalf he's working on, I simply examined the patient and wrote the report based on the facts of the case as I saw them."

"What do you mean you weren't hired, Doctor? He's paying you isn't he? You're not doing this for free are you?"

"No, I'm charging my usual fee, but he didn't hire me. I'm not his employee, and he has no control over what I say."

"Let's get this straight so it's understood, Doctor. Mr. Jones here is defending the insurance company, he hired you to write a report, and you knew that report would be used to defend his case. Yes or no?"

"Again, Sir, I wasn't hired, and as to whether the report helps him defend the case or hurts his case, it doesn't matter to me".

"Doctor, I don't care whether it matters to you or not. What I asked you is whether or not you did this exam on behalf of the insurance company. Did you or didn't you?"

"I've already said that I don't do an exam on behalf of anyone. I'm trying to say....."

"Now look Doctor,..." etc., etc., etc.

Testimony like this is certainly frustrating. At a deposition recently an attorney asked me if the medical records for the past several years used the word "pain". He asked me this 10 or 15 times, trying (it seemed to me) to make it appear that the notes documented <u>continuous</u> pain for five years. He never let me say that the actual notes were: "patient has some pain but better", "patient has had pain but has no problems now", "no pain for one year", "now some pain but minor", etc. Though he was misquoting the records, he never let me correct them. Afterwards attorneys have said thing like this: "No hard feelings, Doctor. I have to do those things in court. It's just part of the game."

WRAP-UP

How to do yourself some favors when you seek legal advice or representation:

1) Examine your situation thoroughly before retaining an attorney. You may not even need one, and you should exhaust all other avenues of recourse first;

2) What's your <u>main</u> goal: return to life and work? Or a one-time financial award? Think twice and advise your attorney accordingly;

3) Get through legal matters as quickly as possible. Don't be surprised to learn that Workers' Compensation can turn immensely more complicated after litigation begins.

K

CHAPTER 26

End Of The Line:
The Rest Of Your Life

"The outlook for the future is most hopeful."
...William Henry Welch

There's a familiar phrase that "Tomorrow is the first day of the rest of your life". It's true, when you close out your Workers' Compensation claim and put it behind you.

Whether Comp has been a brief episode or a major struggle, if you've finished it means you won the match in some way. You conquered the hassles, and now you can get out of the system. This chapter gives you a few pointers that could make your future life easier.

Followup Medical Visits

Stay in touch with your doctor if you had one of the few work injuries (less than 5% of the total) that result in permanent impairment. I recommend patients see their doctor approximately every six months for a year or two and then less frequently if their condition is stable.

This will allow your doctor to monitor your status, check out any new symptoms with testing, and give you the benefit of any new treatments that have been developed. It will also give you some reassurance to know how you're doing.

> *I hadn't seen Margaret for four years, since she settled her case. Now she comes in and says: "My pain never did go away, and for a year I've been getting worse. I figured there wasn't much you could do about it, but now I think I need that operation."*
>
> *The trouble is, because there's no record of Margaret's continuing pain for these years, the insurer won't cover any more care. "This patient hasn't sought treatment for years," their letter said, "she must have had a new injury."*

There's a major value to checking in with your doctor on a regular basis: It substantiates that you still have the problem. Just as Workers' Compensation depends on good medical documentation during the case, good records may be necessary later to reopen or continue a claim. This is easily accomplished by seeing your doctor occasionally.

Physical Activity

If you have been exercising on a regular basis as part of treatment, keep it up even after claim closure--in fact for the rest of your life. Re-read Chapter 16 for all the reasons.

Continue with a walk in the mornings or after work, continue eating right, getting rest, and avoiding alcohol or drugs. If lifestyle changes were successful in getting you off Comp, there's no reason to stop now. Keeping fit will work just as well to prevent injuries in the future.

LOOKING FOR WORK

Patients ask me, "Do I have to disclose my permanent disability on a job application?" The answer is yes. This will cause you inconvenience, even job turn-downs. But that's part of a financial disability "award": It compensates you for loss of earning capacity or other difficulties.

> *I did a pre-work physical examination on a 25-year-old applying for heavy work in a nursing home. On her application she wrote that she had never had any injuries, surgery or physical problems. But I found a surgical scar that could only have been from a low back disc operation. "What's this?" I asked.*
>
> *She turned bright red and stammered: "They told us in school that if we admitted to any back problems we'd fail". I told her that is not necessarily true--I believe she could have been hired anyway--but that lying on the application would almost always keep her out of a job.*

Potential employers deserve to know if you have had a physical problem or injury. If you don't tell them, you can be terminated when they do find out. I just learned of a nationwide data service that provides prospective employers with information on an applicant's credit, drivers' license and criminal record <u>and</u> Workers' Compensation history. This data is available within 24 hours to 2 weeks of requesting it.

The most valuable advice I can give you is to look for work within your physical capacities. There's no point in ignoring permanent limitations. If you're unsure exactly what kind of work is most suitable, ask your doctor for specific guidelines.

When you are hired by a new employer, that employer can "register" your preexisting disability (in most states) with a so-called "second injury fund". This is a state-administered program that lets a new employer off the hook if you have a new injury related to a preexisting disability. Your new employer will have no more financial obligation for you than he would for any other employee who sustains an injury. This is your answer to a potential employer who thinks he would be at increased risk by hiring you.

At Work

You're truly fortunate if you can return to the same job you had earlier. After weeks or months on Comp, most people come to realize how precious their job is: Regular steady work without people looking over their shoulder.

But no matter where you work, put yourself wholly into it. Do your best, keep a positive attitude even if you have discomfort. Keep focused on the good things, the parts of your life and job that you like. Always keep adding new skills so you become more and more valuable to your employer--they'll probably forget about your old "Comp problem".

Many patients ask how to minimize their risk of injury. There are several ways. If you went through Work Hardening (Chapter 16), use all those techniques: Smooth lifting motions, good body mechanics, frequent exercise. If you had a toxic exposure injury, use the methods I suggested in sections E through H to protect against repeat exposures. Stay fit and healthy (Chapter 18) and use techniques from biofeedback training (Chapter 11) or a chronic pain program (Chapter 19) if you attended one.

It may turn out the most rewarding thing you can do is to become active in a safety committee at work. Learn what makes a plant safe and how you can help. If you see another employee going on Comp, give him or her a few encouraging words because he might have to face all the same hassles. Give him this book.

My Best Wishes

I hope this book has helped you make the most troublesome parts of Workers' Compensation less troublesome. Please write to let me know what you liked or didn't like, what I should add or change.

Tell me what helped you the most. I'll try to answer letters as time allows. My sincere best wishes for all the good fortune in the world as you put Comp behind you!

F

William P. Fleeson, M.P.H., M.D.
c/o Med-Ed Books and Publishers
324 West Superior Street, Suite 510
Duluth, Minnesota 55802

26-CHAPTER WRAP-UP

10 WAYS YOU CAN AVOID WORKERS' COMPENSATION HASSLES:

1) *KEEP A RECORD of your Comp claim and doctor visits;*
2) *KNOW AS MUCH about Workers' Compensation as you can;*
3) *ASK QUESTIONS whenever you don't understand something;*
4) *TAKE EARLY ACTION if there's any problem with your claim or treatment or benefits;*
5) *FIND A DOCTOR you trust and follow his advice;*
6) *Make sure EACH VISIT LEADS TO PROGRESS ;*
7) *KEEP YOURSELF FIT with a good diet, plenty of rest and a daily walk;*
8) *GET REHABILITATION ADVICE if it's available to you;*
9) *Keep your FAMILY INVOLVED in your recuperation;*
10) *Don't waste energy on negative feelings or anger--keep focused on POSITIVE GOALS AND PLANS.*

A Final Note
To Workers' Compensation
Reformers

Most states seem to venture into "reforms" of their Workers' Compensation systems every so often. The usual impetus: A sense that Comp doesn't fulfill its goals or simply doesn't work, that it's too costly, it "drives business out", injured employees aren't treated fairly, Comp just creates an incentive to remain disabled, etc., etc., etc.

But such reforms generally produce little overall transformation. The systems remain costly and the popular perceptions persist that Comp is ineffective, or at the very least inefficient.

Those of you who would work to reform Workers' Compensation, and have read this far, must realize that the problem isn't Comp.

Comp is a patient-driven system, yet no-one has worked at the level of this basic unit. You can try to reduce or enhance benefits, change disability or economic recovery schedules, control medical costs or attorney involvement, and all the other measures usually essayed. But nothing much will change. Not until the injured employee who goes on Comp understands what is expected of him, has realistic expectations about what Comp will do for him, and knows he can get through Comp without hassle with a good job waiting.

I'm convinced the vast majority of American workers dislike going on Comp and feeling as if they're on the dole, and earnestly want to reestablish their self-esteem. They want all of us off their backs. They want to return to work. Give them the right info, and they will.

This key--giving the American worker the knowledge to affect his own situation--is the only fundamental "reform" that hasn't been tried. I can't see why it shouldn't have an effect on the problems of Comp: It's worked in every other phase of American life.

Bumps & Bruises, Cuts & Scrapes: The Simplest Industrial Injuries

At the Metro Industrial Clinic two patients wait to be seen. One with a nasty-looking forearm abrasion asks the other, "What've you got?"

"Ahh, it's just a groin pull. They made me come here but it's nothing." Just then, a third man walks in holding a towel to his head, dripping red. The on-duty nurse takes him first.

Through the open door everyone can overhear the nurse saying, "We'd better call Dr. Carlson to suture this, it's all the way down to your skull. But don't worry about all that blood. Scalp lacerations always bleed like stuck pigs. It's really not a very large cut. It'll close up fine."

Most patients with the relatively simple injuries in this section will require little medical care. These minor problems may not even put an employee on Comp because they heal so quickly--in fact with most of these injuries it's unusual to miss more than an hour or two of work. I've included this section so you know how to handle them, and to alert you to the possibility that even a minor injury <u>can</u> become serious in some cases.

The doctor closes the scalp laceration and sends the man back to work. The nurses tell the man with the groin pull to use ice, aspirin, and to avoid heavy lifting for 3 days. The nurse cleans up the abrasion, covers it with antibiotic medication, and dresses it with a bandage. She tells him: "Come back in two days and we'll change the dressing"

Unfortunately, he doesn't tell her that he has diabetes, and they forget to ask him....

If you were to have a single injury like most in this chapter, you would simply go to the nearest medical facility or see the nurse at the plant, have it taken care of, and then go back to work.

CAUTION: Even though all these problems are minor injuries, make sure you report them following the procedures in Chapter 4.

Scrapes And Cuts

Abrasions (scrapes) will usually be minor problems; they're just superficial. Treat them with a simple dressing, usually put on by the plant nurse. Protect them and keep them from getting infected by keeping them clean. They will usually heal within five to seven days. If a scrape does become infected it will get hot, red, perhaps with a gooey yellow pus covering it, and start hurting more. If that happens, get to your doctor as soon as possible because you will need treatment with antibiotics.

A laceration (cut) can be minor, or it can be serious. For a very minor laceration, clean it well, then an adhesive strip or butterfly will keep it together for the two or three days that your body needs to close it permanently.

But if you have a laceration that's more than a quarter or a half inch deep, best to go to the doctor or emergency room. The doctor will numb it up and then clean it out, suture it closed and send you back to work or home depending on how serious it is. The tetanus shot that you get will probably be more painful than the cut itself. The stitches should be removed (by the clinic staff, not by you!) in five to seven days, or two to three days if the laceration is on the face.

If you have a laceration anywhere on your face, make sure the doctor who closes it up is experienced. It's not a matter of healing--there's so much blood supply on the face that almost all facial lacerations will heal easily. It's because you'll have to live with the scar forever if it's a bad result.

And if the laceration is on the palm of your hand, doctors call this area "no man's land" and it had better be taken care of under sterile conditions by a skilled doctor or surgeon. This is an area that can get into big trouble fast even with the best of care in a good facility.

BUMPS AND BRUISES

Suppose a heavy tool falls on your arm, or a large box strikes your thigh, or you strike your leg against a post: Each of these will cause a <u>contusion</u> (bruise). Contusions usually hurt immediately, then they swell a bit and hurt more. Later they turn black and blue for a few days before fading.

A contusion is colored and swells because the trauma breaks open one or more small blood vessels under the skin. Later the blood pigments change color so over the first few days or weeks the contusion fades from blue to green, then yellow as your body reabsorbs the blood.

The treatment for a contusion is simple: Use 20 minutes of ice three or four times a day for the first couple of days, and then leave it alone. Your body's healing mechanisms will take care of the rest.

But suppose you receive a hard impact against an area of your body where there isn't much fat or muscle covering the bone, for example over your elbow or shin. This can cause a painful "bone bruise". It's misnamed because the bleeding and swelling aren't actually in the bone, rather in the tissue just over the covering of the bone.

Bone bruises hurt a lot because the covering of a bone is so tight. The swelling and fluid are trapped and therefore painful. Treatment is the same as for any bruise, as long as an X-ray shows that there's no break in the bone. But bone bruises can hurt a lot longer--weeks to months.

One other type of bruise deserves special mention. A <u>hematoma</u> is a larger bleed under the skin, or even deep in a muscle, caused when larger blood vessels are broken. They can be quite painful, and sometimes last for months. There's really no good treatment but to use heat and wait them out. They usually shrink over time. Very occasionally hematomas should be removed surgically.

PINCHES, CRUSHES, PUNCTURES

Many industrial injuries are classified as "pinched by". This refers to various pinching actions that happen with belts and pulleys, punch and press machinery, moving objects around the shop floor, doors and so on.

When pinches are minor, they're simply painful not dangerous. A pinch is a contusion of skin or soft tissue, such as the pad of your finger or palm. A typical pinch hurts for a couple of weeks and then heals.

But if a pinch is severe it's technically a crush injury. Crushes can cause more deep damage than you would think. Crush injuries can cause severe problems because of damage to the soft tissues, blood vessels and muscles beneath the skin. At best a crush injury will simply be painful and take a few weeks to heal. At worst a crush injury will need surgical attention. Crush injuries can also break bones, so whenever you have a crush injury make sure it's X-rayed.

You should ask to see a surgeon if you have a crush of your hand or foot, if your fingers or toes become extremely painful afterward or they go cold and numb, or if there is a bluish discoloration that would indicate loss of circulation. You should especially watch the healing of crushes to hand or foot if you are over 50 because of possible poor circulation.

Crush injuries to the hand or foot can result in deep bleeding. Because these spaces are tightly packed, this could put pressure on blood vessels and nerves; in the hand or foot watch these carefully.

If you have a crush injury on the back of your hand, there may be associated tendon injuries. You should suspect this if it hurts to open up your hand from a fist. Such an injury should be X-rayed.

Puncture wounds are dangerous if the area that was injured was extremely dirty when injured. If so, this creates a danger of infection. Make sure your puncture wound is cleaned as well as possible. The best place to have it cleaned is at an emergency room or doctor's office. You'll also want to get a tetanus shot if you haven't had one within a year or so.

The reason shot is because tetanus bacteria can thrive where there's no air and puncture wounds are typically airless, being deep in the tissue.

BURNS

You could fill a book--probably a library--with the treatment of burns. The only really simple ones are first degree.

A first degree burn--for example a scald from hot water, steam, or some chemicals--will redden the skin. It will be painful, sometimes very. First degree burns are easily treated with cool water, burn cream and daily dressing changes. The body will heal them quickly with no scar. Really only the simplest first degree burns belong in this chapter; they'll heal fine. Anthing else should have specialty care.

Second degree burns blister the skin. Steam, chemicals, molten plastic or metal, flammable liquids, etc., cause these. So do extreme cold, liquid oxygen, volatile liquids in arctic conditions, etc. Rollers, sanders, and wheels can also cause abrasions and burns, usually first degree.

Second degree burns require more medical care, heal slowly, are very painful, and can be fatal if they cover a large area of the body. (A burn is considered "extensive" if it covers more than 9% of the body's surface area.) Such burns require specialized burn care professionals and facilities. They may require skin grafting.

Third degree burns are the most serious. These are burns where the skin is literally burned away, charring the underlying tissue black and crusty. These are complicated and serious injuries, beyond this book. So are electrical injuries and burns, which are often third degree by definition.

"PULLED" MUSCLES

When a patient complains that he has a pulled muscle, it's basically a strain (see next chapter). These patients have usually used some excessive force or reach or motion on the job, and used their muscles beyond the muscles' tolerance. This "pulls" or stretches them. It's usually painful right at the time of injury or shortly after. Sometimes there will be some swelling, but there will usually not be any bruising.

The best treatment for a pulled muscle is to rest it for a couple of days, and use an ice pack for 20 minutes three or four times a day. Then start using heat and gently move the muscle through its normal motion a few times each day. After two or three days, start increasing the motion and use of the muscle again, slowly increasing to normal amount of activity over a one to three week period.

A pulled muscle is not generally a serious problem. It will heal itself. But it could require an employee to work on a different machine for several days while it heals.

JAMMED FINGERS

The typical cause of a "jammed" finger is having an object strike your finger, such as a baseball at a company picnic. A "jammed" finger is not broken (broken bones are covered in the next chapter) or dislocated. For a simple jamming injury, the best treatment is to gently pull on it once to "un-jam" it. This is not painful if you do it immediately, and of course you should not pull with extreme force.

A typical jammed finger usually heals by being splinted, although sometimes it's enough to simply leave it alone and put it through some gentle motion for a few days. If after pulling on a jammed finger it's still not right, you should go to the emergency room for an X-ray and further evaluation.

A jammed finger can sometimes cause minor dislocation or subluxation, and X-ray should make this obvious. If you jam a finger and over the next few days it seems to be hurting more, or you can't move it without pain, then make sure you see a doctor and get an X-ray.

FOREIGN BODIES IN THE EYES

One of the most common minor injuries in industry is a foreign body in the eye. I must have taken out hundreds of these things over the years. Foreign bodies commonly occur when an employee guides an overhead crane. He's looking up when specks of metal or dirt or grease fall from the tracks overhead. Carpenters frequently have chips or sawdust or metal fly in their eyes. If you have a foreign body the symptoms will be obvious: Your eye hurts, it waters and you won't be able to keep it open.

A simple foreign body can easily be removed in a doctor's office or emergency room. A few anesthetic drops will put your eye completely at ease while the doctor irrigates your eye with sterile solution. This usually flushes the piece away or the doctor may be able to simply remove it with a wisp of cotton.

After removal of the foreign body, the doctor will examine the eye for a scratch or abrasion. He'll usually put some antibiotic cream into the eye and patch it for two or three days, with daily dressing change. These injuries generally heal up perfectly without problems because eyes have good healing properties.

But if a piece of metal or a chip hits your eye at high speed it could puncture the eyeball and these are much more serious problems, potentially blinding. These injuries <u>must</u> be evaluated by an eye specialist immediately to prevent you from losing your vision. <u>Penetrating eye injuries are true emergencies</u>. If you suspect that a high speed object struck your eye you must seek treatment without delay.

COMPLICATING FACTORS

All of the injuries in this chapter should heal quickly. Few of them should limit you in your work, none should result in long-lasting problems. At least this will be the case if you're in normal health.

But <u>if you're not in good health,</u> or if you have a chronic illness or medical condition, it will likely complicate your recovery from even the simplest injury.

> *The employee with the scalp laceration returned four days later. The nurse removed the scalp sutures and sent the employee back to work. He had missed only 2 hours total. The second patient with the groin pull must have turned out fine because he never returned for followup.*
> *But the man with the third injury, the forearm abrasion, didn't do well. It became infected. Because of his diabetes he had lowered resis-*

tance, and the result was a rampant skin infection. It had been inflamed and full of pus only a day when he returned to the clinic, but it was already too late.

"That red streak up to your shoulder is your ticket to the hospital, my friend," the doctor told him. "That and your fever. We'll start I-V antibiotics right away, but you can count on being laid up at least a week...."

If you have diabetes you may not heal as rapidly from a simple abrasion as you should. Contusions may also last a long time, and pinches or crush injuries could be deadly serious.

If you have emphysema, your body tissues are probably not getting adequate oxygen, and may be slow to heal. If you have a chronic heart condition, you may have poor circulation to the lower parts of your legs. So skin injuries in that area, or crush injuries to your feet, may not heal well or even at all.

There are other medical conditions besides diabetes and emphysema that can cause slow healing of simple injuries, though these are the most common. With them, you will have to be more careful than usual to take care of even minor industrial injuries. (Such problems will not ordinarily affect your Comp claim.) Get even the simplest injury evaluated, treated early, and checked often until it's fully resolved.

WRAP-UP

How to do yourself some favors with the simple injuries:
1) Take care of minor bumps, bruises, cuts and scrapes by keeping them clean, resting the injured part, and start to move it gently within two or three days;
2) Any laceration should be cleaned and closed, and if it's on your face have it sutured or closed by a highly skilled professional;
3) Watch punctures or pinches for infection;
4) If you have diabetes, emphysema, or heart disease watch any minor injury for complications and see your doctor more frequently.

J

Strains & Sprains, Bones & Joints

I've been looking at the morning's X-rays with a radiologist and the orthopedic surgeon who'll see one of my patients. We've just reviewed the normal films, some from a patient with forearm tendinitis and another with a knee strain. Those patients will be OK: Time will heal their injuries easily.

But now we're looking at a heel fracture, and it's a bad one. "Ever see so many fragments of the calcaneus? It must have just splintered. How far'd this guy fall, anyway?"

"Twenty-five feet", I say, "and to concrete ... the ankle mortise is involved too, isn't it? Looks unstable." The radiologist nods, then asks "What can you do with this kind of thing, Peter?"

"Well, can't really be sure until I get in there. For sure pin these heel fragments. Probably screws in the tib, plate the fibula. But it's going to be a stiff joint for him. Be lucky if he even has 45 degrees of motion a year from now."

I think about this a few moments and I tell him, "No good, Peter. He needs that ankle. He's a <u>roofer</u>."

For a minute nobody says anything; we all search the films again and then the surgeon shakes his head: "Then this just wasn't his lucky day, was it?"

In this chapter I describe common industrial injuries that occur to muscles, ligaments, bones and joints ("musculoskeletal" injuries). This is hardly a complete list, but it should help you understand the typical symptoms of these injuries, and the treatment you can expect for them. Most of the problems in this chapter, except for the severe joint injuries, should turn out well with the correct treatment.

How You Can Heal Fastest

The human body has built-in mechanisms that heal an injured or torn ligament or muscle tissue of a sprain in four to twelve weeks. A broken bone will knit in a matter of months if it's kept free of stress while it heals. Even many joint injuries will turn out well, thanks to the body's enormous recuperative powers.

The fundamental treatment for all these injuries is to rest the injured part while your body heals it. Basically, the length of time off work with one of these injuries will depend on the severity of the injury and also on the physical needs of your job. Treatment for these injuries can range from a week of simple heat and an elastic wrap to three months in a cast and then daily physical therapy. Some serious fractures or joint injuries can take a year or more to heal.

But one ingredient is key to success in healing these injuries: <u>Keep the rest of your body healthy and active while you recover</u>. I think that any doctor in the world would tell you that the more active you keep all of your non-injured parts, the more rapidly a strain, sprain, bursitis, tendinitis, or fracture will heal.

So if one arm happens to be in a cast, you can start walking several miles each day and swing the other arm while you walk. If it's your legs that are out of commission you can start working out with arm weights. Or if one knee can't be bent or used, then you can start to exercise the other knee. And so on (see Chapter 16, Exercise).

For almost any injury a patient should also get in the habit of swimming daily. Daily swimming is probably the best all-around therapeutic exercise for most injuries, and it's one that I most often try to get my patients to do.

Why Musculoskeletal Injuries Matter

What makes an injury to a bone, muscle or joint a serious matter? Simply that these are the parts of your body that get all the use at work. How serious an injury will be for you depends on a) the type of injury itself and b) what you have to do at work.

For example, if you need your hands every minute, then an arm or hand injury will be more significant to you than to someone who doesn't. If you have to be on your feet all day at work, then a leg or foot injury will be more serious than it would be to someone such as myself.

Most industrial bone and joint injuries are, of course, to an extremity. The upper extremities--arms and hands--are vitally important to virtually everyone who works. Without them most jobs would be impossible.

Because the arms are always being used, they're going to be the most at risk for accidental injury. For example, people use their hands everyplace. They put them into and around punch presses and conveyor belts. They push and pull cables, manipulate controls, and hold or grip heavy tools. If a person ever falls, he'll instinctively put his hands out to absorb the impact. So it's only natural that shoulder, arm and hand strains, sprains, finger crushes, and elbow or wrist fractures are among the most common injuries in American industry.

The lower extremities--legs, knees and feet--are critical too, because everyone constantly needs them to move around, to walk, kneel, stand or climb.

Because people are always on their feet, and often walking in dangerous places, the lower extremities are always at risk. Employees may have to walk over wet and slippery floors, on narrow greasy catwalks or ladders, over or around obstacles, etc. Any of these can trip up a person and cause a leg injury.

Vehicles or carts can bump into hips or knees, legs can bang against corners, anyone could twist a knee when squatting down to work, or a crate or tool could fall on a foot. With the amount of use the lower extremities get, it's a wonder that hip strains and knee sprains, ankle fractures and crushed feet and heels aren't more frequent than they are.

STRAINS

When we move our arms and legs we do it by contracting our muscles. Our muscles move our bones by attachments called <u>tendons</u>. The bones are firmly held together at joints by <u>ligaments</u>.

Overuse of muscles or tendons or ligaments can cause stretching injuries called <u>strains</u>. The places where strains occur are in any muscle that you use--because you can overuse that same muscle.

A strain is a simple stretch of a muscle, tendon, or ligament--but <u>not</u> far enough to tear it. Strains almost always are associated with some pain afterwards.

A strain is usually not a severe problem. To understand a strain, you can imagine stretching a rubber band and then letting it go: It returns to the same shape it was before you stretched it. A strain of a muscle or ligament is essentially no more than a mild stretching. There is no tearing or major damage.

The symptoms of strains are sore, aching muscles, perhaps with some swelling. Diagnosis is usually easy: The history is one of overuse and the examination shows a tender area of muscle or ligament. Treatment is usually ice packs three times a day for a couple of days, then hot packs, then slow reactivation of the muscles. The body's healing mechanisms will easily repair a minor strain.

SPRAINS

A sprain is a bigger problem: A <u>tear</u> of muscles or ligaments beyond their capacity to recover by themselves. The tear occurs when a muscle, tendon, or ligament is stretched beyond its limit of tolerance. The resulting tear can be just a small tear or a complete rupture. To imagine how a sprain happens, think of stretching a rubber band so hard or so fast that it tears and then snaps.

Just as with strains, sprains happen from overuse. Ankle sprains are very common: An employee could slip, fall and twist his foot and tear the ligaments on the side of the ankle that hold it stable. Shoulder sprains are also common: A shoulder could be sprained by pushing upwards with force against a valve or overhead control or by falling on the shoulder. These motions could tear the muscles and tendons in the shoulder called the "rotator cuff" which is the "cuff" of four tendons surrounding the shoulder.

Or an impact against the knee from the side can easily produce a severe tear or sprain of the ligaments along the side of the knee. Any of these spraining injuries exceed the body's ability to tolerate the stress.

Some sprains can even pull a small piece of bone away--called an <u>avulsion fracture</u>. Some sprains can later cause instability of a joint, for example an ankle, if ruptured ligaments heal poorly and remain weakened.

Diagnosis of sprain is made by history and examination, plus an X-ray to evaluate for a fracture. Examination will show a painful, often swollen, area round a joint or at a muscle's attachment to bone. MRI (see Chapter 8) may be needed to diagnose some shoulder and knee ligament sprains.

Sprains will usually be treated with some form of immobilization, either a splint or cast. All we can really do is wait for a patient's own body to heal a sprain. This usually occurs over a six to twelve week period.

It takes this long for a sprain to heal because the only way the body can heal is for the torn parts to grow back together into a tight scar. Sprains need time to heal firmly, but even so the scar may not be as strong as the original tissue.

Sometimes a sprain, for example of the shoulder's rotator cuff, might never heal even with immobilization, and may require surgery to mechanically reconnect the torn tissue so that it can begin healing.

Sprains can be painful for a long time, sometimes months. These injuries can be a long, slowly healing problems. Some sprains can keep you away from work for many months.

TENDINITIS

Tendons connect muscles to bones. Tendons are tough, smooth, shiny and slightly elastic. Tendons are supposed to glide smoothly in their tracks, and when they do we never notice them at work.

But sometimes overuse, stress, or injury can irritate a tendon without causing strain or sprain. This results in a wearing-type of injury. The tendon tissues react by becoming inflamed, swollen, hot, and painful. If a tendon is inflamed it's called tendinitis: The medical term "-itis" means inflammation. Most tendinitis is an overuse phenomenon, like thousands of little injuries that add up to an inflamed tendon or ligament.

Common tendinitis problems at work are in the shoulder, the biceps tendon at the front of the shoulder, or in the forearm or wrist. It's no surprise that these tendon areas are easily irritated, because it's so common to use (and overuse) the arm for work tasks.

Typical jobs associated with upper extremity tendinitis are those that require constant overhead work, lifting, gripping or twisting of tools, wrist motion, pulling or pushing, etc. (There's not much industrial tendinitis in the lower extremities.)

For years doctors have seen and treated "policeman's shoulder", "tennis elbow", and "assembler's wrist". These are versions of industrial tendinitis, and more recently "slot machine elbow" and "video gamer's wrist" have showed up in the modern world.

It's usually easy to make the diagnosis of tendinitis on examination: We look for swollen and tender tendons that are painful with muscle motion. We don't need lab tests or X-rays to diagnose typical tendinitis problems. But some such as in the shoulder may require MRI imaging.

I wish tendinitis were always easy to treat. Sometimes it is, but not always.

Forearm tendinitis usually improves with rest, heat, antiinflammatory medications, and then gentle exercises as soon as it settles down. Shoulder tendinitis may respond to the same treatment, plus physical therapy modalities. But often this is not enough and injections of Cortisone and a local anesthetic along the inflamed tendon sheath provide patients with relief (see Chapter 11).

Tendinitis--especially in the forearm and elbow--can take a long time to heal. Some patients with severe or chronic tendinitis may never be able to go back on their old job. I've found that forearm tendinitis in assembly workers, sewing machine operators, and cooks is always a difficult problem. We don't know why some cases of tendinitis last. But when they do, it can be frustrating for the patient and everyone else.

CARPAL TUNNEL, REPETITIVE MOTION

There's one wrist problem that doesn't fit in any of the categories of strains, sprains, bursitis, or tendinitis. This is Carpal Tunnel Syndrome (CTS). Carpal Tunnel is a collection of symptoms in the wrist and hand, usually beginning with numbness and tingling at night and eventually during the day as well.

The symptoms are caused by overgrowth of a tight band that crosses the inside of the wrist. When the band swells or thickens for any reason, it can compress the nerve below it and that causes the symptoms.

The diagnosis of CTS is made by EMG or Nerve Conduction Studies, as described in Chapter 8.

The treatment of CTS is to splint the wrists, especially at night, use antiinflammatory medications, and try a cortisone injection. If none of this works, surgery is the definitive treatment and is almost always successful.

There's a real controversy over whether CTS is caused by work or not. Some doctors swear it is. Others are just as sure it isn't.

Some doctors feel these types of "repetitive motion disorders" account for over 50% of job injuries. Dr. Jim Cone of San Francisco General Hospital's Occupational Health Clinic recently (1991) said: "People in the past saw this as part of daily life ... These illnesses have been called various things but have not been seen as work-related." Many physicians feel these injuries are the biggest problem in industry today.

But the argument is over whether repetitive motion at the wrist as in using hand tools, in assembly work, etc., is the <u>cause</u>. I'm not confident that anyone really knows the answer about this. In some cases CTS is obviously due to the patient's work, but sometimes it's obviously due to other causes. Sometimes the patient doesn't even have CTS, but rather has tendinitis that was merely misdiagnosed. I expect that over the next few years we'll hear a lot more about this unusual "injury".

BURSITIS

A <u>bursa</u> is a small enclosed sac (like a purse) that lines or surrounds a joint where two bones or other surfaces meet. The purpose of a bursa is to keep the joint smooth and lubricated, so the two surfaces can glide over each other smoothly. You would ordinarily never even think about the bursae in your shoulders, or under your shoulder blades, your elbows, knees or hip joints.

But a bursa can become inflamed from wear, overuse, or other kinds of damage. An inflamed bursa is called bursitis, and the symptoms are a hot, red, tender and swollen area over and around the joint. A joint with bursitis will be very painful to move.

Typical jobs that can be associated with bursitis are those that require repetitive overhead shoulder motion, repeated bumping of the knee (such as carpetlayers, and in the old days "housemaid's knee" was a common injury), prolonged sitting on hard surfaces (from buttock pressure, causing "weaver's bottom") and so on. A recent (1990) study by NIOSH shows, for example, that carpetlayers who use knee kickers have more than 100 times the expected number of claims for serious knee problems. Tile setters and floorlayers have more than 45-50 times the expected rates. All of these people spend much of their time (half to three-fourths) on their knees, and bursitis is the result.

Diagnosis of bursitis is usually fairly easy to make by examination. We look and feel for an inflamed and tender area over the location of a shoulder, elbow, or knee bursa. X-rays seldom are required except to make sure there's no arthritis in the underlying joint.

Treatment of bursitis is similar to the treatment of tendinitis: Heat, rest, antiinflammatory medications, and sometimes physical therapy modalities. Injection is occasionally useful. A few cases of bursitis, especially in the elbow and the knee, can be so prolonged and so bothersome that a surgeon eventually has to remove the bursa to provide relief and a cure.

DISLOCATIONS

Where two bones meet they form a joint. For example, look at one of your "knuckles"--it's the joint of two finger bones. All joints are held together by tendons and ligaments, and are generally quite stable--enough to withstand normal forces of use and even of strain.

But a sudden jerk, fall, blow or an unusual motion can disrupt a joint and <u>dislocate</u> one of the bones out of the joint. This can happen to fingers or thumb, elbow, shoulder, even the knee or ankle if trauma is severe enough.

The shoulders and fingers are the most commonly dislocated joints of the body. This is because they're relatively unstable joints. Because we use the shoulder to produce arm motions in all directions, the shoulders have to be super mobile. They're called "ball and socket" joints, but in reality they're more like a ball in a shallow dish than a true socket. In fact, the shoulder is not even attached to the skeleton except by a small joint at the breastbone. The result is that the shoulder is so mobile it's unstable and easily dislocated.

A fall on the point of your shoulder can dislocate the upperarm "ball" out of the "socket" joint. Or the impact of the fall can widen the joint between shoulder and collarbone and cause an a-c separation or "separated shoulder". Even a fall on your outstretched hand can dislocate your shoulder.

Symptoms of a dislocation are a very painful joint that is obviously distorted and doesn't move. We can usually make the diagnosis by clinical exam. But it's always best to take an X-ray of a dislocation to make sure there is no associated fracture of one of the bones.

Dislocations are treated at an emergency room by "reducing" the dislocation: Putting the joint back in place. Then the joint should be immobilized for several weeks. Later if a joint won't stay in place after appropriate strengthening and tightening exercises, it may require surgery to tighten the joint and keep it stable.

FRACTURES

"I didn't just break my arm, Doc. I think it was fractured."

Any bone can break, and any break is called a <u>fracture</u>. The word "fracture" means nothing special.

But there are several grades of fracture severity: A bone can snap in two like a dry stick (a <u>simple</u> fracture), it can break into pieces (a <u>comminuted</u> fracture), or it can merely crack slightly like a green twig (a hairline or greenstick fracture). A bone can be compressed or compacted (a compression fracture--see next chapter on the spine) or it can splinter and puncture the skin (an open or compound fracture), which makes it serious because of potential infection.

How do industrial fractures occur? Usually from a fall, sometimes from an impact, and of course from vehicular accidents. Fractures can occur to any area of the body: Arm, forearm, wrist, hand, pelvis, hip, thigh, knee, leg or foot. Shoulder fractures aren't very common, because trauma here usually results in a dislocation. Hip fractures are not very common because the joint is well protected. In general, the more exposed and the more frequently used the area or the extremity, the more commonly it will be fractured.

Diagnosis of fracture is usually straightforward. The history gives us a big clue, the examination shows us a very painful and swollen arm or leg, and then X-ray clinches the diagnosis.

As to fracture healing, bones are living tissues and heal themselves, just as any other tissue does. After a few weeks new bone (called callus) starts to surround and bridge the break. This slowly expands and fills the gap, and eventually enough bone remodeling can take place that even an X-ray may not show the old fracture.

Fracture treatment is therefore to let the injured bone rest and keep it stable while the body does the healing.

The specifics of treatment depends on the type and location of the fracture itself. For example, simple finger fractures are reduced (put into good position) and splinted if the alignment is good and remains stable. But more severe finger fractures, or fractures involving a joint, may require pinning to maintain their position during healing. Fractures of the upper arm are treated only with a sling and heal well. Some forearm fractures near the elbow are similar and heal within a few weeks. Most simple wrist fractures heal after six weeks in a cast. Hip and thigh fractures usually require surgery, often with a pin being placed and then casted. So do knee, lower leg, and ankle or foot fractures.

SPECIAL FRACTURES

Some fractures are special because they carry risk of future disability, and they require sophisticated specialty care. For example, if you were to fall on your outstretched hand the force would be transmitted through the hand into the weakest bone on the wrist. This bone, the navicular, has very little blood supply and heals very poorly.

Fractures here are easily missed because in this bone, X-rays may not be diagnostic. Navicular fractures often end up being problem areas for years and may eventually even require surgery to fuse or remove the bone. If you have a navicular fracture you should see the best orthopedic or hand specialist you can find, and see him immediately.

Though industrial hip fractures are uncommon, they do occur in motor vehicle accidents where the impact is transmitted from the dashboard through the knees up into the hips. These are often associated with a hip dislocation, and this can cause nerve or artery injury and usually requires surgical care immediately. The new (1990) OSHA effort to require buckled safety restraints in workers' cars and trucks may help to reduce these problems.

In general, any fracture of a joint is serious and potentially a disabling injury because it can lead to arthritis later. For example, knee fractures-- usually from a fall--can be very serious and require immediate specialist care. The problem with knee fractures is that they can involve the joint surface where all of your weight is carried. If this joint surface remains damaged or develops arthritis after the fracture, it can produce a significant limitation if your job requires walking or standing.

The same is true for other leg joints: Hips, ankles, feet. Suppose you were to fall from a ladder or roof or down into a hole or foundation. Your foot or ankle will likely bear the brunt of the injury. Fractures of the ankle joint range from simple to very severe, depending on whether one bone or two or more are broken. The more severe ones may require open surgery with screws or plates to hold them together. As with any joint, serious ankle fractures can lead to arthritis later with limited motion and prolonged disability.

Fractures of the heel can be disabling because they often heal very poorly, they may require surgery at least once, and many will keep patients from returning to work for many months or years. Heel fractures can also cause permanent loss of foot range of motion. A construction carpenter or a roofer with a heel fracture (and these are the people who often get them) is in a bad spot. It's likely such a person will have to look into a different line of work.

TORN CARTILAGE

One special type of knee joint injury deserves special mention: The meniscus. The meniscus is a small crescent-shaped cartilage between the two bones of the knee. There are two meniscii in each knee. The meniscus is subject to tearing by twisting or other trauma.

Typically with this injury a worker will plant his feet and then rotate his body while he's pulling hard on a load. An example would be a tree trimmer pulling brush, a machinist pulling steel tubing, or a nursing assistant pivoting a patient.

People with tears of knee cartilage typically feel a pop in the knee, and then they fall to the floor with pain. The knee balloons up, and at the emergency room the doctor might remove one to three ounces of bloody fluid.

A torn meniscus may heal on its own with time or at least become asymptomatic. But it will usually have to be removed by surgery, and afterwards the knee usually heals well. Arthritis can occur later.

Therefore, if you have a knee injury with sudden swelling and a meniscus tear make sure that you obtain the best orthopedic specialist care available. You may depend on your knees every day, and it's a very unhappy patient who has a series of two or three or four unsuccessful knee surgeries and can't ever go back to his old job.

"SOFT TISSUE/MYOFASCIAL PAIN"

There are some injuries to "soft tissue" (as opposed to bones which are hard tissue) that are just plain hard to understand and hard to treat. These are the soft tissue problems, and they usually involve muscles and the fascia that covers or surrounds muscles. Because these problems usually involve inflammation of some sort we call them "myofasciitis". These are not simple strains or sprains.

Typically, the patient with this problem starts out with what seems to be a strain. The symptoms are often in the upper back or shoulder girdle and trapezius area. However, to think of these as strains is misleading, because there may not even be an injury. Sometimes patients just come in with pain and say "It hurts when I work, Doctor", and often their job does in fact involve using the upper extremities. But there's no history of strain or sprain or anything else.

At any rate, many of these myofascial problems are between the shoulder blades, in the rhomboids along the upper spine, etc. These patients come in with muscle spasm, a lot of tenderness, and difficulty using their upper extremities.

We treat these injuries at first with the usual methods that help a strain. We use ice and heat, muscle relaxants, antiinflammatories, and time. Often these conditions are accompanied by trigger points, tiny nodules of severe tenderness over the upper back that sometimes we may inject with anesthetic and Cortisone. All the things we do seem to be the right treatment; these conditions clearly aren't tendinitis or bursitis, and they certainly aren't fractures.

But with chronic myofascial pain the symptoms don't get better. The problem lasts and lasts, we try another variant of treatment, different medications, etc., and nothing helps much. The patient may get a little better but then have a relapse. We may try them back at light work but pull them off again when they can't tolerate even light duty.

They go from doctor to doctor, more diagnostic tests are run, they go to physical therapy and then to chiropractors and accupuncturists. Each looks for some unsuspected cause, but all the tests keep coming up negative. The patients try to work again, but they complain of more pain.

Nothing helps, no-one can find much. Eventually someone even starts to suggest they're faking. After a year or two of this, patients with these soft tissue problems are still sort of drifting along, no-one has really known what to do with them medically or otherwise, and they're exceedingly frustrated.

Myofascial pain usually has very little permanent disability, if any, based on the criteria in most states' Workers' Compensation statutes. So eventually these people just drop out of the whole Workers' Compensation system, perhaps with a small financial settlement. Some improve afterwards, some don't, and they keep trying to find jobs within their tolerances.

These are the mysteries of the soft tissue or myofascial problems. If they aren't really strains, if they aren't really sprains, and they certainly aren't fractures, then what are they? The word "Fibromyalgia" is now becoming popular to describe some of these, and so is the phrase "Chronic Fatigue Syndrome". But these are unappropriate diagnoses for most of these patients.

Doctors and insurers often wonder if these myofascial pain problems are all psychological. They probably aren't, although many myofascial pain patients do have personalities that make it appear there is a large degree of emotional overlay in thier problem. And we do know that myofascial pain occurs very commonly in patients on Workers' Compensation or litigation after a personal injury or auto accident. We also know that these people are often employees that don't like their jobs, who have family problems, and who are depressed. But which came first? We often can't tell. I hope that some day we can.

WRAP-UP

How you can do yourself some favors with strains, sprains, bone or joint injuries:
1) If a simple injury isn't healing quickly, suspect something more serious and get further diagnostic workup;
2) If you have an injury to a bone or joint get the earliest and most specialized medical care available;
3) Seek sophisticated specialty care for all joint fractures; the more serious the fracture the more high level the care you should seek;
4) Exercise your whole body to stay physically active while the injured part is healing.

K

Low Back Pain At Work

"I hear you're coming back to work pretty soon, Joe. Feeling better I guess?"

"Sort of, I suppose. But the back still hurts. I thought it was all from the injury, but the doctor says I've got a lot of arthritis in there that I didn't know about."

Low back pain is the most common Workers' Compensation claim, 400,000 cases every year. Low back pain doesn't always come from a work injury, but this chapter describes the dozen or so most common back problems. It should help you make sense out of your own back symptoms and show you what to expect from treatment.

Back problems in the U.S. account for one-fourth of total lost work days every year, more than any problem but flu. Because this is my main field of practice, I'm sorting out complicated back problems every day. I've seen tens of thousands of back pain patients over the years and they all seem to have something in common: They're confused, uncertain about what's wrong or what to do, and scared about their future.

The first step is always to locate just where the problem is and then to determine the actual cause.

"Where's The Low Back?"

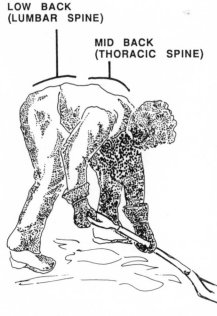

LOW BACK
(LUMBAR SPINE)

MID BACK
(THORACIC SPINE)

Before you see a doctor it may be helpful to use this drawing to locate the site of your own pain.

I've found that patients often have difficulty making a doctor understand exactly where their back hurts. This drawing shows how to describe the various parts of your back to your doctor.

You can help your doctor make the correct diagnosis by describing the right areas. Rather than just pointing vaguely and saying "It's my back", tell him you hurt in the lowest part of the low back on the left, or the right, or whatever, etc. This will help him know where to start looking for the cause of your back pain. Better yet, just draw on this page and show the drawing to him.

Back Injury Or Merely Back Pain?

Though not all back pain comes from an injury, about half of all back pain does seem to start during lifting or with some effort. One problem for doctors who treat back problems is that there isn't always an obvious cause and effect relationship between an activity that brings on pain and the eventual diagnosis. I wish it were always simple, but it's not. There are far too many causes of low back pain.

In particular, just because a back pain comes on while a person is at work does not necessarily mean that the work activity caused the back problem.

Of course, it could have been caused by work. It could have been a lifting strain, a sprain, a joint injury or even a disc herniation. A patient could have leaned over to pick up a part and a heavy box fell on his back: That would also be a definite work injury. But there could be many other reasons: He could have twisted getting out of the shower and pulled a muscle, have gone bowling a night earlier and done the same, etc. Those would be cases of back strain that merely became symptomatic at work later.

Another possibility would be that he could have injured a disc two or three years earlier, then over the years it deteriorated and finally just now became symptomatic. Or it could be that he had arthritis building up in his back for 20 years and it has finally become painful.

Any of these things could cause back pain and most are not "work injuries". Suppose you came in to see me with low back pain and told me it started yesterday after running a bulldozer, or lifting something heavy at work. All I would be able to say is that the preliminary diagnosis is "low back pain". I wouldn't have enough information to conclude it was definitely a work injury.

A doctor always has to figure out the true cause of low back pain before he can conclude that it was caused by work. And because this is often difficult, doctors who deal regularly with back problems often simply describe a problem as back pain and do not label it as an injury until it is proven to be one. This isn't always a popular method with the patient but it's most realistic considering how complex many back problems can be.

Nevertheless, many back pains are obviously due to specific, documentable injuries from work. These include:

Strains;
Sprains, including joint capsule injuries;
Trauma: from bruises to breaks;
Some disc herniations.

Low Back Strains

A <u>strain</u> is a simple stretching injury. A low back strain (lumbar strain) is a stretching of muscles or ligaments in the low back near the spine.

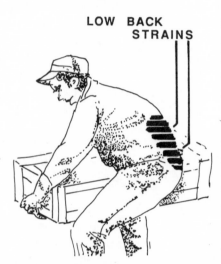

LOW BACK STRAINS

Common causes of lumbar strain are leaning too far forward to pick up an object, or by pulling extra hard on something heavy, and sometimes by a sudden forceful jerking motion.

The symptoms of back strain are a deep aching or "pulling" sensation in the muscles, usually to the side of the spine. This is a deep dull pain because strains are injuries to deep heavy muscles. There may also be swelling and painful muscle spasm or tightening of the muscle fibers.

When you see the doctor with this kind of low back pain, he will palpate (feel) the area: It will probably be tender. He'll ask you to bend forward and backward, then from side to side. He will be looking for limited spine motion and he'll also do tests for nerve or joint damage. But they'll likely be normal.

If he does an X-ray, it may show that the normal curve of the low back is altered by muscle spasm. Otherwise a low back strain has no specific findings on X-ray.

As to treatment for a low back strain, <u>99% heal by themselves</u>. Treatment is usually ice packs for 20 minutes four times a day for a couple of days. Then heat and some muscle relaxants such as Robaxin or Flexeril (see Chapter 11) for five or six days will be all that is needed for a simple strain. Aspirin should be enough for the pain. <u>Two days of bedrest is maximum</u> for a back strain. More than two days inactivity could do more damage than good, because you'll lose strength and become stiff. A simple back strain should be fully healed within a week or two, depending on your overall health.

In three or four days at most you should start light range of motion exercises for the back muscles. If you are a couch potato and have poor slumped posture a strain may take longer to resolve.

Patients ask about future risk. When you return to work you should of course be careful. But a strain probably does not put you at any more risk of another strain than you were at before.

Other than treating a strain with ice, mild medications and back exercise, no medical doctor or chiropractor of any sort can make your body heal a strained back muscle any faster than it will heal on it's own.

But what if you don't improve soon? How soon is soon enough? Suppose after two weeks you feel absolutely no different, or you've felt progressively worse, or you've developed leg pain or weakness. This may be because you're not taking your pills correctly, or you haven't been doing the temperature treatments, or the exercises correctly, or you've been lying around too much. Check these things out.

However, lack of improvement could mean that you have something other than simple strain: You may have a back sprain.

Low Back Sprains

A sprain is a tear of some muscle or ligament near a joint in the low back. A sprain can occur from any of the same motions as a strain: A sudden lift, twist, or pull, a fall, etc.

The symptoms of a low back sprain are similar to strains: Deep pain in muscles along side the spine. The treatment is similar to that for strains. However, low back sprains, being due to tearing rather than stretching, are more serious injuries and last longer.

Facet Joint And Capsule Injuries

The lumbar spine contains small joints, five pairs in all, called facet joints. These interlocking joints allow the spine to bend forward and backward.

Each joint is about the size of your fingernail and each is enclosed by a ligamentous <u>capsule</u> called a facet capsule.

Facet joints--actually their capsules--are particularly vulnerable to sprains. Their capsules can tear when you twist or extend your back sharply, and sometimes they can be injured in a fall. The tear of the capsule causes a "facet syndrome". Such a syndrome can also be caused by underlying arthritis of the facet joint. There may not be anything to see on X-ray unless you do have such arthritis.

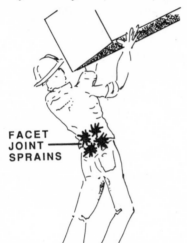

**FACET
JOINT
SPRAINS**

Symptoms of a facet injury or capsular sprain are typically a sudden sharp pain like a knife going into your back, a locking feeling, and difficulty bending. Some patients with these problems find their back shifted to right or left in painful spasm.

If you have a facet injury, the treatment will be different than for a simple back sprain. Muscle relaxants will help some, but you will also probably require physical therapy to increase motion as soon as spasm can be reduced. Specific low back motion exercise may be enough to treat the problem.

I often recommend and perform injections into the facet joints and capsules as part of treatment. A mixture of a local anesthetic (such as Novocaine) and a steroid medication will reduce inflammation. The procedure is done with X-ray assistance and I have found it to be helpful in approximately 60% to 75% of my patients with this problem.

Chiropractors can often treat facet problems successfully, but two to six weeks of treatment should be enough. I've found that many facet problems improve after a few chiropractic treatments but then worsen again after a few more and then stay worse. I think the manipulation stops being effective and can actually weaken the tissues that are trying to heal. That's why I recommend no more than a few weeks of such adjustments.

Facet sprains take some time to resolve, probably at least four to six weeks in most cases. After resolution of a facet injury, when you return to work you'll have to be careful. You are at risk for the same thing happening again because the capsule could still be weak. You **must** avoid twisting, and you must lift by squatting and keeping the load close to you. No more bending at the waist once you've had a facet injury!

Only a few years ago, if you read this chapter and then told your family doctor you had a facet syndrome instead of a muscle strain he probably would have looked at you curiously. Now I think that more doctors are becoming aware that problems in the facet joints cause a lot of low back pain. But I believe that it's still far more common than most doctors realize and it probably accounts for many of the "back sprain patients" who don't respond to treatment.

SPINE TRAUMA: FROM BRUISES TO BREAKS

Some other back problems are clearly due to specific, documentable injuries at work. These are called "traumatic" back injuries.

Traumatic injuries from falls, blows, breaks, wounds, etc., always have obvious causes. They produce acute back pain that has an obvious source and we can direct treatment to them knowing exactly what we're treating.

> *I have a patient who fell off a scaffold and after twelve feet of free-fall his safety rope caught. He was snapped sideways and one of the facet joints in his low back was fractured.*
> *I have another patient who was logging timber and a falling tree struck him across the small of his back. A small part of his spine (a transverse process) was fractured. I have a third patient who was in a truck rollover. He had bruising and bleeding into most of the major low back muscles.*

These three patients all had obvious traumatic back problems. Interestingly, even all three of these patients had very different mechanisms of injury, they all had about the same symptoms: They all had low back pain.

Treatment was very different for each.

> *The first patient, who fell and was snapped by his rope, had the most serious injury: An unstable facet fracture. Unfortunately, now*

two operations and four years later he's still hurting and he's still not back to work. The fracture has never healed well and we probably won't be able to help him much.

The second patient with the logging injury also had a complicated injury because many muscles attach to the transverse processes. Nevertheless there was no true treatment but time: The fracture had to heal by itself and no surgery was required. Eventually he felt better and returned to work after several months. He still has a little discomfort with some motion such as climbing onto his skidder but he is at full duty.

Treatment for the third patient with muscle injuries was quite simple. We did nothing but use ice, then heat and massage and gave him some pain medications. He healed up in a few weeks and was symptom free.

BRUISES AND CONTUSIONS

Bruises and contusions to the low back usually heal in a couple of weeks. They resolve fully afterwards and a patient with a bump has no more risk of back pain later than he did before.

HEMATOMAS

Some contusions are more severe than others and cause bleeding into the underlying muscle tissue. The hematoma (a collection of blood) that results can cause painful swelling with discomfort that can last for months. There is no specific treatment but heat and massage. A very few of these require surgical removal after several months if they are extremely painful.

COMPRESSION FRACTURES

There's one type of spine injury that can occur with severe trauma, falls, auto accidents, etc. This is called a "compression fracture". These fractures are of the vertebral bodies that make up the spine. Because these are chunky solid bones, the trauma "breaks" them by compressing them slightly. (They cannot "break in half" as long bones do).

Vertebral bodies that are compressed never "uncompress", they always stay slightly smaller in height. These can hurt for quite some time, occasionally for years. Most compression fractures require no treatment but a corset or brace and then waiting until they become less inflamed. Symptoms generally do decrease.

But occasionally the injury is a "burst" fracture. In these injuries the vertebral body is broken into a number of pieces. These often require surgery to stabilize them.

DISC PROBLEMS

Disc problems, and whether or not they are related to injury, can be an enormously complicated subject of which we learn more every year. You need to know what discs are to understand how they might cause symptoms.

The spine contains 23 <u>intervertebral discs</u>: Circular ligaments that enclose cartilage in a soft pulpy center. The analogy is a jelly donut sitting between two soup cans. Each of these discs sits between two vertebral bodies and they act more or less like shock absorbers.

As people age their discs naturally start to dehydrate somewhat. Therefore the discs become less resilient. This happens faster in some people than others, for no known reason. Dehydrated discs--sometimes called degenerated discs--are weaker than normal discs and can therefore be more easily injured.

BULGING DISCS

As a consequence of disc degeneration, sometimes the outer portion of a disc ligament weakens. Then, particularly if a person is obese, the pulpy center can "bulge" outward. This may be a normal--or at least natural-- process and not at all related to any trauma or injury. A bulge may not cause any discomfort. In fact if you were to perform CT's or MRI's on 100 people off the street, 25 to 50 of their spines would probably show a bulge. Yet they have no pain, no back difficulties at all.

So why do I mention bulging discs? Because it happens all the time that a patient has low back pain at work, sees his doctor, the doctor does a CT and finds a bulge and says, "There's the cause of your pain--you have a bulging disc!" This leads them both on a wild goose chase because in reality the bulge may be due to degenerative disc disease. The patient's pain may be entirely due to other low back causes. No treatment is required for a simple bulge.

HERNIATED DISCS

Despite all I just said about bulging discs, there is a disc condition known as a disc herniation. This is a serious problem: It occurs when the ligaments of a disc deteriorate over time so that the central "jelly of the donut" can protrude through the tear.

This confuses matters because disc herniation can simply result from plain old degenerative disc disease. In other words, discs may dry out, become weak, deteriorate to a bulge, and then deteriorate further to a disc herniation.

Even more unfortunately for doctors trying to sort out "low back pain at work", disc herniations can also be the result of a severe lifting injury, a fall, motor vehicle accident, or other trauma. To confuse this even further, deteriorated and bulging discs can be injured at work and develop into a herniation. This makes the picture very confusing when trying to sort out the true cause of the patient's problems: Is it a work injury or non-work condition?

SYMPTOMS AND TREATMENT OF DISC HERNIATIONS

Patients with disc herniations usually have severe back pain. The pain is present all the time, though it's sometimes relieved by lying down. There may be muscle spasm, it may hurt to cough, sneeze, or to have a bowel movement.

We can usually diagnose a disc herniation on a CT scan or MRI. These studies will demonstrate a large protrusion and may even show bits (fragments) of the central pulp if any has ruptured out.

The treatment of herniated discs is usually conservative management: Bedrest for two to three weeks, pain medications, and usually physical therapy with daily traction (see Chapter 11). Even if four to six weeks of this treatment does no good, another four to six weeks may be tried unless there are complicating factors (see below).

Usually a simple disc problem will "settle down" with time, though we don't fully understand how and in cases where fragments of the central pulp have extruded, the problem will probably not settle down.

All disc patients still need a lot of careful recuperation, back and abdominal exercises, and probably a long time before they go back to any lifting. Expect two to six months from the first symptoms before you can return to even moderate work, depending on how fast you respond to treatment. After your recovery you'll still have to avoid much bending, twisting, and heavy lifting because you'll be at risk of recurrence for quite a while. If you're obese, soft, out of shape, and have poor posture and smoke it takes longer to recover and you'll stay at higher risk.

In general, if you have a disc injury you should expect gradual improvement. However, if you don't get better at all and have severe leg pain, you probably have sciatica.

SCIATICA

SCIATIC NERVE PAIN

If you develop severe leg pain--like molten metal or a hot poker going down the back of your leg to your foot--and you have difficulty walking, sitting, and standing, you may have sciatica.

Sciatica is an irritation of the sciatic nerve, the one that runs down the back of your buttock down the back of your leg. Sometimes a herniated disc puts pressure on this nerve as it leaves the spine before it travels down to the leg. The pain may be in your leg or foot, but with sciatica the actual problem is in your back where the nerve root is.

If sciatic irritation lasts a long time it may lead to muscle wasting, foot or leg weakness or numbness or loss of a reflex at knee or ankle. When any of these signs show up, we usually expect that the MRI or CT will confirm the diagnosis of disc herniation and entrapment.

Sciatica usually doesn't respond very well to rest, medications, traction, etc. Eventually a patient comes in and says something like, "Doc, fix this or cut my leg off. I can't take this pain any more". Then surgery may be required to remove the portion of the disc that's pressing on the nerve.

If you're in this condition, first read Chapter 13 "How To Decide About Surgery" and then get yourself to the best neurosurgeon you can find and do exactly what he says. In many communities, orthopedic surgeons do low back disc operations.

If you do have disc surgery, will you be able to go back to your old job? It depends on your job, your specific injury, and how well you do in reha-bilitation. You absolutely must have a good rehab program after surgery.

Low back disc surgery does not "repair" the disc. Surgery does not "put the disc back in place" or replace it. It does not regenerate your back to the way it used to be. It does not improve your back. Low back disc surgery removes the herniated disc material and takes pressure off a pinched nerve. It usually helps relieve leg pain, but not in all patients. It often does not relieve all the back pain.

Every disc herniation and surgical result is different. Though many people do go back to their old jobs afterward, not all do. I have patients who are heavy equipment operators, welders, nurses' aides, and bus drivers that returned to work after disc surgery, but generally heavy work is not advisable.

Are post-op back patients at risk for having recurrent disc injuries? Yes. They can help lower that risk by exercise, weight loss, and being care-ful when they lift. Nevertheless, if you are a laborer and you've had disc surgery, there's a very strong possibility you're going to have to look into another line of work where you won't have to use your low back.

SACROILIAC PAIN

Suppose you felt severe pain off to the side of your low back when you lifted or twisted, and you heard a tearing sensation or sound. You may have sacroiliac pain. This is pain between the sacrum (tailbone area) and ilium (the pelvis bone).

This pain may feel like a strain or a sprain, you may have muscle spasm, and it may even hurt down your leg like sciatica. It may hurt to walk, and when you do the standard set of low back exercises they will be painful. All of the tests for disc damage will be normal, the CT and MRI usually will show nothing, and routine low back treatment does not help at all.

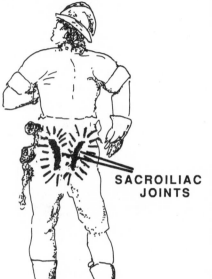

SACROILIAC
JOINTS

Sacroiliac pain is part of the frustrating complex of sacroiliac dysfunction. It is commonly misdiagnosed as a disc herniation. However, sacroiliac pain is usually due to a strain or sprain of the numerous ligaments across the sacroiliac joint. Sometimes it is also caused by a problem--even arthritis--inside the joint itself.

We don't really know enough about this problem, though medical doctors, physical therapists, chiropractors, and osteopaths are always popping up claiming they have a miracle treatment for sacroiliacs. So far I have not found any of these treatments to be consistently better than any other.

We have a lot of trouble treating SI problems. However, some treatments work with some people. You can count on these things:
- SI problems can be diagnosed if the doctor knows where to look and what to test for;
- SI problems can be associated with certain arthritis. Your doctor should do tests for these and treat them if they're present;
- Antiinflammatory pills, certain exercises, biofeedback, and SI joint injections can help. Weight loss helps and so does a positive attitude.
- Chiropractic adjustment rarely helps, it can actually hurt this problem, and I don't think I've ever seen a sacroiliac patient that received long-lasting relief from it.
- About one in six patients improves enough to work at a heavy job again, but it takes a long time, often a year or more.

I hope you never have a sacroiliac problem. I'll keep trying to find better treatments, and if there are any I'll put them in the next edition.

ARTHRITIS OF THE BACK

Arthritis is not an injury, especially when it occurs in the spine. But I'm discussing it in this chapter because it's so common, and because it does complicate many back injuries.

Arthritis is really just a buildup or overgrowth of bone near or in a joint. It can have many causes, many of which are not understood. Typical low back or neck arthritis takes the form of "spurs" or irregularities along the edges of the vertebrae. Any of these spurs can cause pain by themselves, or stiffness in the spine, and some can even cause enough narrowing of nerve canals to pinch or trap a nerve.

In many patients--it seems I see this twice a day--a fall or strain or other minor injury produces pain in either the low back or neck that lasts and lasts, much longer than it should based on how trivial the injury was.

I usually find the cause--arthritis aggravated by strain--but patients don't often accept this for an answer. They'll say, "Why are you saying I have arthritis, Doc? I never had any of this pain until the accident."

But when they fell, or were in a wreck, they had a back strain or sprain and it hurt for several weeks. Their spine got stiff, maybe they were put at complete bedrest without any motion at all (the worst treatment that could be given) or maybe they didn't do their exercises faithfully. And now they're stiffer and <u>any</u> motion hurts, even the therapeutic exercises that should restore motion.

In circumstances like this, all the patient knows is that his back or neck hurts all the time now, it didn't before, and when I show them little spurs on X-ray and tell them those are the cause of their symptoms they don't believe it. The sprain didn't cause the spurs, because they take years to develop. The injury didn't accelerate the spurs either. And the sprain is not still causing their symptoms are limitations. They are having arthritis pain that's aggravated by inactivity.

At this point I know I have to convince these patients to get their low back moving again and get them generally active again also. This is not easy for me or for them, but it does help when they do it.

In some states, the doctor or patient must show that a strain or sprain makes preexisting arthritis demonstrably worse before it's considered a "permanent injury". Wisconsin is such a state: In Wisconsin strains and sprains are not usually considered permanent injuries. But in other states, and Minnesota is notably one, if there is any arthritis on X-ray no matter how old it is, you can have a strain and no matter how minor it is--even if it heals completely in a week--you will be considered to have a "permanent partial disability". This is discussed more in Chapter 22.

Which is a more sensible way of looking at a back injury with preexisting arthritis? Neither one makes much sense medically, because every patient and every injury is unique. Some patients improve after a strain and some don't, and to put them all in the same category is silly.

But the point to remember is this: If you have an injury to your low back or neck and your X-rays show that you have arthritic spurring of any severity at all, you should keep active and do exercises and follow your doctor's treatment. Your best bet is to keep moving and get back to your old life as soon as you can, arthritis or no. There is no other treatment.

QUESTIONS ON WORKERS' COMPENSATION AND BACK PAIN

It would be easy to fill this whole book discussing the common spine problems above, but I can't here. I do want to provide you with answers to some questions I am asked every week.

Q. "Will Workers' Compensation cover any back pain if it starts on the job?"
A. Yes, if there's a clear and definite injury. Perhaps, if there's a possibility an injury occurred. No, if it turns out the symptoms were all due to a non-work injury or personal health problem such as arthritis or a congenital abnormality of the spine.

Q. "Can a person get low back pain from a limp, say after another injury such as an ankle or knee sprain?"
A. Yes, but that kind of back pain should resolve. A few patients develop low back pain when a knee or hip operation causes one leg to be shorter than the other or when a patient favors one side. Correct the favoring or the limp and the back pain should improve. These are not usually back strains, just sore muscles.

Q. "Do chiropractors put "slipped discs" back in place?"

A. I've never seen discs "slip"--that's an outmoded term. Chiropractors will not cure a disc herniation. Occasionally chiropractic treatment makes a patient feel better temporarily. Chiropractic treatment, if you have sciatica, is a bad idea. Most knowledgeable chiropractors would send such a patient to a surgeon.

Q. "Can congenital defects in the spine cause back pain?"

A. Some can. A small defect called spina bifida occulta does not. But a "transitional vertebra" where the transverse process on one side is attached to the pelvis but the other side is free to move, does cause problems. So can facet joint "tropisms", little noticed misalignments of the facet joints. These defects predispose a patient to injury his back. (There are arguments among back doctors about this, but this is my opinion based on what I've seen.)

Q. "Does heavy labor, truck driving, jackhammering, etc., cause arthritis of the back?"

A. Nobody knows for sure, but some studies indicate there may be some connection, as the frequency of back pain in these people is high. However not everyone agrees on this and not all or even most truck drivers or laborers have arthritis. The cause of arthritis is unknown.

Q. "What about sex?"

A. A happy and normal sex life (whatever that may be for each individual) is important for well-being and recovery. For many back patients, pain interferes with intercourse and this is one of their biggest irritants. There is a short booklet (Sex and Back Pain) available that gives some solutions. You can obtain it by writing to Educational Opportunities, 7750 West 78th Street, Minneapolis, Minnesota 55439. It costs $3.00 and it's well worth it. (Tel 1-800-654-8357)

Q. "Should my doctor take an X-ray if I hurt my back?"

A. Definitely. I can't conceive of a medical doctor in the 1990's not taking X-rays when an employee complains of back pain from a work injury. In Workers' Compensation a doctor needs to do everything he can to make an early and correct diagnosis and start appropriate treatment.

I had a back patient who had been told by her doctor she should simply rest. After six weeks she was worse, I saw her and an X-ray showed the obvious problem was unsuspected scoliosis. With treatment including back exercise, she improved. If X-rays had been taken earlier, treatment would have been more effective.

Q. "What's the best treatment for back pain?"
A. Each injury is different so each injury needs different treatment. Most back problems need gentle range of motion, medications, eventually exercises, and also the simple passage of time.

Weight loss is critically important, tightening of the tummy muscles is important, and after a back injury you will have to learn how to prevent recurrent problems by lifting correctly. You should keep yourself fit, do the right back exercise, and so on. This will mean a good physical fitness program for many years to come, Something we all should be doing whether we've had a back injury or not!

> I saw a policeman recently with low back pain. There wasn't much seriously wrong though his problem prohibited him from some of his work. Unfortunately, some doctor had told him: "You're just one surgery away from a wheelchair" and recommended that he retire on disability.
> I found that this patient hadn't had physical therapy, antiinflammatory medications, injections, a TENS unit, corset, exercise, CT or MRI, or even a good surgical opinion. He hadn't even been worked up and his doctor told him to retire.

There's no such thing as a disability retirement for this or any other back problem until at least these treatments have been tried (see Chapters 11, 13, & 16). If you're in this situation, make sure your doctor exhausts all these therapies before giving up.

WRAP-UP

How you can do yourself some favors with low back pain:
1) Locate your own low back pain and give your doctor accurate information about your symptoms;
2) Follow recommended treatment;
3) Seek advice from a back specialist or surgeon if you have leg pain;
4) Make sure conservative treatment with medications, exercise, physical therapy, and the passage of time are all tried before giving up.

K

Neck And Upper Back Pain

"You still having problems from that injury?"
"Yeah, it just keeps on and on. I'll tell you, it's a real pain in the neck."

Neck problems at work aren't as common as low back problems--after all, nobody lifts things with their neck. The injuries that do occur are mostly from strains and motor vehicle accidents.

This chapter describes symptoms and causes of the most common neck and upper back problems, tells you how they're treated, and advises you what results you might expect from treatment.

WHERE'S THE "NECK"? WHERE'S THE UPPER "BACK"?

The neck (cervical spine) is the top part of the spine, the approximately 6 inches from the skull down. It's made up of seven vertebrae and it merges with the thoracic spine just below the prominent bump that you can feel at the back of your collar.

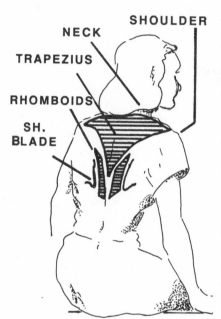

When you see the doctor it may help you to use this drawing to show him the location of your symptoms. And if you use the correct terminology, it will help your doctor make the correct diagnosis.

I've had many patients tell me they have "back pain" when they really meant cervical spine pain. I've heard many patients say they have a "shoulder problem", but it turned out they meant pain in the upper back between the shoulder blades. And many patients have trapezius muscle pain, but they call it their shoulder, neck or back and this misleads a doctor.

So I recommend you use this diagram, draw your own problem area right on it, and show it to your doctor.

TRUE NECK INJURY OR JUST NECK PAIN?

Just as with low back symptoms (see last chapter), not all neck symptoms are necessarily from an "injury". Many things cause neck pain, and many have nothing to do with on-the-job injuries.

For example, you may have neck pain and tell your doctor you assume that it came from your job. But other things could cause you to have that pain: An old injury, an injury a week ago at home or work, cervical arthritis, even something as simple as sleeping on the wrong pillow.

So any doctor's first job when an employee comes in with neck pain should be to sort through the symptoms, look for all possible causes, and then make the diagnosis. That diagnosis might in fact turn out to be work injury: Neck trauma, neck strain, neck sprain, or even a disc herniation. But you and your doctor will usually have to go through a full workup to find out for sure.

STRAINS AND SPRAINS: NECK

A lot of neck strains and sprains do occur at work. A mild stretching is only a strain. A more severe injury causes tearing of the ligaments: A sprain. The most severe neck injuries are generally from work-related auto or truck accidents.

A neck strain or sprain in a motor vehicle accident occurs when the vehicle is hit from behind, with the injured person's neck extending backwards and then flexing forward. Some people (mostly attorneys but also some doctors) use the word "whiplash" for this. Though I dislike the shock-value of this word, whether the injury is called a whiplash or an "extension cervical strain" it does often cause stretching or tearing of the ligaments and tissues along the spine.

Neck strains and sprains can also involve the muscles on the sides of the neck or those in the back of the neck. The symptoms of a neck strain or sprain will usually be painful muscle spasm, pain with neck motion and a rigid neck. When the muscles in the back of the neck become tight they pull on the scalp. This causes headache pain from irritated scalp nerves. With strains and sprains usually nothing much shows up on X-ray other than a straightened (rigid) cervical spine. Fractures are possible but uncommon in these injuries.

The treatment is muscle relaxants, applications of ice and after a few days heat, and early gentle physical therapy for massage and range of motion. A cervical collar for 24 to 48 hours--maybe 72 hours--can take some of the load off the neck. Chiropractic may help make a few of these patients feel better, though in my experience it doesn't really change over-all recovery. Biofeedback therapy (see Chapter 11) can help when discomfort is prolonged.

But the only thing that makes any real difference with severe neck strains or sprains is usually the simple passage of time. Minor strains will resolve with a few days or a week or two. But it can take months, or sometimes even years if the injury is severe. As neck strains and sprains heal you have to be very careful to avoid injury. In many cases I recommend a change to restricted work for several months.

Once a neck sprain has fully healed, you won't be at any higher risk of recurrence. But if your symptoms persist for three years, and you've had all the appropriate treatment but it hasn't helped, the symptoms are probably going to be permanent. At that point the best recommendation will be to get on with your life as best you can.

Could strain or sprain be the wrong diagnosis? Yes, it could if you have any of the following: Severe deep pain--not a superficial muscle type pain--that's constant, if even a tiny motion of your neck produces severe pain, or if you have pain or numbness shooting down your arm. These can be symptoms of cervical radiculopathy (see next page), and they usually indicate a disc problem.

CERVICAL DISC PROBLEMS

The cervical spine is made up of seven vertebral bodies with discs between six of them, with eight spinal nerves that exit from the spine through eight small openings on each side.

In some severe injuries, the soft central part of a cervical disc can "herniate", or protrude out of the disc itself. This is similar to the herniations in the lumbar spine that I wrote about in the last chapter. A herniation can occur after a severe fall, a heavy lift, an auto accident, etc.

A herniated cervical disc can cause severe pain deep in the spinal tissues and also spasm in the neck muscles with an immobile or rigid neck and pain on motion.

These symptoms of cervical disc herniation sound similar to a severe neck sprain, don't they? In fact they are, and sometimes it's difficult at first to distinguish between the two.

One thing that differentiates a sprain from a disc injury is that a neck sprain will often settle down within a few weeks but a disc problem will not.

RADICULAR ARM PAIN

However, the most important signs pointing to a probable disc herniation would be pain or numbness shooting down one arm, weakness in part of the arm or hand or some fingers. These symptoms are clues that the disc is pressing on one or more of the nerves that pass out of the cervical spine on their way down the arm. This is called cervical <u>radiculopathy,</u> which means an injury to the nerve root (radicular injury). The pain is in the arm, but the injury is in the neck.

Cervical disc problems sometimes get better on their own. But usually the best treatment is to put a patient at bedrest and start cervical traction. Traction reduces the pressure on the nerves by "stretching" the spine slightly. Traction treat-ment is done at least once a day in a physical therapy department.

A better way to use traction is to do it two or three times per day at home with a home traction apparatus that hangs over a door. Sometimes muscle relaxants and gentle range of motion exercises will also help a bit with cervical disc herniations.

But if this conservative treatment doesn't produce improvement or resolution of the symptoms--in other words if neither arm pain nor arm weakness resolve after six weeks or so of treatment--you may need surgery to remove the portion of the herniated disc that is pressing on the nerve. So if you have unrelenting neck and arm pain and your doctor thinks you need an operation, first read Chapter 13 and then see the best neurosurgeon you can find. With cervical disc surgery you have a good chance of making a full recovery.

After cervical disc surgery, I've found that a program of rehabilitation is essential. This will mean neck exercises, physical therapy, and appropriate physical activity. Most people with simple cervical disc operations eventually return to their regular work, usually after three months or so. But depending on how heavy your work is, you may have to modify it to avoid heavy lifting, bouncing in a truck, constant neck flexion, and so on.

Will you be at higher risk of injury after one neck operation? Probably some, but not dramatically so. Just be prepared to feel like a barometer--you'll probably be able to predict the weather by your neck.

STRAINS AND SPRAINS: UPPER BACK

Upper back strains and sprains usually occur in the trapezius--the large muscle that covers the upper back like a cape--or between the shoulder blades in the rhomboid muscles. They can be caused by overuse, by a fall, or by a contusion. I often see upper back strains in nursing assistants who have lifted a patient that suddenly fell or went dead weight, in dockworkers who pushed hard against large objects, and in welders from heavy overhead work.

Symptoms of upper back strains can be muscle pain or spasm, swelling, and pain with overhead arm motion. As with neck strains, they usually improve slowly with medications, physical therapy, and the passage of time. Though most upper back strains get better, some go on to become cases of "chronic myofascial pain".

MYOFASCIAL PAIN OF THE UPPER BACK AND NECK

Some patients develop a frustrating, long-lasting and unexplainable pain in the soft tissues--muscle and fascia--in the upper back. I already wrote about this in Special Section B. It seems that most cases of this chronic inflammation of soft tissues, this "myofasciitis", occur in the upper back between the shoulder blades or over the trapezius. Sometimes it occurs in neck muscles.

This problem usually follows some upper back injury, usually a sprain from lifting or pulling, but often there's no obvious injury at all. Myofascial pain is often associated with severe cervical arthritis. It is usually <u>not</u> associated with a disc injury or radiculopathy.

We don't know what makes myofascial pain last and last, but it certainly does. I've seen many patients who are chronically uncomfortable with this problem, who have had all of the right therapies--and some of the wrong ones--and still don't get better except very, very slowly. These myofascial pain patients are often misunderstood, mistreated and misdiagnosed. They go from doctor to doctor, each trying something else that doesn't work. They get frustrated and discouraged. They feel no-one can help them.

Many of these patients have to change jobs to accommodate their symptoms and limitations.   For example, I saw a cement finisher that had to go into estimating and supervising because of it. I've seen machinists that had to go into light assembly, nursing assistants that had to become ward clerks, and so on.

Some doctors have suggested that stress is really the cause of myofascial pain. I think they're only partially right. Stress is certainly not the sole cause. A few insurers and attorneys have come right out and asserted that desire for financial compensation is the cause of myofascial pain, and that these patients are just out-and-out faking.

But they're wrong, too, at least in 95% of these cases. In fact in many cases much of the problem of stress with myofascial pain comes from the frustration of going through the medical care system without relief.   Art White, M.D., the noted spine surgeon at the San Francisco Spine Institute, has said "These people aren't crazy--we <u>drive</u> them crazy".

I have a patient, Marvin, who's been unable to lead his usual life, let alone work, for several years because of this kind of problem. After I tried all manner of treatments without success, I did ask a surgeon to see him. I hoped that he might be able to recommend some relief for this man's terrible arthritis and myofascial pain. On the day of the consultation his symptoms were particularly severe, and he had to turn his whole body to face the surgeon. He swears the surgeon took one look at him and his rigid neck, said "You're faking--There's nothing I can do for you!" and walked out of the room. The poor patient was naturally devastated. He knew how real his symptoms were then, and he still has them to this day.

Eventually I gave trial testimony about this same patient. After the testimony one of the attorneys said to me: "He'll get better as soon as he gets his money. Six months from now his symptoms will all be gone."

Well, I told that attorney he was wrong when it happened three years ago and he's still wrong. Marvin still has every bit as much pain as he ever did. I don't know everything about what causes the myofascial pain in this man and patients like him, but I do know he would gladly give it all away to that surgeon and that attorney.

I've found that the majority of these people still have this pain, as Marvin does, long after their case has been settled. Those few insurers who think all myofascial pain is make-believe should have the pain for a while. Most of these patients aren't faking.

ARTHRITIS

Arthritis is not an "injury", especially in the neck. But because it's so common, and because it complicates so many injuries, it's important to understand it.

Arthritis is really just buildup or overgrowth of bone near or in a joint. It can have many causes, many of which we haven't sorted out yet. To understand how arthritis affects the neck, read the section on Arthritis in Special Section C. Everything there applies to the neck and upper back as well as the low back.

BRACHIAL STRETCH INJURIES

One type of neck injury deserves special mention. This is a stretch or strain of the brachial plexus. This plexus is a complex bundle of large nerves where they leave the neck and join together to go down the arm. The plexus is located just above your collarbone at the side of your neck. These nerves can be injured by a forceful stetching motion, for example if your arm is jerked downward suddenly or perhaps forced behind you and upward. The symptoms of a brachial plexus stretch can appear to be radiculopathy: Pain, numbness, or weakness in one arm or hand.

Sometimes diagnostic tests such as an EMG (see Chapter 8) will demonstrate the problem, but they can also be negative. Often the diagnosis must be made by exam only--the trouble is that sometimes a doctor might not think of this injury because it can be quite obscure or subtle.

The treatment for a brachial stretch is simply patience and waiting. There's nothing a doctor can do to make your body heal faster than it will on its own. Keep healthy, keep your arm flexible with gentle exercises. If the injury isn't too severe, about six months to a year later the pain will probably start to fade away and the strength will return.

MID-BACK (THORACIC SPINE) INJURIES

There are fewer industrial injuries to the mid-back than to the neck and upper back. This is partly because the thoracic spine is kept rigid by the rib cage. It doesn't move much, but it still can be damaged. Most mid-back injuries at work are either strains or sprains or trauma, including fractures.

A thoracic strain or sprain occurs from lifting, usually when an employee is leaning far out in front of himself--for example reaching across a counter to pick up a heavy object. Symptoms are the same as in most other back strains and sprains and so is the treatment. Some of these injuries are more severe, however. If so they can be very symptomatic and last many months.

In severe trauma to the mid-back, such as in a fall or in a motor vehicle accident, one or more bones of the thoracic spine can be fractured. The fracture is usually a "compression" fracture (see last section). The symptoms of thoracic spine compression fractures are usually local pain, and sometimes pain upon taking a deep breath.

There's not much treatment for a simple thoracic compression fracture other than wearing a corset and taking antiinflammatory medications. The simple passage of time helps the most. A few of these fractures are extremely severe and cause the spine to be unstable. For these immediate surgery is necessary.

Occasionally a thoracic spine injury will cause thoracic radicular pain. This is pain around the chest that comes from pressure on a spinal nerve, usually from a disc injury or a severe fracture. Treatment for this is complex and beyond this book, but may include surgery.

FINAL RECOMMENDATIONS

I listened to Dr. White talk about some of the neck problems we see every day, and about the fact that they seem to baffle some people: Doctors, patients, claim adjusters, and rehabilitation consultants. He concluded: "Neck pain isn't a mystery. Conservative care works for the cervical spine, and we just have to use it more extensively than we do."

Conservative treatment for neck sprains, chronic soft tissue pain and cervical arthritis should always start with a brief period of resting the neck. It may be appropriate to use medications to relax the muscles and decrease inflammation (see Chapter 11).

Then gentle range of motion and flexibility treatment should be started. Some physical therapy may help with ultrasound and massage, and sometimes manipulation helps. At least these things help patients feel better while their necktissues begin to heal.

Then if there's still discomfort and muscle spasm, other medications may be needed as well as injections to painful areas. Biofeedback treatment is helpful in chronic problems.

No course of treatment for continued neck pain should be considered complete until <u>all</u> these have been tried. Dr. White felt strongly that too many people have jumped into surgery, and the results weren't good. He emphasized over and over that "Surgery is not the answer. It may be the answer sometimes. But the emphasis should start first with accurate diagnosis, and then use of good conservative management for as long as it takes."

WRAP-UP

How you can do yourself some favors with neck problems:
1) <u>Show</u> your doctor exactly where your symptoms are;
2) Strains and sprains usually resolve on their own, but if you have arm pain along with neck injury let your doctor know right away;
3) Range of motion and stretching exercises, and other conservative care, should always be tried before jumping into surgery. J

Occupational Respiratory Injuries

"We saw him going down slow, kind of falling. He was driving his deck crane--you know, with the low cab?--and he'd just got inside one of the sheds. Right away, he just went down to the ground. We ran over and yelled "Carl, you all right?" but he was already out."

"Then we smelled it too--rotten eggs, you know, real strong, like they tell us about? So we run back to get our respirators. He looked pretty blue when we dragged him out. Suppose we could've ended up the same way if we'd just run in there, right?"

They were too right. Many rescuers in cases of H_2S asphyxiation have ended up needing rescue themselves.

Occupational lung injury is hardly rare. Literally hundreds of thousands of employees have daily exposure to potential respiratory irritants, toxins, and allergens.

If you're reading this because you have symptoms of lung disease and think they came from a work exposure, <u>this chapter will help you recognize the common occupational respiratory injuries</u>.

I'll describe symptoms, typical causes, and the occupations or industries most likely to carry risks of exposure. I'll describe how doctors make the diagnosis, typical treatment, and tell you what to expect if you have one of these illnesses.

WHEN YOU SUSPECT A LUNG INJURY

In most cases Workers' Compensation will cover obvious occupational lung injuries. Payments for medical care, loss of earnings, and permanent partial disability if it exists will all be part of your coverage. But you'll only receive this coverage if you can prove there was a damaging exposure at work and that it caused your problem.

If you suspect you have an occupational lung (pulmonary) problem, first talk to your foreman or supervisor. They may recognize the problem and immediately send you to a physician who can diagnose and help you. But if they don't, then you should see your own doctor (or see Chapter 4 on how to choose a doctor), tell him your symptoms, and ask him to evaluate you for possible inhalational exposure or injury.

Ask at your workplace for the MSDS (Material Safety Data Sheet) for each compound you might be exposed to. By law the MSDS has to be available. It lists the chemical properties of a toxic substance, the toxic effects, and the dangerous doses. Show it to your doctor--this may be enough information to make the diagnosis, or he may need to send you to a specialist for further evaluation.

If the medical opinion is that you have sustained a work-related lung disease or injury, then report it to file a claim.

But be prepared for some difficulty. Only the easily-proven or documented lung injuries will be covered without any questions or investigation. If the exposure wasn't obvious, if your symptoms don't match the expected pattern, or if you have other reasons to have lung disease you may have to work hard to prove your case. If you have confounding factors (see the end of this chapter) you'll have even more difficulty. For example, a heavy smoker with emphysema who tries to prove that dust at work caused his shortness of breath has a tough case to prove.

THE CLUES TO DIAGNOSIS

Almost any occupation can carry some risk of lung injury. There are exposures in American industry to everything from coal dust to chlorine, papaya dust to platinum. Any of hundreds or thousands of substances could be the cause of respiratory symptoms in any given employee.

Many different chemicals can cause similar or different symptoms when they affect the lungs. For example, workers in refrigeration are likely to be exposed to toxic ammonia which causes one kind of lung damage. Workers in printing shops are more likely to be exposed to tragacanth or gum arabic, and from this they develop respiratory allergies. Even the correcting fluid I use as I rewrite this line carries a warning that "Inhalation can be harmful or fatal."

Fortunately the human body has superb defenses against most exposures. And modern workplaces offer far more protections against toxic chemicals than ever before. But lung injuries do still occur, and when they do the symptoms can point the way to the correct diagnosis.

Diagnosis depends not only on the chemical itself but on symptom onset (immediate or delayed) and symptom type (irritating, asphyxiating or allergic, high in the mouth and nose or deep in the lungs). These are all very different and reflect the different modes of action of the toxins.

Doctors get a clue to diagnosis from symptom onset because it shows us whether the toxin is a) acting like an asphyxiant by immediately stopping your breathing, b) is immediately irritating to the lining of your respiratory tract like a soluble chemical, c) is causing a delayed sensitivity reaction, or d) causes symptoms only after years and years of exposure.

The second clue to diagnosis is to look at the symptoms themselves. Was the injury characterized by nose and mouth and throat irritation? That would suggest a soluble irritant. Or were they deep in the chest such as a deep heavy cough and shortness of breath? That would suggest a less soluble irritant.

On the other hand, were the symptoms asthmatic breathing and a tight chest that got worse with every exposure? These would indicate an allergic mechanism. And coughing every day and getting more and more short of breath over the years would suggest chronic lung disease or emphysema due to years of daily exposure to some dust or particle. Examples would be silica, talc, and asbestos. Their action is slow because they aren't soluble at all.

Because there are so many possible exposures and respiratory effects, your doctor will probably use several tests, including chest X-ray and lung scan, breathing tests and some lab work, etc. (see Chapter 8) to help him make the diagnosis.

Still, the information that you can provide will probably turn out to be your doctor's most important clues. Be prepared with notes so you can provide an accurate history to tell the doctor just what happened to you, when it happened and how you felt. Know your exposure history in detail.

If all a patient says is: "My lungs bother me from work, Doc", the doctor has to start working with a hopelessly wide field of possibilities.

But a doctor can do a lot better when a patient tells him something like: "For the past six months every Monday morning when I start work at the cotton plant my chest tightens up. Now it's lasting all week, and I feel like I just can't get enough air. I do get better on the weekends, though". We wouldn't even have to look farther to know this patient probably has bysinnosis: Sensitivity to cotton dust. A good history usually leads to a good diagnosis.

IMMEDIATE LUNG SYMPTOMS: ASPHYXIATION

The patient, Carl, at the beginning of this chapter described a typical H_2S (hydrogen sulfide or sewer gas) exposure: Asphyxiation. H_2S is heavier than air so it collects in low places, it has a rotten egg odor, and it causes symptoms immediately by simply shutting off respiration. It has no irritant effects.

Symptoms can be mild, or they can be fatal depending on the dose and the duration of exposure. A worker exposed to H_2S may recover in the emergency room but then have more serious symptoms starting 24 to 48 hours later. This is what happened to Carl.

> When I saw Carl in my office several weeks later he was slowly recovering, but he still wasn't a well man. He told me how he'd been overcome:
> "I was going in after a load, when I smelled the egg odor. I knew I had to find my mask, 'cause I was already kind of low in the building area. But it was down behind me, and the lower I bent to reach for it the stronger the smell got. I tried to hang on, keep my head up as high as I could, but I guess I started to pass out.
> "I've been weak ever since I got out of the hospital. I still can't breathe right. They told us that sewer gas was heavier than air, but I didn't realize how fast it hits you. It can really do a guy in, can't it"

Carl had acute asphyxiation symptoms. His body's respiration mechanisms were simply shut down by the H_2S. Of course he would have died quickly if he hadn't been rescued by his two buddies who put on respirators to pull him out. He did recover somewhat in the hospital. But then he developed bronchitis, and then later severe pulmonary edema and pneumonia (fluid in the lungs). He was also bothered by chronic fatigue, and was barely recovering six months later. Unfortunately he was then also having heart trouble because of the strain that had been put on his heart.

The industries with exposures to asphyxiants such as H_2S are gas fields, coal mines where it's called "stinkdamp", tanneries and breweries, sewer and liquid manure tanks, felt making, smelters, paper mills and rubber or nylon manufacturing processes.

Almost every agricultural community knows of cases where a farmer is overcome by this gas. His children see him fall and run to help him, yelling to their mom. She calls the rescue team and then goes to help too. But when the team arrives they find all dead of asphyxiation, victims and rescuers alike.

Cyanide gas is another asphyxiant. Cyanide exposures can occur in gold extracting, and the chemical is used in the metal plating industry, in nitrile manufacturing, and in fumigation work where it's used to kill pests. Carbon monoxide is another well-known asphyxiant, found wherever motors are running.

There are specific treatments for some of the asphyxiants, including immediate removal from the toxin and administration of oxygen, but that is too complex a subject for this book.

IMMEDIATE LUNG SYMPTOMS: SOLUBLE CHEMICALS

Soluble toxins' symptoms can be mild in the case of brief exposure or small concentrations, but severe or even fatal in heavy exposures.

They had poured in panic out of the cooling rooms, a few with hastily-donned respirators but most of them coughing, gasping for air, unable to see.

A few made it out with nothing more than stinging eyes and noses. A couple didn't make it out at all. The newspaper headline the next day read: "26 hospitalized, 2 dead from ammonia tank rupture".

History records hundreds of fatal <u>ammonia</u> eposures in ice cream factories and fertilizer plants, and ice skating arenas and refrigeration plants have the same risks. Modern dye, explosives, plastics and chemical factories utilize ammonia and it's also generated in tanning operations.

The human respiratory tract includes mouth, nose, sinuses, throat, trachea and lungs. The tissue in all these areas is moist. A soluble toxin such as ammonia affects these areas immediately. The more soluble and irritating a toxin is, the more it will cause an immediate injury in the areas closest to nose and mouth. This means that if you inhale a strong soluble toxin your sinuses, oral cavity, and throat will be injured immediately.

There are other kinds of immediate irritants that cause severe symptoms. <u>Hydrochloric</u> (muriatic) acid is used in chemical manufacturing and plating, fertilizing and ore refining, metal pickling, textile making, paint and dye making and photography.

<u>Chlorine</u> forms an acid in contact with the respiratory tract and causes choking, coughing, shortness or breath and severe pneumonia. Bleaching processes use chlorine and it's also used in drycleaning, textile making, and water treatment plants.

<u>Hydrofluoric acid</u> is similar in its toxicity. It's used in glass etching, fluorocarbons and plastic manufacturing, making of aluminum and pesticides and in smelting. <u>Hydrogen fluoride</u> is also a primary irritant. So its toxicity is to nose, eyes and lungs with bronchitis, sinusitis and even pulmonary edema.

<u>Sulfur dioxide</u> or SO_2 has a pungent taste because it forms sulfurous acid when it touches the moisture of mouth and moist respiratory tract. It's so soluble that almost all of the symptoms will be high in the mouth, throat and nose. But patients with asthma may be especially sensitive. In all patients there can be an immediate tightening of the upper respiratory tract with a severe shortness of breath. If you work in the woodpulp or smelting industry, with fumigants or disinfectants, or around burning coal you can be exposed to SO_2. In fact 500,000 workers are potentially exposed to this every year.

<u>Nitrogen oxides</u> also form acids in contact with the moist mucus membranes of the respiratory tract. They're found in metal cleaning, welding and explosives or fertilizer making, making of rayon, plating, and

are present wherever auto or truck engines are running. Pulp and paper mills have nitrogen oxides around also.

Most farmers know about silofiller's respiratory injury from silo gas: Nitrogen dioxide and CO_2 are common in a silo and can be extremely toxic to anyone exposed. Most nitrogen oxide compounds produce cough, shortness of breath, headaches, and sometimes very severe symptoms of respiratory distress up to two weeks later. Every year there are a million to a million and a half workers potentially exposed to this toxin.

There are many other irritant compounds with immediate or early toxic effects. <u>Arsenic</u> in pesticides, <u>beryllium</u> in ceramics and ores, <u>boron</u> and <u>cadmi um oxide</u> in welding and smelting, <u>manganese</u> and <u>nickel</u> in chemical plating, <u>phosgene</u> in plastics and pesticides, and <u>xylene</u> in paints, solvents and resin manufacturing all produce varying degrees of upper and lower airway disease. Any can be fatal with severe burning and bronchitis and pneumonia.

For all the simple irritants, the first treatment is immediate removal from the gas. Oxygen is usually necessary depending on the symptoms, hospital observation is usually a good idea and is critical in the more severe pneumonia and pulmonary edema cases.

If you have a lung injury from the more powerful irritants and acids, your body is just going to have to heal on its own with little help from doctors but medical support and treatment of infection or pneumonia.

Needless to say, the healthier your lungs are before such an injury, the better and faster your healing will be. Smokers do exceedingly poorly with irritant respiratory injuries.

If you already have chronic obstructive lung disease (emphysema) and then have a severe inhalational exposure you could get into deep, deep trouble.

ALLERGIC LUNG SYMPTOMS

There is a whole class of occupational respiratory problems that result from an employee being allergic to a substance at work. This type of lung injury or disease is called <u>occupational asthma</u>.

Many things can cause occupational asthma, from red cedar dust to chromium, from <u>teas</u> and <u>spices</u> to <u>TDI</u> (<u>toluene diisocyanate</u>). Some common diseases that are now easily recognized by most everyone affected by them are bird-breeders lung, maple bark stripper's disease, and cheese-washer's lung.

> *Jackie felt like she couldn't breathe. Her chest was getting tight again and she started wheezing. She was shaky, every breath was an effort. This time she went to the doctor.*
>
> *"I can't take much more of this,"she told him. "I get this now every time I walk into the plant. It wasn't this way till a couple of months after we started using that new adhesive. What is this, asthma or something?"*

The way occupational asthma usually develops is as follows: An employee may have no allergies of any sort, or have some minor allergy that's under control. He or she may work with a potentially allergenic substance every day for a while, and still have no problems. But then with repeated exposure the body develops a sensitivity to the chemical and reacts to it.

The two most common parts of the body are those in closest contact with the environment: Skin and lungs. The skin often reacts because of its high surface area and daily exposure (see next chapter).

The lungs have such reactivity because with every breath a person takes in gases and dust and particles. At 15 breaths per minute for eight hours a day, that's 7,000 times every work day, one and half million times every year, that you expose delicate respiratory tissues to potential allergens.

When you become allergic to a workplace chemical, the symptoms could be mild with only a runny or irritated nose or scratchy throat. But with increasing sensitivity you can experience chest tightness, constricted breathing, and on up to a full-blown asthma attack with wheezing and secretions and extreme shortness of breath.

These symptoms may occur immediately after an exposure, which makes the diagnosis easy. But some of these problems are difficult to diagnose because they're delayed reactions--they occur many hours after exposure. One typical delayed type is Farmer's Lung. Six or seven hours after exposure to moldy hay, a farmer will come down with shortness of breath and cough and symptoms that are indistinguishable from a pneumonia. The symptoms go away after several hours or a couple of days, even without treatment. Often a doctor may even think he's treating pneumonia without ever making the true diagnosis.

Treatment for occupational asthma is two-fold. First the symptoms can usually be alleviated with medications, bronchodilators and anti-asthmatics. But second, the obvious and most important treatment is to avoid exposure.

You should also be aware that repeated long term exposure can result in chronic obstructive pulmonary disease or "emphysema".

Some of the substances and typical industries where occupational asthma is a frequent problem are: Aluminum soldering flux in electronics. Flies, insects, and animal hair or dander in outdoor animal processing workers. Hops, tea, sugar cane, castor bean meal, soybean dust, flour or grain dust, malt dust and mushroom compost in the food industry and spices in spice workers. Chromium in casting and chemical manufacturing, nickel and platinum processing. Wood dust--western red cedar, walnut, and the exotics--in furniture making. Pyrethrins in insecticides, proteolytic enzymes in detergent manufacturing or use, orris root in cosmetics, and gum arabic in printing. Epoxy resins in glues, phthalic anhydride in plastics work. Cotton, flax and hemp dust in textile industries.

One of the worst substances for allergic exposure is toluene diisocyanate (TDI) used in polyurethane foam and insulation manufacturing, as coating agents, in upholstery and tentmaking work, paint and linoleum work and industries. After sensitization, exposure to even undetectable amounts of TDI causes severe allergic symptoms. These patients simply have to work elsewhere forever.

Workers' Compensation will usually cover inhalational injuries when the symptoms clearly indicate occupational asthma.

However, even though you may be certain that it's a work injury, the insurance company may not see it your way and the burden of proof that your symptoms come from work exposure is going to be on you. If you have a preexisting history of allergy, particularly if you had asthma or sinusitis in the past, these are called confounding factors. Because of them you will probably face an argument from the insurer. They may point out that you had similar symptoms before, and conclude that the work didn't cause your problems with certainty, and didn't necessarily accelerate your disease. They will be especially adamant about this if you are a smoker.

Depending on how strong the medical evidence for your case is, you might eventually get some compensation for medical care and lost time. But if you also claim permanent damage, be prepared to prove that you had a bona fide injury, that it was solely from work, and that nothing else contributed to your symptoms.

CHRONIC LUNG DISEASE FROM OCCUPATION

Most people have now heard of <u>asbestos</u>. Most people know that exposure to asbestos can cause lung disease, but that it only occurs 20 or 30 years after exposure. Asbestos dust or fiber should no longer be in construction use anywhere. But it is involved in demolition and cleanup where exposure can still occur.

There are actually a number of other dusty or particle type compounds that, with repeated exposure, will eventually lead to one of the chronic obstructive (emphysema) lung problems.

> *Maggie had been in pretty good health most of her life. Occasional bouts of bronchitis, a little smokers' cough, nothing much more. She never had any injuries on her job in the foundry where she'd worked for 30 years.*
>
> *But in her early 50's she had noticed a little less stamina. Then shortness of breath in her late 50's. By retirement she was huffing and puffing most of the time. "You've got emphysema", her doctor told her, "probably from all those cigarettes.*
>
> *"But couldn't it be the sand at the foundry?" Maggie asked. "I breathed that stuff for years. And we never wore masks back then."*

<u>Silica</u> is a dust which causes silicosis, and it's found in mining and outdoor work, stone cutting, and anyplace there is a dusty or sandy enviroment such as farming. <u>Kaolin</u> or china clay is found in quarrying, milling, bagging and loading of the clay; <u>iron oxide</u> plus carbon plus free silica from jewelry making causes silver-finishing disease, and iron oxide is found in welding and steel or foundry work. <u>Beryllium</u> was used in the past in manufacturing fluorescent lamps and caused berylliosis. Lung disease also has come from <u>aluminum</u> in smelting or abrasive manufaturing; <u>tungsten</u> or <u>titanium carbides</u> in cutting tool manufacturing; <u>talc</u> in

the cosmetics or rubber industries; and of course coal dust in coal mining (coal miner's lung or black lung).

The actions of each of these compounds is slightly different. But most cause disease by being inhaled deep into the lungs where they set up a reaction in the lung tissue. Some diseases look worse than they are: Arcwelder's lung causes a frightening picture on X-ray, as does stannosis from tin exposure, but both cause relatively minimal symptoms if any and may never be a problem to the patient.

But with most of the other compounds, over a long time the reaction deep in the lungs leads to scarring. The scarring is at first microscopic, but then increases in size and spreads. The result is called pulmonary fibrosis. This is a thickening and hardening of lung tissue. Fibrosis causes symptoms because it prevents good oxygen uptake and exchange. Long-term occupational asthma with repeated allergic episodes can also cause this "chronic" lung disease.

With dusts and progressive scarring, symptoms usually don't develop till many years after exposure and then get worse with time. Asbestosis can take 20 to 30 years, others take 20 years, some less. The result is usually chronic bronchitis for several years and then ultimately chronic obstructive pulmonary disease (COPD) caused by the fibrosis and reduced breathing and pulmonary function. Symptoms are shortness of breath with exertion early in the bronchitis stage, and then eventually shortness of breath even at rest, accompanied by cough and weight loss. Some occupational respiratory exposures also carry an increased risk of cancer as a delayed effect. These include exposure to asbestos, arsenic, chromium, osmium tetroxide, and coal dust.

Is there any good treatment for these chronic pulmonary problems? You should cease the occupational exposure, of course. You should also improve general physical fitness. These are about all that we can offer.

Smokers naturally have much greater problems with these exposures. For a smoker the risk of cancer from asbestos is multiplied over 100 times. So if you are a smoker and have any suspicion that you have an occupational lung disease, stop smoking today.

Workers' Compensation should cover many pulmonary exposures. But you will likely have a battle on your hands to get much compensation (unless you're a coal miner where the Black Lung Act covers you) because there are so many confounding factors in chronic pulmonary disease.

For example, suppose you have smoked for 30 years and now you have emphysema. How could you prove that your emphysema came from exposure to silica sand in a foundry 15 years ago? Or to the tungsten carbide back when you made cutting tools? You probably won't be able to. Because it's the rule that in Workers' Compensation you as the employee must prove the disability and the cause, you may not have a successful claim.

If you have asbestosis, you may have another kind of wait before your claim is settled. Since there's a latency period of at least 15 years and more like 25 years before symptoms develop, and because you may have many worked in several locations, how can you ever pinpoint which period of exposure was the most responsible for the disease? Asbestos cases often are extremely complicated, they involve dozens of employers and insurers and years of medical records. Right now in the U.S. there are at least 20,000 new asbestos cases filed each year, with hundreds of thousands pending. Some patients may have to wait until 2015 to receive their compensation from one company, Manville.

WRAP-UP

How you can do yourself some favors with occupational lung disease:
1) If you have respiratory symptoms, find out what your exposure is and give your doctor a specific history. You may have occupational lung disease or you may not, but the doctor will need an accurate history to find out;
2) Get away from any serious respiratory exposure. Of course you need your job to put food on the table. But you can last for weeks without food, and your lungs keep you breathing--you have to do that every 14 seconds;
3) If you work where there's any exposure at all, don't smoke!

J

Occupational Skin Injuries

A patient shows the doctor his itching hands. He holds out his fore-arms covered with red bumps, some of them infected: "I've got it on the front of my legs, too, Doc".
"Hmm, I'd say you work as a machinist, don't you?"
"How'd you ever know I do that, Doc?"

Skin injuries are extremely frequent occupational medical problems, almost half of all Workers' Compensation claims for occupational disease according to some authorities. This chapter describes the most common work-related skin conditions, their diagnosis and their treatment.

Though almost any occupation could have associated skin problems, some have more than others by the very nature of the work exposure. The largest of these occupations in terms of numbers of employees in-volved are outdoor work, food and foodstuff handling, and machining or plating work. This chapter describes the skin disorders and exposures of these occupations separately.

WORKERS' COMPENSATION AND SKIN DISEASE

Workers' Compensation benefits will generally cover occupational dermatitis (work-related skin disorders) and pay for treatment, medications, and lost time from work.

Any specific case may not fit the category of "injury", but may not be a typical "illness" either. Some cases are difficult for Workers' Compensation to categorize, and the actual label used will probably depend on what the doctor calls it and on the details of exposure.

Whichever way your dermatitis is classed, it should make no difference to you as long as you are covered by Comp, and Comp will usually cover occupational exposures if they are obvious.

Your employers may prefer to list your problem as an injury rather than an illness, as this will help them keep their occupational illness reports to OSHA in the low numbers. For example, an obvious severe acid burn would undoubtedly be termed an injury. However, delayed basal cell carcinoma on the nose from years of sunlight exposure would more likely be termed an illness.

But just as with any Workers' Compensation injury, the most important thing is to get a firmly established diagnosis. More than with almost any other disease, the diagnosis is the key to treatment and to preventing future problems.

THE FIRST STEP: LOOKING FOR CLUES

The place to start with a skin injury is by attempting to discover the cause of the problem, by narrowing down the list of possible sources. Skin irritants and toxins can occur literally anywhere, in any occupation, to any employee. You and your doctor may have to become detectives to pinpoint the exact cause.

Clues to the diagnosis will come from 1) the location of the rash; 2) the history of the exposure; and 3) the actual symptoms and appearance of the rash itself. The diagnosis can be difficult because many problems look alike.

If you have a rash, where is it? Is it on the arms, hands, face, or legs? The most common areas for occupational dermatitis are on hands and wrists--half of all industrial cases are in these areas. You would expect this, because these areas are exposed often and repeatedly at work.

Forearms and face are second in frequency. The areas with the thinnest skin such as eyelids and face are generally the most susceptible to injury. Genital skin is also thin and sensitive but that area is protected somewhat by clothing. Covered skin areas are last.

It is possible for a doctor to diagnose a few occupational dermatoses merely by their appearance. Skin ulcers that affect chromium workers are called "chrome holes" and are easily recognized by anyone familiar with them. Some patterns of reactions such as rashes that follow clothing lines can also tip off a well informed doctor.

Next clue: What's your exposure history? If your rash is on your hands and forearms, is it because you are up to your elbows in detergent all day? When did you first notice it--what had you been doing just before? The previous day? The previous week? Sometimes an accurate exposure history may be all that's necessary for diagnosis, such as when a patient comes in and says: "Doc, I walked through a thicket of poison ivy and now look at me," or: "I never had a rash in my life until last week when we started doing nickel plating in the shop".

If your rash is on your face, could it be because you've been exposed to irritating dusts or powders at your job? Have you been wearing protective caps? Was there an accidental spill or vapor release? What's the recent history--have you just started using plastics or epoxies?

Are other employees complaining of rashes lately? What job exposures do they have--the same as yours? It could be helpful to simply ask co-workers. If compounds in the workplace have caused skin injuries before, other people will probably remember. Sometimes a union officer will have the same information.

You can help a doctor immensely by knowing the details about exposure. If you do, I recommend you start with your family doctor. If a problem is severe you might ask to see a dermatologist, a skin specialist. He will probably be quite familiar with many workplace skin disorders in the local community.

Third clue area: The symptoms themselves. For almost any skin injury the first symptom will likely be a red and itchy or burning rash. The skin erruption or "dermatitis" (itis means inflammation, derm means skin) will probably be on one of the exposed or sensitive areas.

But the important thing is what the rash looks like. Is it in streaks like poison ivy? Is it red and itchy like an allergy or burning like a burn? Do you have infected pustules, for instance on your forehead? If so the doctor might look for a sunlight and chemical combination or an oil mist at your workplace. Is your skin dry and cracked? If so the doctor would consider daily solvent exposure.

Your doctor will take all the factors of your exposure history, location and appearance of the rash and attempt to combine them into one correct diagnosis.

DISCOVERING THE CULPRIT

It can be quite difficult to sort out all possible toxic skin exposures because there are so many candidates. For instance, if your job brings you into contact with organic or inorganic chemicals they can cause skin damage. But so can animal and plant products, metals, dusts, even light or cold or heat. Home can also carry toxic skin exposures, from kitchen, garage, garden, sports, or hobbies.

> *"Occupational dermatitis": An inflammatory reaction of the skine caused by some agent--chemical, biological or physical--in the workplace. Exposures to a host of various agents may cause identical-appearing reactions.*

To complicate matters further many different toxins or substances can produce identical skin rashes or pustules or ulcers. The symptoms or appearance of the lesions themselves may not provide enough information to make the diagnosis. Usually getting the diagnosis will require more information.

You can help the doctor most by knowing the names of the chemicals and other substances you come into contact with at work. If you can tell the doctor: "I work with light cutting oils on my machining job and we clean up all our tools in trichloroethylene twice a day", it gives him a lot more information than if you just say, "There's some kind of liquid at work that bothers me".

To locate chemical names, the most valuable source will be Material Safety Data Sheets (MSDS's) These sheets list the known toxic effects and chemical names of all substances used in your workplace. You can get MSDS's from your foreman or employer by asking for them--by federal law they must be readily available. MSDS's may also be available from some unions. An MSDS can help your doctor by describing possible skin toxicity damage and will list the concentrations and doses of the substances that are toxic to skin.

Even with all this information, a dermatologist may still do further studies to finally nail down the diagnosis. The most likely will be <u>patch testing</u>: He'll apply tiny amounts of several potential skin toxins, including the ones you've been exposed to, to your skin. This will probably be on your forearm, thigh, or upper back. The test areas are then covered.

Patch tests are read in one or two days. The doctor will look for redness, irritation, or a rash that signifies a positive patch. This identifies the substance as one that does in fact cause dermatitis on your skin. If it matches a known exposure at work, and your history also matches, you almost surely have found your culprit.

The only remaining tasks are to treat your symptoms and to find out how or why the substance injured your skin.

WHY SKIN IS INJURED

Skin acts as a barrier between the inside of our body and the whole world outside. It serves us pretty well in this capacity: Liquids flow off us because skin has an oily component that repels water. Almost no fluid can get through skin easily. Skin covers a huge area, many square feet in surface, and absorbs some excess heat and cold rather than allow inside tissues be damaged.

Skin is a barrier to most natural substances. It grows by itself and you almost never have to even think about it. It stretches in every direction and enlarges (or shrinks) as you do. Skin doesn't really wear out; in fact it's self-renewing. Skin even regenerates itself quickly when it's damaged.

In fact it's precisely because skin has such a large surface area and performs all these barrier functions that skin problems are so common: Skin always takes the brunt of the injury so the rest of the body doesn't have to. If it weren't there as a guardian, any toxic substance could burn, blister, dry, irritate and destroy all your internal tissues and be a treat to life.

But because skin is available to take the hits, occupational dermatitis is common. It's exposed to the environment from every angle. Oils, dusts, tars and smoke settle on it. The sun shines on it. Toxic plants rub against it. We plunge our hands and arms into our work. We let our clothes accumulate chemicals and metal dusts and powders and wear them all day or longer, letting them chafe against our skin.

We use solvents that defat our skin, robbing it of its barrier properties. We spill caustic acids or alkalis on it that cause burns. We expose our arms and hands and face day after day to substances that eventually set off an allergic reaction. It's hardly any mystery why skin injuries are so common.

In fact one way to think about any occupational dermatitis could be: "Great! My skin did its job. It kept me safe".

Even though the skin is subject to such varied exposures, it generally responds with only a few basic patterns of injury: Inflammation, burning and scarring, infection, or long-term effects such as cancer.

There are four fundamental mechanisms by which toxic substances can cause dermatitis:

1) Simple irritation (contact dermatitis);
2) Absolute irritation with destruction (also contact dermatitis);
3) Allergy formation (allergic contact dermatitis);
4) Cancer formation.

CONTACT DERMATITIS: IRRITANT

The simplest mechanism of skin injury is by irritation and is called contact irritant dermatitis. This is caused when chemicals or other agents simply irritate the skin but do not destroy it.

"Well, now that you mention it, Doctor, I have been doing an awful lot of overtime work in the processing room. Do you think it could be those fluids on my arms all the time that are causing this?"

Agents that can cause contact irritation and dermatitis include <u>resins</u>, <u>mild acids</u> <u>and alkalis</u>, <u>nuts and fruits</u>, some metals such as <u>antimony</u> and <u>zinc chloride</u> and <u>chromium</u>, <u>gasoline</u>, many <u>woods</u>, <u>poison oak</u>, <u>solvents and oils</u>, etc. (Some also cause skin allergy: see next page.)

These things are all "relative irritants", which means that the amount of damage will be related to the amount of exposure, and repeated or heavy exposure causes more irritation. The problems of contact dermatitis account for at least three-fourths of all occupational skin disease. They are fairly easy to treat, see below.

Contact Dermatitis: Destructive

There are also more severe skin injuries from "absolute" irritants: Compounds that will always and immediately damage human skin. Examples of absolute irritants would be strong acids such as <u>sulfuric acid</u> and strong alkalis such as <u>lye</u> and <u>lime</u>. These compounds can produce disease similar to a severe thermal burn, they can destroy skin by their action or dissolve the fatty layer of the skin itself. <u>Mercury, arsenic and chromium salts</u> can also destroy the skin and produce ulcerations.

The usual medical treatment for both relative and absolute or destructive contact dermatitis is to treat the injury, with a steroid cream or ointment. If an infection develops, antibiotics may be required. A severe burn may necessitate skin grafting.

However, the most important treatment is to prevent repeat injury by avoiding exposure.

You can avoid exposure to irritants and destructive chemicals several ways. You could work in another area or on a different process. You could wear protective clothing, gloves, or shields. For example if your job requires you to use cutting oils you could try wearing impervious aprons or smocks. You could even consider changing clothes once during the day. I know this sounds like a bother, but it will keep your exposure to oil-saturated pants and shirts at a minimum. And in some jobs you could perhaps find substitute products or compounds.

ALLERGIC CONTACT DERMATITIS

The third type of occupational dermatitis is <u>allergic contact dermatitis</u>. It's possible to become allergic to almost any substance on earth. The process goes like this: Some substance gets on your skin and causes no initial reaction. But that substance may be an allergen, which means that with repeated contact your body develops an allergy, or hypersensitivity, to it. Eventually every time you come in contact with it there's a reaction, a skin eruption which gets more severe every time.

> *"No, I never had anything like this before. I think it's because I've been around the new adhesives so much in the plant. It seems to be getting worse each time I go in there."*

These allergic problems are often called occupational eczema. When they occur, you remain sensitized for life. If you are what doctors call an atopic individual--a person who already has allergy problems such as eczema--your risk of developing true occupational allergic dermatitis may be greater. (However, there is controversy over this.)

<u>Nickel</u> allergy is the most well-known example of occupational skin allergy. But the list of other offenders is literally endless: <u>Other metals, woods and wood dust, plant and animal tissue, cheese, fungus, oils, rubber, plastics, cosmetics, shampoos</u>, etc.

Treatment for allergic dermatitis is to first treat the skin injury itself, usually with appropriate creams; and to avoid repeat exposure afterward. Ways to avoid exposure are to change job processes, change job locations, wear impervious clothing, etc. Keep the allergenic substances from building up on your skin and clothing. Wash off every trace of chemical or dust and change clothes frequently. And of course make sure you are not actually allergic to something from some home, recreation, or hobby exposure. Some people, such as hairdressers, must simply change occupations.

SKIN CANCER

Skin cancer can result from exposure to several chemicals and ultraviolet light. The classic occupational skin cancer was first discovered in 1775 by Percival Pott. He found that young chimney sweeps in London were developing cancer of the scrotum. It turned out this was from daily heavy exposure to soot and coal tar in the chimneys. Anyone who works with coal tar, creosote, heavy mineral oil or similar products is at some increased risk for eventual skin cancer. Some oils and greases, exposure to ultraviolet light, and in particular the combination of UV light plus grease also potentially cause cancer.

Most substances that are carcinogenic to skin, like coal tar, probably have a latency period of six to ten years before they produce symptoms. Long-term exposure to coal tars produces "tar warts" on hands, forearms and face and these may result in cancer after several years. Tars are also likely to cause cancer problems when there is long-term exposure to sun or ultraviolet light.

Most occupational skin cancers are basal cell carcinomas, though a few are the much more dangerous squamous cell cancers.

Cancer-causing agents often found in industry are benzo(a)pyrene and dibenz(a,h)anthracene. Exposure to arsenic (which enters the body in drinking water rather than through the skin) could cause skin cancer also. Excessive industrial X-ray exposure can also cause skin cancer.

Occupations that carry exposures to skin cancer-causing agents are work in refineries, coke ovens, and with asphalt. In addition machinists, agricultural workers, brick makers and dye makers, drug manufacturers, employees in the tobacco industy, and plastics workers are at risk.

Treatment of occupational skin cancer is usually surgical removal of the cancer. This is usually successful if performed early enough.

The most important treatment is preventive: Avoiding exposure. Because of the long latency period of carcinogens you should prevent exposure over the years by avoiding repeated contact with these materials, especially in combination with the sun.

SPECIAL PROBLEMS OF OUTDOOR WORK

Outdoor work contains numerous potential toxic skin exposures. Poison oak or poison ivy is the most common skin injury, in fact it causes up to 50% of the industrial skin cases in agricultural states such as California. About two-thirds of the population of the United States is sensitive to poison oak's irritating and blistering oils.

Diagnosis and treatment of poison oak is usually easy: There's usually a clear history of exposure, and all the doctor has to do is look at the red and raised lines along the patient's scratch marks!

Treatment of poison oak is usually fairly easy: Steroid creams and antihistamines, or perhaps steroid pills by mouth if the case is severe or near the patient's eyes. Naturally, the best treatment is to prevent the exposure by learning to recognize the leaves and avoiding them or wearing protection.

There are zillions of other agricultural sources of skin irritation: Chrysanthemums, primroses, tulips, tree bark and lichen, sagebrush, nut and fruit tree bark. Forestry workers and furniture makers know that cedar, redwood and walnut are often irritating and sensitizing but that exotic imported woods with their dusts and oils can be worse.

Outdoor farm and agricultural workers can also receive severe burns from lime or strong disinfectants and some pesticides. A daily part of outdoor work also includes heavy exposure to sun and wind which results in dried out skin, chapping, sunburn, and blistering. Construction workers can develop skin burns from sun or from the alkalinity of cement or by becoming allergic to the chromium in some cement preparations. Fiberglass insulation particles can irritate skin.

Other risks of outdoor work include skin infections from tiny mites in grain, barley cuts from the sharp parts of barley that act like fiberglass, and skin cancer from chronic sun exposure.

Treatment is usually fairly straightforward: Treat the skin damage and then avoid exposure.

MACHINING, MANUFACTURING AND PLATING PROBLEMS

Cutting and lubricating oil dermatitis is probably one of the most common industrial skin injuries. These fluids are used in large volumes, spattered around, and they often saturate the workplace and the employees' clothing. The symptoms are an irritated red pustular skin eruption over the hands and forearms and thighs where the clothes are soaked and the skin stays in constant contact with oils. The disease is called "oil folliculitis" because the oil plugs and then inflames the skin pores or follicles.

Other oils, tool cleaners, and solvents may produce drying and chapping or blistering of hands because they defat the skin and take away its resiliency and its imperviousness. Most solvents cause a contact dermatitis by simple primary direct irritation, not by allergy.

The most common irritant solvents are gasoline and kerosene, diesel fuel, coal tar solvents such as xylol and toluol, turpentine, alcohol and ketones, methylene chloride and trichloroethylene.

In manufacturing processes employees can be exposed to ethers which cause burns and blisters or phenolic resins that sensitize the skin and lead to allergic dermatitis. The phenolic resins are found in brake linings and clutch parts and are often used as a binder in foundry sand. Other manufacturing processes utilize carbolic acid or phenol and these act like any acids and produce burns. Acid cleaners and etchers such as hydrochloric or hydrofluoric acid also cause severe chemical burns.

Employees in the plating industry probably are alert to the fact that chromic acid produces a contact dermatitis and ulcers known as chrome holes. These may not be painful but are slow to heal. Chromium also can cause an allergic reaction. So can nickel. Plating operations also utilize acids which cause burns.

Some workers with antimony, particularly antimony miners, will develop a typical skin irritation in sweaty areas of clothing friction and this disease is known as "antimony spots". Antimony is also used in rubber compounding, flame proofing, and as an alloy of tin, copper and lead. Employees who manufacture dyes or paints also can be exposed to antimony.

Treatment is to use creams or medications for the skin problems and then avoid repeat exposure.

DERMATITIS OF ANIMAL, PLANT, AND FOOD PRODUCT WORKERS

Workers in these areas are exposed to a host of potential skin toxins, all the way from the most basic production of the foodstuff to its kitchen preparation.

Animal carcasses and pelts can expose employees to parasites, anthrax spores, infections, and other irritating or allergenic substances. Meat and fish protein can cause skin allergies. Poultry processing produces frequent minor skin infections. Fish and shellfish workers in processing plants and restaurant kitchens can become allergic to this material.

Cheese makers can develop skin irritations from rennet, and cooks can become sensitive to spices, garlic, onions, and flours. A fungus infection (candida) is common with kitchen employees, dishwashers and bartenders, etc. Landscape and nursery workers have exposure to other kinds of fungus (for example with roses), and anyone working with live animals is exposed to ringworm.

Any employee who spends much time washing can develop irritation from the alkalinity of detergents and can become allergic to them. Sometimes these employees will wear rubber gloves to protect their skin, but then they can develop a sensitivity to rubber gloves as well. Those who can't avoid soap exposure should use low temperature water and should avoid prolonged contact with the material that is irritating and should never allow detergents or cleansers to remain on the skin.

Plant and animal substances can cause occupational dermatitis by the irritant phenomenon but more commonly it's by causing an allergy.

Treatment is to use skin creams and medications to cure the rash. The best treatment is always to prevent the problem by avoiding repeat exposure.

WRAP-UP

How to do yourself some favors with skin injuries:
1) There are hundreds or thousands of potential occupational exposures to skin damaging substances. Get as much information as you can to track down the one that caused your symptoms;
2) If your skin problem doesn't respond to basic treatment, or the diagnosis remains elusive, get medical specialty help from a dermatologist;
3) Keep your workplace, clothes and skin clean and free from the offending agent;
4) Try not to scratch!

L

Toxic Work Exposures

The emergency room radio came to life, the nurses heard the siren over the paramedic's urgent voice: "Base, Unit 6. We're transporting an approximately 18-year-old male in profound coma, vomitus in the oral cavity. Cardiac rhythm regular at 150, blood pressure 40/0, respirations irregular and now approximately three per minute. We have oxygen running."

"THIS IS A PRESUMED TOXIC EXPOSURE. We're proceeding Code 3. Our ETA your facility is six minutes. Request you have full cardiac arrest team standing by."

The nurses looked at each other as they hurried to prepare: "Wonder if we'll be able to pull this kid through?"

Many workplaces contain materials that are potentially toxic if used without protection or if there is accidental exposure.

In this chapter I'll show you how to recognize some of the more common workplace toxins and describe typical symptoms of exposure to them.

Workers' Compensation And Toxic Exposures

Workers' Compensation will usually cover a toxic exposure, especially when it's obvious and causes a dramatic toxic illness. For example, an acute case of pesticide poisoning or solvent coma will be obvious. The Workers' Compensation insurance carrier will probably consider this kind of exposure an "injury" rather than an illness. Benefits will pay for medical care, medications, hospital stay if any, and lost time from work. This kind of an exposure problem fits the compensation model of an injury event.

> *An employee is discussing the denial of his claim: "My buddy got poisoned at work and he got his benefits all right. But now I've got this liver problem, and they're denying my claim. How come?"*

Workers' Compensation may not cover more subtle illnesses, the ones that could come from chronic low level toxic exposures. For example, exposures to low levels of lead over several years might finally become symptomatic. But in such a case of toxic illness (as opposed to an acute injury), compensation coverage may require that the patient prove the exposure caused the illness. It may be difficult to do so, and benefits may therefore be hard to obtain.

There are several reasons for toxic illness claims not being accepted. The most common is just plain uncertainty as to whether there really was an exposure or not. With other illnesses, especially when the toxic effects take a long time to develop, there may be a question of which insurer was covering the workplace at the time of most significant exposure.

In addition, some toxic exposures may be chronic and never documented. Comp benefits would be very difficult to obtain for such cases. Some toxic illnesses only develop in a few workers out of several thousand exposed, and Comp carriers are (understandably) reluctant to provide benefits to every employee who has symptoms that only might be related to the exposure.

And some individuals may actually have a bona fide toxic illness, but they also have "confounding factors" that make it impossible to determine whether a personal health problem caused a portion of their symptoms. For example, an employee may have liver disease and feel it is from exposure to Carbon Tetrachloride. But if the compensation carrier feels the liver problem may actually be due to alcohol abuse, they may not cover the claim.

A 1991 study showed <u>four and a half times greater claim rejection</u> for occupational diseases than for injury. Nevertheless, almost all states' Workers' Compensation laws do include coverage for some, most, or even all occupational illnesses. The way to find out if your state has coverage is to call or write your state Workers' Compensation office, using the telephone numbers and addresses in Chapter 24.

IF YOU SUSPECT YOU HAVE A TOXIC EXPOSURE

Follow the steps I recommended in Chapter 4 about reporting your injury. If you experienced an obvious toxic exposure and there's no doubt that it caused your symptoms, report the injury to file your claim, just as you would with any work injury.

But if you only suspect you have become ill from a toxic exposure, I recommend you see your doctor first. See the doctor as early as you possibly can. The more days and weeks that go by after a toxic exposure, the harder it will be for him to pick up the trail. The more time it takes to get the diagnosis, the less likely your chance of getting Workers' Compensation coverage.

Tell the doctor your symptoms and your reasons for suspecting a toxic injury and use the information in this chapter. He may be familiar with the more common toxic exposures in your community. If he confirms that you do in fact have an occupational illness, then go ahead and report the problem as soon as you can.

> *"I saw the doctor and told him about my exposure. But I don't think he had any idea what I was talking about, even what chemicals we use. Said he'd look it up if he could find a book that had it. I don't think I'm going to get anywhere this way."*

You may need to ask your own doctor for a referral to a physician familiar with toxic problems. This could be an Occupational Medicine specialist, or in larger cities it could be a toxicologist. Such physicians are hard to find because toxicology is a complex and specialized field and the possible number of exposures and combinations of exposures is so immense.

It can almost require a small reference library even to evaluate one patient.

When you see the doctor, bring him a list of the chemicals and metals and other compounds that you are exposed to most often at work. You can get these lists from your foreman or your employer by asking for the MSDS (Material Safety Data Sheet) for every substance you work with. The employer must by federal law have this material available. A union will probably also have MSDS's for your workplace.

An MSDS will show you and your doctor the chemical names of the toxic materials in your workplace. It will also describe the chemicals' properties and the forms in which they are usually encountered. The MSDS will describe the compounds' toxic doses and the effects on humans. If you can give your doctor all relevant MSDS's for your presumed exposures, they will be an immense help to him as he tries to find the diagnosis. MSDS's will also help you back up a compensation claim later.

Your doctor will try to track down the correct diagnosis through a combination of your history and MSDS information, his physical examination, and undoubtedly some lab tests. The effect of some toxins, for example lead or organophosphate pesticides, can be tested for specifically by blood work. For many other toxins, no tests are available. However, some blood tests might provide indications that some internal damage has been done, and from that information your doctor may be able to make the diagnosis.

But I still often have to warn patients with mild symptoms and an uncertain exposure history that we may never be able to find any effects of toxic exposure. I have to tell patients with some presumed toxic illnesses that there may be no lab procedure that will show what happened to them, and that we may never be able to document either their exposure or their illness. I have to tell some patients that they may feel toxic effects, the most common being dizziness or mild nausea or fatigue, but that the human body is far more sensitive than many lab tests and their exposure may simply go undocumented.

THE BROAD RANGE OF TOXIC EXPOSURES

You could divide toxins into two basic types: Those that cause sudden and acute symptoms as opposed to those that work slowly or cause delayed symptoms. (The fact is that toxicology is hundreds of times more complicated than this, that <u>anything</u> could be toxic in large enough doses--even water for example--and that even the most potent toxin isn't a bit of hazard as long as it's safely contained, that toxicity of any compound depends a great deal on the health of the exposed individual and the properties of the toxin at the time, that toxins can have multiple effects, and so on. But for the purposes of this chapter we'll describe toxins only this way: Immediate versus slow or delayed.)

ACUTE OR IMMEDIATE SYMPTOMS

These are the toxic poisonous exposures that sound so scary to people, that send people to the hospitals, that lead to damaged eyes or livers or bone marrow or that cause fatalities. Newspapers report these in big print: "Hundreds Hospitalized When Storage Vat Leaks"; "Toxic Gas Causes Evacuation of Entire Factory"; "Deadly Chemical Found in Runoff"; "Workers Exposed, Three Injured Seriously"; and so on.

These exposures produce immediate signs and symptoms, patients feel faint or nauseated, dizzy or in extreme cases develop lethargy and coma or even death.

People are frightened of this kind of toxic exposures and with good reason. There are plenty of industrial chemicals that will cause serious injury or death in a sudden massive exposure. <u>Methylene Chloride</u>, <u>Carbon Monoxide</u>, <u>Hydrogen Cyanide</u>, <u>Organophosphates</u>, and many solvents are in this category.

Symptoms of this kind of toxic exposure can range from mild to severe to fatal, and these exposures can affect virtually any area of the body depending on the substance. For example, Carbon Monoxide causes asphyxiation, solvents cause neurologic symptoms of sluggishness or coma, etc. (See Special Section E).

SLOW OR DELAYED SYMPTOMS

This kind of toxin shows no immediate signs after exposure. Rather they manifest their symptoms slowly or after accumulation of the toxin over years, or even after a long latent period in some cases. These toxic exposures are more difficult to document because an employee can continue his job for years and then develop symptoms that are related only to an exposure many years earlier.

"I saw this article, Doc. It said there's a higher amount of heart disease in people who do my kind of work. It said that chemical exposure years ago caused it. Do you think that could be my problem?"

Lead is the classic example of a slow-acting toxin. Daily very low exposure to lead causes a buildup of the toxin in the body, and symptoms eventually become noticable after many months or even years.

A few massive exposures to some carcinogen, or perhaps to radiation, might not cause any symptoms until eventually the exposed employee develops cancer. Arsenic is another slow-acting substance that builds up in the system and eventually causes symptoms. Mercury and Manganese are others that manifest their effects slowly or late.

A MULTIPLICITY OF TOXIC SOURCES

Almost any industry--heavy or light, low tech or high tech--can involve potential toxic exposure. Chemicals, dust, metals, fumes and gases are everywhere in our world of work.

A recent (1990) study by a private research organization in Chicago, The National Safe Workplace Institute, reported that in one year there were 390,000 job-related illnesses. Using figures from the U.S. Office of Technological Assessment they concluded that these occupational illness result in as many as 100,000 deaths every year, nearly twice the number from all motor vehicle accidents.

It's virtually impossible to list all the effects that industrial compounds could have, partly because there are so many and partly because we don't know. There are more than 50,000 chemicals "in commerce" (used commercially in the U.S.). Every year approximately 5,000 are discarded but 5,000 new ones take their place, so the list is always changing.

Unfortunately, toxicologists can't keep up with it and we only know the toxicology of a couple of hundred of the chemicals at most. Rather depressingly, we know little or nothing about the possible effects of mixtures of these 50,000 chemicals.

Toxins can affect any area of the body: Lungs (see Section E), skin (see Section F), the nervous system, blood or bone marrow, kidney, liver, bone, reproductive organs, etc. Some chemicals and metals are carcinogenic: Causing cancer after a latency period.

The rest of this chapter describes a few of the major kinds of toxic illnesses, in particular the ones that affect the nervous system, and lists some of the more common toxic substances found in industry.

NEUROTOXINS

It's been known for years that toxins at work can affect behavior. Back in the 19th century the phrase "mad as a hatter" was common because the making of felt hats required mercury, and mercury exposure causes mental abnormalities. It causes people to act oddly, sometimes timid and sometimes bizarre, and causes sensory and vision disturbances as well.

There are hundreds of other industrial chemicals that affect the nervous system. In the past 50 years grain fumigaters and viscose rayon workers have been exposed to arsenic and Carbon Disulfide, another chemical that can cause damage to almost every part of the nervous system. Employees exposed to Carbon Disulfide experience numbness, weakness, confusion, and they can even develop psychosis or suicidal tendencies. Many were considered mentally ill for years because their toxic exposure was never suspected.

Methylene Chloride is another neurotoxin, nearly ubiquitous in industry. It's used as a cleaner and grease remover, in hair sprays and aerosols. In any year there are approximately 600 million pounds of Methylene Chloride manufactured, 200 million pounds for paint stripper alone.

Methylene Chloride exposure is usually a case of a worker breathing fumes in a poorly ventilated area and being overcome. Depending on the degree of exposure, the symptoms can be similar to being very drunk: Dizziness, headache and nausea. Too great an exposure and these symptoms change to respiratory depression and then unconsciousness and eventually coma. In addition to these neurologic effects, a worker could fall unconscious in the fluid and suffer extensive first and second degree burns. Death is not uncommon from severe Methylene Chloride exposures, but neither is full recovery.

Dramatic symptoms but full recovery is typical of many neurotoxic exposures. They can be severe or even deadly in the acute phase but recovery can also be complete with no lasting effects that can be seen. Many times employees return to work as if nothing ever happened, though they are of course usually very careful to avoid any repeat exposure.

Carbon Monoxide is another well-known poison which can cause sleepiness, unconsciousness or death. It's found wherever internal combustion motors are running, but also can be found in any industry that involves flames, burning, smelting, etc. Carbon Monoxide can cause severe illness or even death, but individuals can also fully recover from Carbon Monoxide exposure.

Many other common solvents and chemicals also affect the nervous system. Some of these can cause long-lasting neurologic damage also. Organophosphates are such. These are common insecticides that cause acute poisoning that can be fatal to severely exposed agricultural workers. Recovery can be extremely slow, taking months.

Compounds causing neurologic damage are found in occupations as diverse as auto painting and tool making, ink and cosmetic manufacturing, rubber making, etc. The list of possible neurotoxins is so long and varied that I can only mention a few more here: Lead causes headaches, seizures, muscle weakness and abdominal symptoms. Methyl n-butyl ketone causes muscle weakness and cramps and fatigue. Manganese toxicity causes Parkinsonism, as does Carbon Disulfide. DDT, Kepone and others can cause tremors. Toluene, Chlordane, and Acrylamide can cause a staggering gait. Arsenic and Styrene and many solvents can cause irritability and sensory damage.

LIVER, KIDNEY, REPRODUCTIVE SYSTEM, BLOOD, CANCER

Some toxins cause damage to systems other than the nervous system. Carbon Tetrachloride is used in dry cleaning plants and in many other industries as a solvent. It is a liver-damaging toxin and is most commonly is used as a model for liver damage in lab experiments. It also can cause cancer after a latent period. Other liver toxins are vinyl chloride, Dioxin, TNT and epoxy resins.

Kidney toxins include Ethylene Glycol, found in antifreeze, and also Mercury, Chloroform, Chromium, Cadmium, and Uranium. Many solvents and alcohols and other compounds can cause damage to reproductive organs and reproductive tissues: The result is infertility. This can affect males as well as females, depending on the toxin.

Other toxins have effects on the blood system. These cause loss of blood cells, anemia, and some even cause leukemia. Chronic <u>benzene</u> poisioning causes leukemia, and other common blood system toxins include <u>Nitrofurans</u>, <u>aniline dyes</u>, <u>naphthol</u>, <u>quinones</u>, and <u>quinine</u>. There are some metals that also cause blood damage including <u>mercury</u>, <u>copper</u>, <u>lead</u>, and <u>arsine</u> vapor.

Carcinogens (cancer-causing agents) are another huge group of chemicals that include <u>Dioxane</u> and <u>Benzene</u> which are solvents, <u>Thioamides</u> which are food additives, <u>aflatoxins</u> that occur in certain moldy grains, the metal <u>nickel</u> found in nickel mining and jewelry making, and others. Some industrial processes, for example those that use <u>radiation</u>, can be carcinogenic as well. In fact a recent (1990) study by Dr. David Garabrant at the University of Michigan reported that men who work with metal and wood dusts had higher risks of bowel cancer.

TREATMENT OF TOXIC EXPOSURES

As to treatment of toxic illnesses, unfortunately there is no way I could list here the management of all these problems. The chemicals and the diseases are so numerous and varied that there's not one overall type of treatment for all toxic exposures.

Some toxins do have specific treatments: lead poisoning can be countered, there is an "antidote" for some organophosphate poisoning, carbon monoxide toxicity can be "treated" with oxygen, etc. But there are many other toxic exposures that just have to be treated by supporting the injured employee and waiting until his body recovers.

And some toxins have no treatment. For example there is nothing to do for massive liver damage due to carbon tetrachloride exposure.

The most important part of treatment is prevention. Always be alert for any potential work exposure and stay away from it if you can. Make sure you use fume hoods and exhaust ventilators whenever you use solvents. Wear respirators or supplied air face masks when you work with any toxic liquid or dust.

Cover your exposed skin to prevent absorption of toxins from all kinds of metals, dusts, liquids, and volatile compounds.

Some other precautions are simple but effective: Don't eat in the same place you work, wash your hands to remove toxic chemicals or metals or dust and then eat in a clean place. Leave your work clothes at work. I've seen patients' families become sick because of coveralls saturated with pesticides and hung in the kitchen or front hall to "air out".

If you believe there is a problem with toxic exposure in your workplace that is not being addressed, or if you need more information about some toxicity you might be able to get some information from your local OSHA (Occupational Safety and Health Administration) office by calling them for advice. Every state has an OSHA office, and their personnel be extremely helful to you. But I recommend that before you ask OSHA for information, work with your foreman, union, and employer to sort out whether or not there is any toxic exposure present.

WRAP-UP

How to do yourself some favors with workplace toxicity:
1) Take workplace exposure seriously. If someone says "I've been using that chemical for years and I never had any problems", he probably does have a problem but he just doesn't know it yet;
2) Use ventilated areas, wear protection, leave toxic materials where they are: At work. Eat in a separate area from your work. Change clothes and wash off toxins before you go home;
3) An MSDS can help your doctor more than almost any other information you can give him. Take an MSDS for each chemical with you when you seek medical care.

J

Noise, Heat, Cold, Radiation, Infection

"I never realized how close to the environment we are. It seems to be all around us!"

...Anonymous

Some physical environments are potentially injurious. Environmental injuries can occur from too much noise exposure, radiation exposure, extremes of heat and/or cold, and from infectious contacts.

This chapter describes jobs and environments that could have significant exposures to these physical agents. This chapter also describes the most common injuries and treatments.

Workers' Compensation & Environmental Injuries

The problems in this chapter blurs the line between <u>occupational injury</u> and <u>occupational illness</u> perhaps more than even the toxicity problems in Section G. Environmental "injuries" are much more difficult to document--or to prove--than strains and sprains and even the occupational back problems I described in other chapters.

These problems blur the line because there is often no clear-cut injury, nor often an obvious cause-and-effect relationship between the work and the illness. There may be years after an initial environmental exposure before the illness shows up, and even then the illness might be one that occurs from other causes, without any relationship to work exposures.

In addition, historically Workers' Compensation laws were written to provide benefits for work <u>injuries</u>--obvious traumatic events--and work illlnesses were left out of coverage. Because of all this blurring, Workers' Compensation may not cover some of the problems in this chapter.

> *"But Doctor, of course this thyroid cancer is because of my exposure on the job. It must be--I don't think it could be from anything else. No-one in my family has cancer."*
> *The doctor, however, knew it was much more likely a non-work problem.*
>
> * * *
>
> *"Doc, I <u>know</u> my hearing's bad, but it's because of the presses I worked with 20 years ago. We didn't wear protection back then. It can't be just because I'm getting old."*

The blurring of the line between injury and illness is also due to "non-specificity of disease": This means that people can have conditions (such as hearing loss) that <u>seem to</u> be the same as symptoms from work exposure, but that simply come naturally with age or from other causes we don't understand yet. When similar problems also naturally, it could be even more difficult to get Workers' Compensation to cover a problem as work-related.

Most physical/environmental problems lack the cut-and-dried simplicity of a work injury. To put it most bluntly, it would be an obvious occupational <u>injury</u> if a patient is hit on the head by a falling tool, or if he's in an explosion and his eardrum is ruptured, or he walks into a nuclear reactor and dies of radiation sickness two days later.

But it's not at all so clear in occupational <u>illness</u> if a person claims his hearing loss is due to 30 years of machine noise, or if he has cataracts that he claims are due to infrared exposure, or he has some cancer that he thinks is due to 20 years of industrial X-ray exposure. These problems <u>might</u> be occupational, but that will have to be proven by the patient before he can get benefits.

The critical factor is often primarily one of time: If a physical or environmental exposure produces problems in a short time (or instantaneously) then it's an obvious occupational injury or illness. But if it takes months or years it could in fact be a naturally occurring condition and Workers' Compensation may balk at covering it.

There's yet another reason that causes difficulty with Comp coverage: <u>Confounding factors</u> that confuse the issue. A confounding factor is a personal health problem or disease that could also cause the same problem as the occupational exposure. For example, suppose an employee claims hearing loss from punch press exposure but also is an avid hunter. The hearing loss could be due to either noise exposure, so Workers' Compensation may deny the claim. Or suppose a patient claims occupational cataracts but is also 75 years old. The cataracts could simply be due to age. Or suppose a patient claims occupational hepatitis but also used intravenous drugs in the past. Either could cause the disease.

Follow the same guidelines as in Sections E, F, and G on helping a doctor sort out these issues of causation.

Each case of possible occupational environmental exposure will have to be decided on its own merit based on the symptoms, history, and the Workers' Compensation laws in the state. Some occupational environmental illnesses will eventually be covered, but others will not be. This may not seem fair if you have one of the problems, but this is how it often is.

NOISE

Noise (an annoying or injurious sound level) is a common work problem. The usual difficulty is that there's too much of it.

Surprisingly, there are really almost no natural sounds that cause hearing damage. All the damaging sounds have man-made sources such as manufacturing, transporting, blasting, hunting, recreation, racing, chainsawing, etc.

The most common noise injury is <u>hearing loss</u>. Prolonged noise can cause damage to the inner part of the ear, the sensory fibers or possibly the blood supply of the inner ear (the cochlea). This usually causes a temporary decrease in hearing activity. If noise is loud enough, if exposure is frequent and long enough, permanent hearing loss will be the result.

OSHA allows 85 decibels (dB) exposure before jobsite measurement and personal protection is required. The eight-hour time-weighted average can be 90 dB. But there can be no human exposure of 115 dB for more than 15 minutes, and there can be no impact exposure (sudden or sharp sounds) greater than 140 dB.

By contrast, rustling leaves are 20 dB, average speech is 45 dB, traffic noise is 75 dB, and presses are 100 to 115 dB.

Noise-induced hearing loss is painless, insidious, and not even noticed until several low frequencies are affected. But by then the higher (4,000 Hz) frequencies are also gone and it's too late for prevention or treatment.

The symptoms of noise-induced loss are decreased ability to hear speech, particularly when there is background noise. Later effects include perception of <u>increased</u> loudness of <u>loud</u> sounds. The latest stage is tinnitus (ringing in the ears). Unfortunately, this type of hearing loss may not be helped by hearing aids. The problem is actually one of perceiving the clarity of speech, rather than the sound itself.

Other noise-induced problems might include hypertension, generalized muscle contraction, and psychological effects including anxiety, annoyance with the noise, a sense of isolation and also a feeling of danger when unable to hear warnings or instructions.

Treatment for noise-induced hearing loss includes trial of a hearing aid to see if it helps. But there is little else to do once it occurs. Treatment is primarily preventive: Wearing personal protective equipment in noisy areas.

The preferred method of control is to decrease the noise generation first. If controls are ineffective, workers should wear protection.

RADIATION

When we use the term radiation we usually mean what scientists call "ionizing" radiation: Radiation that causes injury by changing the atomic or electron structure of a tissue. X-rays, cosmic rays, radon, and nuclear power radiation are in this category.

The notable occupational sources of radiation are mining of uranium or thorium, deep drilling or mining, industrial laboratory X-ray use, medical and dental X-rays, and nuclear power reactors.

Radiation injury can be acute: Causing radiation burns or skin ulceration of varying severity, nausea or vomiting, temporary decrease in blood cell formation in non-fatal cases, or severe hemorrhage, loss of gastrointestinal lining, coma and death in massive exposures.

Radiation illnesses can also be of delayed onset. There are several types. One type is an exposure that results after months or years and produces cancer of the bone marrow (leukemia), or of bone, liver, thyroid or lungs. Other delayed effects are genetic, affecting the baby of a pregnant employee who sustains an exposure, or causing abnormalities in exposed male or female employees' reporductive cells.

Treatment of a radiation injury may require blood count monitoring for several weeks but no other active treatment. The more severe injuries (rare in peacetime) might require a blood transfusion, antibiotics, medical support, and a long recovery. But treatment for a very mild radiation injury may not even be necessary as the body will recover in a few weeks with no symptoms.

I want to mention two other kinds of non-ionizing radiation: Infrared and ultraviolet. Large amounts of infrared (IR) are given off by hot objects such as heat lamps, molten metals, welding operations, etc. Long-term exposures to large amounts of IR appear to cause cataracts in exposed workers.

Ultraviolet (UV) comes primarily from the sun but also from hot metal, arc welding, and some lights. Exposure to UV can cause skin burns (typical sunburn), burns of the retina in the back of the eye, photosensitivity of the skin, and possibly cataracts. Treatment is preventive.

HEAT AND COLD

Temperature variations in American industry can be wide, from loading a flatbed truck in a northern blizzard at -35 F to pouring brass in a foundry at somewhere near 115 F. The human body can tolerate and adapt to even this 150 degree range.

But several occupational problems can occur with temperature variations. These range from minor to very severe (burns from hot and cold are covered in Sections A and F).

HEAT

Heat rash is a relatively minor problem, most common in hot and humid areas and easily treated by cleaning and drying the skin. Heat fatigue is a syndrome of decreased ability to concentrate, anxiety, and a feeling of decreased physical performance in a hot environment. Acclimatization is usually all that's necessary for this problem. Heat faints are fainting episodes caused by the body's attempt to get rid of heat by sending blood to skin, arms and legs--which takes it away from the brain. Treatment is simple: Take the fainter to a cool location.

More dramatic is heat exhaustion which is similar to a heat faint but complicated by decreased blood volume due to sweating and dehydration. A patient with heat exhaustion feels weak with headache and muscle cramps but has a clammy skin and no increase in body temperature. Treatment is urgent but simple: A cool place, lots of fluids including slightly salty solutions.

The most severe heat problem is heat stroke. These patients collapse and may have convulsions, their skin is dry and hot, and their core body temperatures rise quickly because their temperature regulation is not working properly. Immediate treatment is necessary to avoid a fatality: A cool area, immersion in a tub of cold water or ice chips, and vigorous massage of arms or legs. Heat stoke is a true medical emergency.

COLD

The most significant problems from physical cold are hypothermia and frostbite. Hypothermia is common in cold wet weather when the body loses heat quickly. This is most common in outdoor workers and usually goes along with exhaustion, which accelerates the problem. Patients with hypothermia experience coldness, shivering, convulsions and later exhaustion with coma. Hypothermia can be fatal if not treated. Treatment is a warm place and warm fluids.

Frostbite is a simple injury--freezing of tissues such as facial skin or fingers or toes--but not easy to treat if severe. Treatment is gentle warming (not use of snow or ice as many people seem to mistakenly believe) but amputation is occasionally all that can be done.

INFECTION

There are so many possible occupational exposures to infectious material that it would require a book to describe them fully. In this section I only want to point out that these risks are in basically two areas. Employees in medical situations are at risk of contagious infection and employees who work with animals or animal byproducts are at risk for several diseases carried by animals but transmittable to humans, who contact them.

Medical personnel (surgeons, nurses, anesthetists, custodians, lab workers) are at risk of contracting hepatitis from patients' blood or excretions, tuberculosis from patients' coughing or sneezing, and AIDS from blood samples or secretions. These people are often amply given information about these problems through in-service training and may not need this chapter.

Of course medical personnel are also susceptible to more colds, herpes, skin infections, strep throat, flu, measles, mumps and chickenpox because of their daily contacts with sick people.

Workers with animals can be exposed to a vast number of diseases. Anthrax (woolsorter's disease) is a severe skin disorder that also occasionally affects lungs and can be picked up from pelts, carcasses or live animals. Tularemia (rabbit fever) is a skin or lymph node disease that can be picked up from infected animals and flies, ticks, fleas and lice. This puts trappers, vets, meat processors and the like at risk.

Brucellosis (undulant fever) comes from livestock--though most livestock is now tested on a regular basis--and can affect vets, butchers and farmers who come in contact with the animals. Psittacosis (parrot fever) is a lung disease picked up from poultry and pet birds. Plague is transmitted by fleas in certain plague areas and affects outdoor workers, trappers, etc.

Rabies is uncommon in humans. It is a virus carried by skunks, raccoons and bats and thus risky for vets, trappers, outdoor workers, etc. The main problem associated with rabies is that exposure requires a painful series of rabies vaccinations which can be dangerous in themselves. Otherwise the clinical disease is quite rare.

TREATMENT OF INFECTIONS

Treatment for each type of infection is by antibiotics that are specific to the disease itself. The best treatment however is, as usual, protection: Wear protective coverings and especially gloves when handling carcasses, wash your hands frequently, and don't wear work clothes when you eat.

WRAP-UP

How to do yourself some favors with environmental illness problems and exposures:
1)   Realize that Workers' Compensation may not automatically cover these problems;
2)   Wear hearing protection around high noise levels. Try a hearing aide if you have lost some sound perception;
3)   Beware of other physical hazards--heat, cold, radiation, infection--in your workplace. Know how to prevent problems and how to treat the simplest cold and heat injuries.

G

INDEX

To Order *Going on Comp*

Telephone Orders: 1-218-726-0581; Have credit card ready.
FAX Orders: FAX # 1-218-726-1566; FAX this form.
Mail Orders: Complete card information or enclose check and mail this form to address below.

Book		Price	Quantity	Total
Going on Comp	Softcover	17.95		
	Hardcover	26.95		
		Subtotal		
		MN residents add 6% sales tax		
		Shipping & Handling: $3.00 on orders under $50.00 No charge on larger orders		
		TOTAL		

Payment method: ☐ Check enclosed ☐ Visa ☐ MasterCard ☐ Discover Card

Card Number: _____ Expiration Date: _____

Name on card: _____

Signature: _____ Phone Number: _____
I hereby authorize my credit card to be charged for this purchase.

Med-Ed Books Order Dept.
324 W. Superior St. # 510
Duluth, MN 55802

Ship To: _____

_____

_____

_____

Discounts for multiple copies on pre-paid orders.

5-10 books – 20% off
11-100 books – 30% off
101 books and up – 40% off

To Order *Going on Comp*

Telephone Orders: 1-218-726-0581; Have credit card ready.
FAX Orders: FAX # 1-218-726-1566; FAX this form.
Mail Orders: Complete card information or enclose check and mail this form to address below.

Book		Price	Quantity	Total
Going on Comp	Softcover	17.95		
	Hardcover	26.95		
		Subtotal		
		MN residents add 6% sales tax		
		Shipping & Handling: $3.00 on orders under $50.00 No charge on larger orders		
		TOTAL		

Payment method: ☐ Check enclosed ☐ Visa ☐ MasterCard ☐ Discover Card

Card Number: _____ Expiration Date: _____

Name on card: _____

Signature: _____ Phone Number: _____
I hereby authorize my credit card to be charged for this purchase.

Med-Ed Books Order Dept.
324 W. Superior St. # 510
Duluth, MN 55802

Ship To: _____

_____

_____

_____

Discounts for multiple copies on pre-paid orders.

5-10 books – 20% off
11-100 books – 30% off
101 books and up – 40% off